Sandra Kurfürst
Dancing Youth

Global Studies

For Anton and Nikolai

Sandra Kurfürst is Professor of Cross-cultural and Urban Communication at the Institute of Social and Cultural Anthropology, University of Cologne.

Sandra Kurfürst

Dancing Youth

Hip Hop and Gender in Late Socialist Vietnam

[transcript]

Excellence Initiative by the German Federal and State Governments, Global South Studies Center – University of Cologne, Female Professors Program of Federal and State Governments

Bibliographic information published by the Deutsche Nationalbibliothek
The Deutsche Nationalbibliothek lists this publication in the Deutsche National-bibliografie; detailed bibliographic data are available in the Internet at http://dnb.d-nb.de

Cover concept: Kordula Röckenhaus, Bielefeld
Cover illustration: B Nashor
Proofread by Jonathan DeVore, Miriam Laage

Print-ISBN 978-3-8376-5634-3
PDF-ISBN 978-3-8394-5634-7
https://doi.org/10.14361/9783839456347
ISSN of series: 2702-9298
eISSN of series: 2703-0504

Contents

Acknowledgements

First of all, I would like to thank Mai, Nguyet, Hoang Phuong, Thanh Phuong, Yen Hanh, Kim, Max, Thanh, Vy, Tien, Hien, Cuong, Cong, and Duong for introducing me to their world of hip hop, and their cordial support of my research.

My gratitude also goes to Bui Van Tuan, Pham Hong Tung, Hoang Anh Tuan, and Nguyen Ngoc Binh at the Vietnam National University Hanoi, for sharing their knowledge on youth, public space and Vietnamese sociolinguistics with me. I also want to thank Do Kien for his assistance during my research in Vietnam. Without all their help this research would not have been possible.

I would like to thank Tamaki Endo, Tomonori Ishioka, Tomohiro Machikita, Ivy Wilson, Tracy C. Davis, and Paul Kockelman for discussing my initial ideas for this book.

At the University of Cologne, I want to express my gratitude to the members of the research area "Communicative Repertoires" at the Global South Studies Center (GSSC) as well as my students for fruitful and interesting discussions.

I want to thank the GSSC and the "Professorinnenprogramm des Bundes und der Länder I-II" for funding this research.

I am also thankful to Phuong Glaser for assisting me with Vietnamese language translations, Eva Fuhrmann for her research assistance, and Miriam Laage for her assistance with the layout of this book. A special thanks also goes to Jonathan DeVore for editing this book.

Finally, I would like to thank Nils, Anton and Nikolai for their patience and encouragement, and for travelling together to Vietnam with me.

Hip Hop, Youth, and Urbanism

"Hip hop is from the United States. So, in Vietnam they copy from gangster rap videos, right?" "Hip hop is violent and misogynistic. So, why should it be a good thing for young Vietnamese people to engage with hip hop?" These are some of the many concerned questions that I am often confronted with when telling people about my research on youth and hip hop in Vietnam. What these questions imply, among many other things, is what Jenny Mbaye (2014: 396) refers to as an overt focus on hip hop's origin, which results in a very specific "geohistorical understanding of hip hop." According to such thinking, all appearances of hip hop outside the setting of its particular geohistorical origin are considered to be mere appropriations, a mimicry of what is estimated as an original culture. In order to overcome such single referentiality, Mbaye (2014: 396) suggests that we think of hip hop as multi-polar and multi-referential. Meanwhile, such multi-referentiality has been acknowledged by many scholars, who conceptualize hip hop as an idiom or cultural form that travels transnationally, is locally adopted and integrated into local practices and materials, thereby creating new identities (Alim 2009; Androutsopoulos 2003; Pennycook 2007; Schulz 2012). Generally, the idea that boundaries between nations, cultures, and other forms of social organization are becoming more and more fluid, and that "flows" should be given much more analytical attention, are claims that have surfaced among scholars interested in culture, and particularly popular culture (Appadurai 1996; Condry 2001; Gupta and Ferguson 1992). Yet, latent in many accounts of cultural flows, is a division between centre and periphery within globalized cultural networks. Since the United States is considered the cultural and commercial centre of hip hop, other localized hip hop markets, such as in Vietnam, remain at the periphery of the international music and dance market, struggling for international recognition.

Hip hop is comprised of four elements, including MCing, DJing, graffiti writing, and break(danc)ing,[1] and is often discussed in connection with social inequalities. Halifu Osumare (2001: 173) identifies hip hop as a "global signifier for many forms of marginalizations," while Mbaye (2014: 398) views hip hop as emerging from a "southern positioning," situated at "the margins of an assumed sociality and urbanity." This book takes the trope of southern positioning as a starting point for investigating how hip hop practices, and embodied dance practices in particular, have the potential to cross, subvert, and otherwise permeate seemingly fixed geographical, linguistic, bodily, and gender boundaries. The analysis is situated at a particular moment in history, 30 years after Vietnam's integration into the global economy and the rise of its private sector economy during the so-called Doi Moi period. In academic literature, Vietnam's current political economy is referred to as "late socialist" or "postsocialist" to indicate its transitional form. Both terms are used to capture tensions between the persistence of a one-party-rule authoritarian state on the one hand, and the introduction of a free market economy on the other (Harms 2011; Hue Tam Ho Tai 2001). Li Zhang (2012: 661) uses the term post-socialism to "refer to *conditions* of transformation and articulation of socialist and nonsocialist practices and logics regardless of the official labeling of the state." Both China and Vietnam have embraced market reform, commodification, and consumerism, while officially insisting on socialist ideology and one-party rule. By delving into dancers' everyday lives, this book aims to provide insights into "postsocialist assemblages from the margin" (Li Zhang 2012: 662).

Referring to Brian Larkin's (2013) work on uptake and desire of images and cultural forms, this research started out by asking why hip hop was taken up in Vietnam in the first place, and why young people particularly (although not exclusively) seem to enjoy hip hop. Hip hop began to be practiced in Vietnam in the early 1990s, shortly after the introduction of economic reforms. With the introduction of a privatized market economy, and the country's integration with the world economy, the circulation of people, commodities, and cultural artefacts—such as music, dance, film, art, and so on—began to intensify in unprecedented ways. Students began to study abroad in France, Australia, the

---

1   Breakdance is a commercialized term for breaking or b-boying/girling. As I will show in the following, the fourth element of hip hop is much more diverse, comprising diverse street dance styles. In Vietnam, breaking, popping, locking, waacking, hip hop and house dancing are subsumed under the umbrella term of hip hop.

United States, Germany, among other places, and later returned to Vietnam with "information artefacts" (Star et al. 2003: 44), storage and display devices, such as music and video tapes. One of the first b-boys in Vietnam, b-boy LionT, recalls how, in the beginning, no one really knew what they were doing. He remembers that he and other young people merely mimicked the moves they saw on TV or abroad. This memory is one shared by many dancers. Many of the dancers I talked to were either the first to practice a particular style in Vietnam, or they referred to a teacher as the first to learn the bodily practices with which they were so fascinated. Hip hop appeals to young people, as its bodily practices offer room for creativity, innovation, and self-development. Another pioneering b-boy, Phuong Silver Monkey, who like LionT has been a practitioner of hip hop since 1992, explains that "in this music genre, you are free to develop yourself."

Historian David Marr (2000) contextualizes this yearning for development of the self and individual freedom in his work:

> "The trend in the 1990s has been towards diversity and freedom of choice, certainly in comparison with the Stalinist command and control environment of earlier decades. In particular, young men and women are departing the village, loosening family ties, choosing their own occupations, and joining voluntary associations to a degree that would have been unthinkable only ten years ago. How persons in these uncharted waters proceed to look upon themselves is one of the important questions for the twenty-first century." (Marr 2000: 796)

This book provides insight into the uptakes, desires, and aspirations of young people, focusing on diverse street dance styles that are all in local terms summarized under the umbrella term "hip hop culture" (văn hoá hip hop). Analysing the actors, spaces, and infrastructures coproducing Vietnam's hip hop community of practice (Lave and Wenger 1991), this book embeds dance practices within larger contexts of socioeconomic transformation, urban restructuring, and changing gender relations. Each of the book's chapters introduces a hip hop dance style, its practitioners, and the spaces that are coproduced in collective practice. The young street dancers whom I have met so far are all aware and fond of their particular dance style. Therefore, the reader will engage with breaking, popping and locking, waacking and hip hop dance, while considering each style's local underpinnings in Vietnam. Participating in dance classes, battles, and crew practices, as well as interviewing young street dancers, I found that, for many dancers, participating in hip hop culture meant leading a good life. Hip hop serves as a vehicle for developing the self, while simultaneously dealing with uncertainties of late socialism. Living a dancing life has implications far beyond the body and self, as it calls into question and simultaneously adheres to an ethics of striving identified by social anthropologist Minh Nguyen (2019). The ethics of striving is comprised of personal achievements, which finally materialize in the accumulation of private wealth, while at the same time receiving social recognition. While indulging in hip hop may not be the conventional lifestyle aspired to by youth in contemporary Vietnam, it becomes clear from the ethnographic evidence that striving in hip hop culture is as much about self-development as it is about creating community and achieving recognition from one's peers. To be sure, the dancers' parents often imagined more conventional lifestyles for their children. Yet, notwithstanding quarrels with members of the older generation, and obstacles presented by the economic precarity of dancing labour, young people between the ages of 20 to 40 continue to follow their passion for dance. Accordingly, I will discuss the overall meaning(s) of hip hop in Vietnam, including dancers' aspirations as well as the anxieties and obstacles they face for doing what they love most: dancing. While I talked to male and female dancers, my research has a gender bias, as I was particularly on the lookout for female protagonists – perhaps owed to my own biography as a lover of hip hop ever since my teenage years. That is why each chapter dedicated to a particular dance style also includes a section on gender performance and relations. Apart from my own intimate relationship with hip hop, my interest in the topic in a Vietnamese context resulted from attention to intersections of embodied practices, performance genres, and gender identities. The hip hop genre is generally considered masculine, occurring in men's spaces, and shaped by norms of aggression and fierce competition – as seen in battles. Women who come to inhabit such spaces are too often viewed as deviating from the norm, especially in dance, as the aesthetics of many dance styles presented in this book are most often assigned to young, energetic, masculine bodies. However, when female artists "comply" with the genre, and adapt to norms of the genre, they radically challenge the masculine domination in hip hop (Berggren 2014: 245), overcoming the binary view of gender altogether. However, as a female participant to this research rightfully pointed out: "I don't think it's about young women, but about people who want to enjoy their life and develop themselves (...). My passion is for dance and I want to do what I want. I want people to know what I need for myself." Accordingly, this book is about young people of diverse genders following their passion. Over 15 years of conducting field research in Vietnam, I noticed the diversification of life styles, fashion, music, and dance styles among urban youth. Over the last decade, Hanoi's youth seems to have become more visible in public spaces, more diverse, and, in a way, louder and more tangible than the first time I visited Vietnam at the turn of the millennium.

Who is young in Vietnam?

The United Nations defines youth as persons aged between 15 to 24 years old (UN 2018). The Vietnamese term for youth, *thanh niên*, originally only denoted young men, but later came to include young women, as well. The Vietnamese dictionary, *Từ điển tiếng Việt*, published by the Institute for Foreign Languages (*Viện Ngôn ngữ học*) in 2003, defines *thanh niên* as "young people, who find themselves in the stage of maturation (Pham 2011: 38). In his book *Thanh Niên*, historian Pham Hong Tung (2011) explains that, according to the Youth Law, individuals between 16 to 30 years old are considered youth. According to this law, the age of 16 is considered the age of criminal responsibility (Drummond and Nguyen 2008). Apart from legal age indices, family status is another determinant of youth in Vietnam, as unmarried and single persons are typically classified as youth. In fact, in a study of youth in Hanoi, many respondents mentioned marriage as marking the end of the stage of youth (Valentin 2008: 80). However, law and regulations are insufficient frames for understanding youth, especially as the experiences of those designated "youth" often diverge from the legal contexts. Karen Hansen (2008) reminds us that, both in the Global North and South, people younger than the legal age work for wages, have sexual relations, and bear children. At the same time, many people stay in their parents' or relatives' homes far beyond legal age of adulthood. In urban Vietnam, young people do not necessarily intend to establish their own independent households before or after marriage, as many instead seek to reside with their extended families for various economic and cultural reasons, such as to fulfil socially assigned rules as daughters, sons, in-laws, and so forth (Hansen 2008) – not to speak of the exorbitant rents they would have to pay for small apartments of their own in the city. In her study of youth in urban Vietnam, Karen Valentin (2008: 79) found that, although youth is a category generally denoting both social constraint and freedom, young respondents mostly referred to the responsibilities they had as young Vietnamese. For instance, they mentioned preparation for professional careers, marriage, financial support for elders, and law-abiding citizenship, while contributing to the development of the nation. The responsibilities cited by these young Vietnamese people align with the ideal of the socialist moral subject (Nguyen 2019; Schwenkel and Leshkowich 2012), which will be discussed in-depth in chapter 8, "SELF-ENTREPRENEURISM AND SELF-FASHIONING."

With over half of the population being younger than 25, these young people have not experienced the hardships of the Indochina Wars or the famines of the 1980s. All they know from this period derives from stories told by their parents and grandparents, as well as from diverse media reports and school curricula. In contrast to the previous generation, the younger generation born after Doi Moi grew up in the context of accelerating economic growth. As a result, Vietnamese youth, like youth in many places around the world, has been accused of an overt focus on consumption. However, Christina Schwenkel (2011) cautions against assumptions often made by government officials and members of older generations, who believe that young people who grew up in times of peace and prosperity do not understand, nor recognize, the older population's sacrifice to liberate the country.

In fact, young people in late socialist Vietnam experience the war's enduring aftermath, too. Schwenkel reminds us that Vietnamese youth embody values central to the revolution, such as betterment and development. Yet, in contrast to older generations, they draw on capitalism as a tool to achieve the ends of national sovereignty, prosperity, and progress. With her argument, she already alludes to the dovetailing of authoritarianism with neoliberalism, which she later discusses in a special issue on neoliberalism in Vietnam (Schwenkel 2012), situating her findings within the larger context of late socialist societies (Ong 2008; Li Zhang 2012). Further, Schwenkel considers young people's conspicuous consumption not so much an indicator for the loss of cultural values and norms, but rather as an engagement with capitalism and the global market that is a more effective way to fulfil their familial and national duties (Schwenkel 2011: 133). Making use of the newly gained freedom of movement within Vietnam, and migration abroad, many young people have departed for the cities. The result is a pluralization of destinations, and sources of income in the cities, as well as multiple trajectories toward the future (Simone 2019; Skelton 2002). The socialist state has always had an eye on youth, trying to mobilize young people for its own ends. The Communist Party regards youth as the pillar of the Vietnamese nation (*Thanh niên là giường cột của nước nhà*). The political legacy of the youth dates back to the revolution and the independence movement. In 1925, the Revolutionary

Youth League of Vietnam (*Việt Nam Thanh Niên cách mạng đồng chí hội*), was founded in Canton by old emigrants, including former followers of Phan Boi Chau and communists like Nguyen Ai Quoc, who became renowned as Ho Chi Minh. The Revolutionary Youth League was founded at a time of great political turmoil in French Indochina. In the same year, the elderly Phan Boi Chau was arrested by the French in Shanghai and brought back to Hanoi to stand trial, while Phan Chu Trinh passed away shortly after, with his funeral attracting thousands of people (Chesneaux 1955: 70-71). Prior to the founding of the Revolutionary Youth League, both Phan Boi Chau and Phan Chu Trinh had already engaged in intellectual movements and political actions. Both scholars had turned from Confucianism to Western rationalism. Informed by the writings of Rousseau and Montesquieu, they preferred the republic over the monarchy and the Romanised Vietnamese script, *Quốc ngữ*, developed by Roman Catholic missionaries in the 17th century, over the Chinese script.

In 1905, Phan Boi Chau decided to migrate to Japan where he founded the League for the Renewal of Vietnam (*Duy Tân hội*) (Chesneaux 1955: 68). Eventually, the movement was comprised of educated middle-class men. As a consequence, the Revolutionary Youth League set itself apart from previous movements owed to its social configuration and political goals. The league aimed at gaining independence, while simultaneously seeking to improve people's livelihoods. This latter goal won the movement support from the industrial working class, which had emerged at the beginning of the 20th century due to the expansion of mines in Tonkin (Northern Vietnam) and plantations in Cochinchina (Southern Vietnam). Eventually, members of the Revolutionary Youth League led the waves of 1928 and 1929 strikes in Tonkin's major cities, Hanoi and Hai Phong (Chesneaux 1955: 70-71). From Vietnamese independence in 1945 until today, the youth has constituted an enduring focal point in the country's political rhetoric, beginning with the writings of Ho Chi Minh, which are cited time and again. During the Eleventh Party Congress, held in 2017, Nguyen Phu Trong—the former general secretary and president of the Socialist Republic of Vietnam since October 2018—called the youth "the masters of the future, the pillar of the country" (*Thanh niên là người chủ tương lai, là giường cột của nước nhà*) (Doanthanhnien 2017). The importance ascribed to Vietnamese youth is also indicated by the existence of the Ho Chi Minh Communist Youth Union, which claims 3.5 million members. Under direct control of the Communist Party, the Youth Union serves as a preparatory school that grooms young people for future party membership. Membership is only granted upon a selection process that considers school performance, family background, as well as behaviour and morality (Thayer 2009; Valentin 2008).

The socialist state's focus on urban youth has also been outlined by Jennifer Cole's (2010) research in Madagascar, where urban youth are sent to the countryside for one year. In Vietnam, the Ho Chi Minh Communist Youth Union regularly organizes trips to visit "heroic mothers" in faraway places, bringing them food and gifts for their service to the country. At the same time, the Youth Union involves urban youth in urban development projects focusing on environmental and social issues, seeking to provide members with "meaningful" social activities in their leisure time (Valentin 2008: 91). In general, many students regularly engage in youth volunteer activities, such as charity and volunteer work for those who have made sacrifices for the nation (Schwenkel 2011). Apart from mass organizations, various universities clubs and volunteer organizations offer students activities to occupy their spare time, creating a collective identity by serving the nation. Recently, the state has taken to promoting popular culture in order to attract more young people, such as inviting famous singers to national celebrations. Likewise, the Youth Union organizes popular events, such as dance competitions, or singing contests in semi-public places such as stadiums, schools, and cultural centres (Valentin 2008). Apart from these mass organizations, universities and high schools increasingly offer dance clubs, as well. Beside these organized activities aimed at structuring young people's spare time, the urban youth increasingly organizes itself. After school or work, young people often meet in Hanoi's public spaces to meet friends and to participate in diverse sports activities and street dance. They make use of a wide array of resources, knowledges, and sources of income generation. In his account of young people in a precarious urban environment, Abdoumaliq Simone (2019: 27) explains that they "decouple themselves from a fixed set of aspirations and development trajectories and instead use the infrastructures of the city as a means not so much to 'settle' within as to 'traverse' territorial and institutional boundaries." They transgress such boundaries, for example, through their dance practices. A mapping of the dance events that I encountered during my field research in 2018, together with events that I followed on social media, reveals the dancers' high mobility and territorial flexibility. Almost all of the events took place within the administrative boundaries of the city of Hanoi. Only one of the events was organized outside of Hanoi, in the neighbouring Hung Yen Province. Interestingly, this event was not organized by a particular crew, as were many other events that I joined, but was rather coordinated by a private company and sponsored by the Austrian energy drink company, Red Bull (see chapter 4, "BREAKING"). What particularly struck my interest was how young people traversed institutional boundaries, in particular as young women negotiated and transgressed normative gender roles. Although in their mid- to late-twenties, most of the women I met were single or in relationships, but few had married and none of them had children. Due to the emphasis placed on women's reproductive role – as literal bearers of the nation – women in Vietnam are expected to marry in their twenties, and quickly thereafter bear children (Drummond and Rydstrøm 2004; Schwenkel 2011). Consequently, many female dancers explained that their decision to dance did not always align with their parents' expectations, as they were critical of their children's participation in street dance. Nonetheless, many of the female dancers were finally able to gain their parents acceptance, and sometimes even their recognition.

So, who then is "young" in Vietnam? The discussion of youth in Vietnam shows that legal or age-based definitions are insufficient to explain what is going on *in situ*. Youth is a fluid category, culturally contingent, as well as relational. Who is considered youth varies according to the local context, is highly contested, and constantly changing (Durham 2004; Hansen 2008). Drawing on linguistics, Deborah Durham (2004) suggests that youth is a social shifter. In linguistics, the term shifter denotes something that has both a referential and an indexical or deictic function (Jakobson 1971; Silverstein 1976). Referential meaning points to something in the world that is independent of a particular use. By contrast, the indexical aspect of a shifter can only be comprehended in the context of a particular use in a situated social interaction. With each use, the meaning of the shifter changes. Deictic terms establish a variety of relationships, for instance, determining the spatial relationship of a speaker to an object, temporal relations among parts of an utterance, social relationships between a speaker and listener, and so forth. In sum, social shifter denotes young peoples' changing positions in relationships with others as well as in space. Moreover, shifters allude to the fact that youth is a category always under construction. While "youth" might be stable as a signifier, the signified to whom it can be assigned, including those who understand themselves as such, remains highly contested, political, and is constantly negotiated (Durham 2004: 591-593). As shifters work meta-linguistically, they draw attention to particular relations within a structure of relations, and moreover, to the structure itself (Durham 2000: 116). This idea of a shifter pointing toward the overall structure also emerges in the Vietnamese community of practice and speech community. In Vietnamese, terms of self- and second person address are defined relationally, and vary according to the age, gender, and status of interlocutors, as well as the context of the speech act. From a sociolinguistic point of view, whomever is considered young in Vietnam is decided on *in situ*, in relational, mostly asymmetric, terms. Consequently, youth as a social shifter is highly dynamic, constantly changing, and yet referential as in the state rhetoric outlined above.

Of course, age has a lot to do with the definition of youth. Accordingly, Durham (2004: 601) suggests putting age at the centre of social analysis, since

> " (...) in arguing over youth, or age, people must address not just the relationships themselves but also the nature of sociality as it is envisioned and made to matter in their lives. Finding youth, or maturity, involves exploring what it means to be a person, what power is and how it is exercised, how people relate to one another, and what moral action might be and who may engage in it and how."

The questions of personhood, morality, and social embeddedness are central to inquiries into the subjectivities of hip hop dancers in the city. In a similar vein, in his monograph, *Spaces of Youth: Work, citizenship and culture in a global context*, sociologist David Farrugia (2018: 111) considers youth cultures as representing relevant sites for understanding shifts in the articulation of social subjectivities and collectivities through culture. He points to the modes of youthfulness that are valorised and devalorised by economies of symbolic prestige across and within different spaces and places. Farrugia identifies a bias in the research on youth culture towards Northern experiences, since the basis for youth cultural research is the notion of subculture, most prominently put forward by scholars from the Chicago School, and subsequently the Birmingham Centre for Contemporary Cultural Studies. Scholars from the Chicago School already related the idea of subculture to the urban, while identifying deviance, or divergence from what was regarded as the norm, as the guiding principle (Cohen 1955; Gordon 1947). In the 1970s and 1980s, scholars from the Birmingham Centre for Contemporary Cultural Studies became increasingly concerned with the working-class youth. The notion of subculture in relation to youth considers young people's cultural practices and identifications as a response to the structural dynamics of post-war industrial capitalism. In particular, it relates young people's tastes and styles to their changing position within the class structure relative to their parents (Clarke et al. 1997; Cohen 1972; Farrugia 2018). Subcultures offered an alternative to class-based analysis and thus were considered as transitional states, shifting from their parents' class-based identity toward commercialized mass culture. According to Gelder (1997) subcultures emerge as a means of resolving and expressing the crisis of class.

Apart from such post-war experiences in the Global North, the concept of subculture has been criticised for presupposing a "mainstream" culture from which the subculture diverges. Another point of critique is the idea that subcultures constitute socially enclosed totalities with clear boundaries, demarcating the difference of one subculture from another. Furthermore, the Centre of Contemporary Cultural Studies' focus on subculture failed to address dimensions of gender, internal stratification, upward social mobility, as well as cultural production (Gelder 1997; Farrugia 2018; Jacke 2009; Schulze 2015). Later on, the academic field of Post-Subcultural Studies or Popular Cultural Studies emerged, situating subcultures in their heterogeneous and hybrid environments, while considering them as temporally limited social phenomenon, without a necessarily enduring nature. Moreover, such studies considered fluidity and mobility as characteristic of subcultures (Jacke 2009; Schulze 2015). In *Hardcore & Gender*, Marion Schulze (2015) chooses a processual approach to the study of subcultures. Choosing an emic perspective, Schulze is interested in the subculture's "doing." Accordingly, she focuses on how actors create social cohesion within the group, and demarcate the group's boundaries in relation to others. Overcoming the assumed linkage of subcultures to territory, moreover, Schulze suggests that subcultures act translocally and transnationally, while taking up elements from diverse social worlds. According to Farrugia (2018), the emphasis on the mobility and fluidity of cultural flows signifies a general shift in social theory. With respect to subcultural theory, this means an "emphasis on the contingent articulations of aesthetic styles and collective identifications through the deterritorialisation of cultural symbols in an era of globalization" (Farrugia 2018: 112). As stated earlier, hip hop has been recognized as involved in cultural flows, being taken up and integrated locally, creating new identities. For instance, the idea of the Global Hip Hop Nation is an imagined community of hip hop practitioners and peers, in which nation still refers to a territorial or at least political-administrative entity.

In this book, instead of referring to the notion of subculture outlined above, or sticking with the term Global Hip Hop Nation, I consider practitioners of hip hop's diverse dance styles as constituting communities of practice. Etienne Wenger (1998) defines a community of practice as a group that develops through mutual engagement in a joint enterprise, creating a common repertoire. In contrast to the term community, which usually suggests a unity, a degree of social cohesion, or sameness (Cox 2005: 532), the community of practice does not necessarily imply "co-presence, a well-defined, identifiable group or socially visible boundaries" (Lave and Wenger 1991: 98). It may or may not be spatially contained. Accordingly, a community of practice forms around a certain practice rather than a particular locality. Still, communities of practice are situated and local insofar as any activity is situated (Cox 2005; Lave and Wenger 1991; Star 2003). Situated learning and the sharing of knowledge, including the rapid flow of information and the propagation of innovation, are important features of communities of practice. Against this background, this book examines the community of practice emerging around the embodied practices of diverse hip hop dance styles in Vietnam. Apart from focusing on the embodied practice of dance, this book also engages with a sociolinguistic understanding of language as social practice. Language in dance co-constitutes and communicates belonging to a particular community of practice (Bucholtz 1999; Eckert and McConell-Ginet 1992).

Infrastructures of circulation

Technology and economics significantly contribute to the development of cultural forms, such as hip hop (Rose 1994). The hip hop practices of breaking and rap became known and practiced in Vietnam around the 1990s, shortly after the country's integration into the world economy. The country's economic opening, as well as technological progress, significantly contributed to the circulation of hip hop to and within Vietnam. In more recent years, the connection to social media, such as YouTube, Facebook, Instagram, and the like, facilitates the exchange of music, videos, dancers, and knowledge about hip hop.

Before the country's opening-up, music primarily had a political and educational function, culminating in the creation of red music, and its counter-currency, yellow music, which was considered the deviation from the norm and the materialisation of capitalism, such as disco or funk music. After the end of French colonialism, a period in which the urban middle class particularly referred to French cuisine, fashion, and music as markers of social distinction (Dutton 2012; Peters 2012), and the First Indochina War, two regimes with different political orientations developed in northern and southern Vietnam. The Democratic Republic of Vietnam, with its capital in Hanoi and Ho

Chi Minh as its first president, was first oriented to China and since the 1970s toward the Soviet Union. Like many countries of the Eastern Block, the arts had a political function, and were aimed at addressing the masses rather than the small educated elite. Artists and musicians were required to adhere to this political orientation and adopt the style of socialist realism (Huynh 2005). In public spaces, socialist propaganda posters, the rhetoric of the mass organizations, and state media all propagated the ideal image of socialist man that the nation was supposed to follow (Drummond 2004). In this context, revolutionary music (*nhạc đỏ*) developed in the north. *Nhạc đỏ* literally translates as "red," which is also the colour of the Vietnamese national flag. Southern music prior to 1975, by contrast, was referred to as *nhạc vàng*, yellow music. In his monograph, *Fragments from the Present: Searching for Modernity in Vietnam's South*, Philip Taylor seeks to understand the meaning and origin of these two terms. He recalls how few people he spoke to were actually aware of the meaning of *nhạc vàng* and its origin. While most considered its origin Chinese, others thought it meant 'weak,' one 'feudal,' and another 'sick.' Yellow music had been influenced by French and American post-war pop music as well as rock ballads. Themes of yellow music were mostly focused on love as well as the enduring war. Red music, by contrast, was seen as borrowed from the Soviet bloc, Chinese, and Cuban music repertoires. Red or revolutionary music featured tropes of war, the longing for liberty, the collective fight for freedom, and the patriotism of the population (Taylor 2001: 39, 150). With the reunification of the country and the founding of the Socialist Republic of Vietnam in 1976, yellow music became the sonic icon of decadence and U.S. occupation. Consequently, yellow music was prohibited and confiscated when detected during any police searches. After the end of the Second Indochina War (1955-1975),[2] and following the country's reunification, many people, mostly from southern Vietnam, fled the country. Many found refuge in the United States and Europe, particularly in France and Germany, where they constituted a Vietnamese diaspora. The so-called *Việt Kiều* initially had little relation with their home country. Parcels and letters that they sent to relatives and friends back home often did not reach their addressees as they were often considered subversive materials (Taylor 2001). Simultaneously, citizens from northern Vietnam migrated as contract workers or students to countries of the

2   In Vietnam the war is referred to as the American War, whereas the war is globally known as the Vietnam War.

Soviet Block.[3] Along the way, contact to other cultures and forms of thought were established. Although in line with socialist ideology, the government yet again sought to control these outside influences.

At the same time in the 1980s, political songs became less and less popular in Vietnam, particularly with the youth. Concerned with the crisis of popular music in Vietnam, a conference was held on the topic of "Youth—Music—Our Time" (*Tuổi Trẻ—Âm Nhạc—Thời Đại*) in 1982. The aim of the conference, which was attended by senior members of the Musicians' Union and the performing arts, was the development of a vibrant popular song culture in order to attract young people. A major debate evolved around the question of rhythm without mimicking neo-colonial music from the West, such as disco music. In response, Do Nhuan, the general secretary of the Musicians' Union, suggested that musicians draw on the nation's rich rhythmic repertoire (Norton 2015: 13).

The Doi Moi reform of 1986 not only brought a shift in economic policy, but also in the cultural sphere. One year after the party congress, Nguyen Van Linh frankly acknowledged during a meeting with writers that the party leadership acted in an authoritarian manner when it came to literature and the arts, calling on writers to criticize negative aspects of society. As a result, more and more artists and writers began to develop a more critical stance (Norton 2015: 14). Moreover, Vietnam's opening toward the world economy also facilitated the circulation and import of cultural artefacts from non-socialist countries, mostly through networks of the Vietnamese diaspora. Critically observing the influx of Western popular culture to Vietnam, the party-state returned to antagonizing what it referred to as "Western" cultural influences. Finally, in 1996, the VIII Party Congress initiated the "Foreign Social Evils Campaign" (Logan 2000: 254). Western influence was believed to result in a deterioration of cultural norms and traditional values – a discourse that was shared widely across Southeast Asia at the time.[4] Among other problems,

---

3   Vietnamese soon to depart for Eastern Europe imagined what their life there would be like, and upon their return told their friends and families what they had encountered. A common trope in these memories is the scent of the West (*mùi Tây*) (Nguyen Thu Giang 2019b).

4   Main proponents of the Asian values debate, Singaporean and Malaysian Prime Ministers Lee Kwan Yew and Mohamad Mahatir propagated that Asian values were not necessarily coherent with Western ideals of democracy and called for a specific political order of Asian societies (Croissant 2015).

state authorities identified premarital sex, prostitution, drug addiction, gambling, and crime as social evils that negatively affected the moral traditions of the country. In other words, social evils were understood as a "dirty" external influence on the (inner) moral order, brought about by globalization. Accordingly, the Foreign Social Evils Campaign particularly became a means for regulating female bodies, gender, and sexualities (Tran 2014). In terms of media and popular culture, the Foreign Social Evils Campaign prohibited the adoption of the English language on billboards, and the consumption of Western music and media. Instead, Vietnamese folklore, including traditional songs and dances, were broadcast on national television (Valentin 2008; Logan 2000; Nguyen 2019). Further measures included raids against entertainment venues, such as karaoke bars and dance halls (Tran 2014). In other words, it became more difficult to physically encounter foreign cultural artefacts, and even more difficult to share musical preferences with others. This stands in stark contrast, for example, to Japanese hip hop, which actually flourished in Tokyo's club culture (Condry 2001). However, the Foreign Social Evils Campaign did not prevent the circulation of cultural commodities into and within Vietnam. In the circulation of hip hop music and artefacts, individuals, most of them Vietnamese exchange students abroad, took on particularly important roles. Studying abroad in Germany, France, Australia, and Great Britain, on their return back home to Vietnam, they brought "information artefacts" (Star et al. 2003: 244) with them, including storage and display devices, such as video tapes and mix tapes. In sum, hip hop artefacts circulated in Vietnam through the mobility of youth cultural symbols and practices, as well as spatially distributed economies of symbols, tastes, and distinctions, operating through flows that transgressed both territorial boundaries (Farrugia 2018) as well as efforts to police what were perceived as negative foreign influences. Translocal connections between otherwise distributed actors emerged in the process, including actors situated at the peripheries of metropolitan centres of the production and consumption of hip hop.

Uptake and desire in the circulation of cultural artefacts

Larkin (2013: 241) considers circulation "not simply as the unfettered movement of objects disseminated instantaneously and globally by new digital technologies, but as involving complex acts of identification and translation, dependent on the fragile, uncertain nature of uptake." Accordingly, Larkin not only considers the material infrastructures of cables and wires as mediating circulation, but also the meaning-making that occurs in local contexts, through which objects and subjects enter into and engage circulation. With respect to subjects and subjectivities, Larkin urges analysts to consider practices of uptake and rejection. Drawing on the example of Hindi film entering into Hausa culture, he argues that uptake is always driven by desire. Circulation then involves "complex acts of identification and translation," as well as commensuration, as these images move across cultural differences (Larkin 2013: 241, 245). As a consequence, the uptake of hip hop in Vietnam was and still is not only mediated by technical means, such as mix tapes and video cassettes, and social media more recently, but also by individuals' desire and willingness to take on new cultural practices. When recalling her musical influences from the USA, a female rapper Suboi says "I listened to Pop, Rock, Rap, Blues, Jazz, but I stopped at Hip Hop. This is, you know, the music of rebellious people, you know, I need that in my life" (Interview Viet Talk 2015). In a similar vein, male hip hop dancer Phuong Silver Monkey, who is considered an "OG" (*đại*) on the Vietnamese hip hop dance scene, says "Hip hop is very free. In hip hop music, you can easily create with all the skills that you have... In this music, you are free to develop yourself" (Hanyi 2014). In other words, hip hop appears to cater to the desires and aspirations of young people in late socialist Vietnam. Such aspirations concern the two concomitant processes of developing the self, and being a social person, creating (new) forms of sociality that often depart from collectivist socialist ideals.

Dance scholar Thomas DeFrantz (2016: 71) discusses the uptake of dance styles in relation to the circulation of theatricalized social dance forms, such as krumping, waacking, or voguing:

> "These forms emerge in local public spheres, where music and dance arise together, each driving the other to light. Some dedicated dancers practice the emerging style until a repeatable basic form solidifies with a name everyone can remember; this simplified dance travels from neighborhood to neighborhood, until landing, inevitably, in some national media orbit. After being exposed on a national stage, expert practitioners develop incalculable choreographies of the form: advanced versions of the movements that extend its expressive capacities. Meanwhile, most of us do a very simple version of the dance for a few months. Some forms become more extravagant in their theatrical capacity, though, and even more expert dancers realize even more eccentric embodied possibilities previously unknown. I say eccentric to underscore the hand-made, extravagantly detailed, expert versions of Black

social dances that inevitably develop. These versions bear little resemblance to the dance that was briefly practiced by a larger population."

According to DeFrantz, these expert demonstrations of the dance style enter the archive, coming to represent the dance in later generations. DeFrantz alludes to two processes. The first is the process of circulation. Arjun Appadurai (1996) describes the movement of media away from the publics for which it was created into different arenas of social life as the "disjunctive" nature of media. This movement and redefinition of media from one place, situation, and community to others is characteristic of hip hop. Second, DeFrantz refers to the process of archiving. The practices of what Gates (1988: 51) calls "Signifyin(g)" and sampling are crucial elements of Black expressive culture generally, and in hip hop particularly. The constant referencing of texts, body postures, lyrics, and beats constitute an intertextuality and referentiality characteristic of hip hop culture. The practice of Signifyin(g) refers to "the manner in which texts seem concerned to address their antecedents. Repetition, with a signal difference, is fundamental to the nature of Signifyin(g)" (Gates 1988: 51). Building on Gate's definition of Signifyin(g), Andrew Bartlett considers sampling a form of highly selective archiving, linking, and digital sampling to the "African American diasporic aesthetic of careful selection of media, texts and contexts for performative use" (Bartlett 2004: 393). In other words, through the repetition of basic elements, such as beats, rhymes, and dance basics, dancers are able to innovate, and achieve a personal style. Innovative creation in hip hop is thus closely linked to the Deleuzian (2007) understanding of repetition as being inherently about difference.

Moreover, DeFrantz (2016: 72) scrutinizes the "slippery nature of Black expressive culture's archive." The movement of dance forms out of their originary social circumstances ultimately alters their capacity to underscore emergent social relationships, as exemplified in Madonna's appropriation of voguing, or krumping in her videos and stage tour choreographies. Put differently, Madonna's appropriation of these Black social dance forms indicates their common decontextualization, which occurs after the revelation of excellence in their performance. Such movement out of the publics in and for which such forms were created undermines the dances' capacity "to highlight individualized non-normative, resistant expressive modes." (DeFrantz 2016: 72). Finally, with regard to the uptake of performative forms, such as dance by new publics, power differentials and the transformation of meaning need to be examined.

Hip Hop in Vietnam: multiple communities of practice

Hip hop originated in the United States, and comprises four elements, including MCing, DJing, breaking, and graffiti writing. These practices quickly began to circulate after their emergence, and where taken up by practitioners around the globe. Such circulation leads Mbaye (2014) to shift the analysis away from an overt focus on the United States, and to consider the multipolarity and multi-referentiality of hip hop. The gerund form of the four elements already signifies the active practice of each specific discipline, which have been recognized in Hip Hop Studies as distinct cultural practices (Brunstad et al. 2010: 240; Cutler 2009: 331). Rose (1994: 26) attests to the coherence of hip hop style, pointing to the intertextuality between graffiti, rap, and breaking. In this book, I draw on the community of practice concept to illustrate how communities evolve around particular practices. The community of practice concept has been applied to the study of hip hop, but rather vaguely in the sense of an already existing entity. For example, Cecilia Cutler (2009: 81) refers to one hip hop community of practice, and Sarah Simeziane (2010: 96) to a cross-cultural community of practice. Elizabeth Betz (2014), in reference to Tony Mitchell (2007), includes some scaling when referring to an Australian hip hop community of practice. Yet, the term community of practice has been applied to hip hop with little differentiation and elaboration.[5] Rather than thinking of a singular hip hop community of practice, I suggest that distinct communities of practice have evolved around the four practices of MCing, breaking, graffiti, and DJing in Vietnam. In fact, the four elements show distinct trajectories and involve different infrastructures. Moreover, the particular infrastructures for each practice require different kinds and degrees of economic investment.

In the 1970s, MCing or rap evolved among the turntables of the first DJs who practiced in New York basements, clubs, and at block parties. The first MCs (Masters of Ceremony) animated the crowd, talking over the DJ. Aiming to raise the crowd's energy level, they called out rhymes: "Hip Hop y'all, and ya don't stop, rock on, till the break of dawn," thereby baptizing the term hip

---

5   An exemption is Love (2014), who uses the concept of community of practice in the context of hip hop-based education in early childhood and elementary education. Accordingly, the term community of practice is applied in its original form as rooted in social learning theory (see chapter "URBANISM AND HIP HOP COMMUNITIES OF PRACTICE").

hop (Bradley 2009; Chang 2006: 19; Price-Styles 2015). In Vietnam, the MCing community has developed since the 1990s, having been introduced through transnational networks, and particularly by those in the Vietnamese diaspora. Lee 7, a Vietnamese rapper who has lived most of his life in the German city of Munich, claims to be influenced by the track *Đời Anh Thanh Niên* (Life of a young man) by rapper Khanh Nho, a Vietnamese American from Portland, Oregon. In the track, Khanh Nho refers to the movie *Green Dragon* (2001), directed by Timothy Linh Bui. The movie depicts the experiences of Vietnamese refugees arriving in the United States after the fall of Saigon in 1975. Having himself experienced the hardships of leaving his home country, and being a rightless migrant together with his mother on their journey to Europe, Lee 7 can easily identify with the rap track. In 1997, together with another Vietnamese American rapper named Thai Viet G, Khanh Nho released what is regarded by many as the first Vietnamese rap track, "Vietnamese Gangs." Khanh Nho raps in Vietnamese, while Thai Viet G raps in English, thereby expressing their dual modes of belonging, both to their new home in the United States and to their natal country, Vietnam.

At the end of the 1990s, the first rap crew to form in Vietnam was known as VIETRAPPER.com. Rapper Andreee belonged to this collective. From 2002 to 2005, the rap collective known as Rapclub.com was very active in Hanoi, featuring some of the most well-known Vietnamese rappers, such as Lil'Knight (aka LK). Apart from LK, other members included Eddy Viet, Young Uno, Lil' BK, Chip Nho, and Ca Chep. Together, they formed the main hub of what is referred to as "Northside rap," meaning rap originating from Hanoi and Northern Vietnam, more broadly. By contrast, "Southside rap" refers to rap from Ho Chi Minh City and other cities in southern Vietnam. Southside rap only became prominent in 2006, when the rapper named VTA formed the FanHipHop (FHH) collective (Norton 2015). From 2006 to 2010, GVR became a major collective. While its main protagonists, including Lee 7 and Gizmo, originally come from Northern Vietnam, a rapper named Nah, who collaborated together with Lee 7 on various tracks, as well as a female rapper named Linh Lam, both come from Southern Vietnam. Accordingly, GVR unites rappers from both the North- and Southsides.

The ongoing increase in hip hop collectives shows that hip hop is becoming more and more popular in Vietnam, although they are subject to strict censorship. Rap lyrics that make reference to explicit violence, sex, and sensitive political issues are censored (Norton 2015). This is not surprising given that the first Vietnamese rap track mentioned above made explicit reference to gang violence in the United States. Contributions on "Vietnamese gangs" on the Urban Dictionary website describe them as the most violent gangs with its members carrying weapons. One contribution characterizes "Vietnamese gangs" as consisting of small groups of close friends, being non-territorial, and resolving conflicts with their fists in the first round and with weapons in the second.[6] The trope of violence also shaped imagery of the MCing scene early on. Initially, Vietnamese rap was known to be obscene and insulting. Confrontations between rappers often turned violent (Margara 2014). However, this violent image of Vietnamese rap has recently been challenged by the success of female rappers, such as Suboi. Through their rap lyrics and videos, they appropriate male-dominated hip hop space. Suboi, a 29-year MC from Ho Chi Minh City, has been tagged "Vietnam's queen of Hip Hop" by foreign media. This self-address as "royalty" can often be found among women rappers in the United States. In her analysis of black female identity as expressed through rap performances in the United States, Cheryl Keyes (2004: 266) explains that self-reference as "Queen Mother" is used by female rappers in their lyrics, who consider themselves Africa-centred icons embracing black female empowerment and spirituality. That is how they identify themselves as African, woman, warrior, priestess, and queen. Yet, Suboi does not adopt categorizations derived from United States rap, but instead presents herself with her stage name, which combines "Su," a nickname given to her by her family, with "boi," a name that her friends gave her due to her "tomboyish" nature. She began singing in a high school rock band when she was 15 or 16 years old. After graduating from high school, she became a solo performer as a rapper. Initially, she produced tracks on her own by downloading beats, writing lyrics, and rapping to them. When she turned 19, she signed with a Vietnamese music label called Music Faces, which promoted Vietnamese artists (Viet Talk 2015). Working with the Dutch producer Gremlin, she released her first album *Walk/Bước* in 2010. By 2012, she founded her own company, Suboi Entertainment. Two years later in 2014, she released her second studio album, *Run*, this time only using an English album title. The transition in her album titles from *Walk* to *Run* symbolizes the dynamics of her professional and personal development. Opening her own label, she has become a self-entrepreneur, giving her the freedom to choose her own staff and to write her own lyrics.

---

6   See urban dictionary: http://www.urbandictionary.com/define.php?term=vietnamese
+gang.

Suboi raps both in Vietnamese and English, and claims to be influenced by Eminem, Kendrick Lamar, Will Smith, Erykah Badouh, but also by Le Huu Ha, a Vietnamese composer, and Elvis Phuong, a former star on *Paris by Night*. Having grown up in Saigon, she raps about her childhood, family life, and struggles she faced by not following the "conventional" respectable path for a young urban middle-class Vietnamese woman. Suboi is commercially quite successful, with a recent club tour through the United States.

Apart from commercially successful rappers, MCing is also practiced by young people at home and in public space. On YouTube, several videos have been uploaded showing Vietnamese kids gathering in groups on the streets, especially at popular ice-tea stalls (*trà đá*) where they freestyle rap lyrics. MCing requires the least economic investments for participation, as most young MCs play the music to which they rap on a mobile phone,[7] while in some cases another member might beat box. Moreover, they access the infrastructure necessary to produce rap tracks through digital networks, such as by downloading drum loops and autotunes from the internet (Norton 2015). Other than this minimal technical infrastructure, MCs also require practical knowledge in order to participate in the community of practice. MCing also differs from dancing in terms of the infrastructure necessary to practice rap. While face-to-face interactions in public spaces and dance studios are crucial to the sharing of knowledge and membership in a dance community of practice, rap battles and collectives mostly exist in the digital sphere, connecting actors from places around the world as diverse as Germany, the United States, India, and Vietnam. Nowadays, such connections are mostly built on social media platforms, such as Facebook and YouTube. Before these platforms were available however, the early Viet rappers used to connect via digital platforms such as Soundclick and Forum.

Compared to MCing, graffiti writing only became popular in urban Vietnam much later, beginning in Hanoi between 2002 and 2004. Only later would the arts, including dance practices, move to Saigon (Margara 2011). However, in the early 2000s, only a few pieces and tags marked the urban landscape. When I was living in Hanoi from 2005 and 2006, and again from 2007 to 2008, there was hardly any graffiti to be found in Hanoi's city centre, except for a few tags along Ly Thai To Garden. By contrast, six years later, in 2014 and

---

7   The rate of mobile phone users in Vietnam makes up approximately 139 per cent of the population, with 127,318,045 mobile phone contracts counted in 2012 (Wearesocial 2012).

Piece on a wall in Tay Ho District

Source: Sandra Kurfürst (2018)

2015, graffiti and prints could be found on the walls of Ho Chi Minh City's major streets as well as in the West Lake District of Hanoi. Today, along construction sites and major streets, large pieces can also be detected. Daos501, a popular sprayer from Ho Chi Minh City, explains that soon after graffiti had been introduced to Vietnam, it seemed to disappear again. But around 2008 and 2009, his current crew members increasingly engaged in graffiti writing. In 2009, they founded "The Saigon Projects" to promote graffiti projects. The aim of The Saigon Projects is to connect graffiti practitioners so that they can achieve more visibility in the urban landscape.

Nonetheless, the community of writing practice appears to be much smaller, and expanding much more slowly, than the dancing community. One reason for this might be that the community of practice is still operating in the sphere of informality (as in many other parts of the world). As for breaking, the materiality and accessibility of space matters. Urban space provides the infrastructure for both practices. Yet, while breaking is socially accepted in public space, and tolerated by the late socialist state, drawing in urban space is punishable under the law. Sprayers will have to pay fines of up to 5 to 10 million Vietnamese Dong (177 to 354 Euro) if caught drawing in public (Margara 2011).

A further reason for the different trajectory might be the higher economic and social investments needed in order to participate in graffiti writing. Graffiti requires particular writing materials, such as spray paints and markers, which for a long time were quite difficult to acquire in Vietnam. Even if available, the colours often lacked quality. This changed with the opening of the online store NCStore in 2012, which sells inks, markers, as well as magazines and ballcaps in Vietnam (Margara 2015). Organizing colours and collectives, Vietnamese writers engage in infrastructuring work. Geoffrey Bowker (1994) refers to infrastructuring work as a set of techniques – administrative, social, and technical – that assist completing certain jobs, in fact institutionalizing particular manners of doing things. In the community of writing, infrastructuring work involves both processes of institutionalization and commoditization. First, institutionalization refers to establishing regular meeting points, the exchange of techniques among practitioners, and the organization of graffiti events, such as *Style Jam* organized by The Saigon Projects. Meanwhile, dedicated hip hop dancers have organized dance battles, which have also included graffiti writing sessions. Second, graffiti tools and writing materials are made accessible in Vietnam through the expansion of consumer commodity markets. This process of commoditization involves a social dimension, as well. Members of one crew will chip in on costs in order to purchase the colours (Zink 2013: 109), thus making the practice affordable to all the members.

DJing constitutes an emerging community of practice in Vietnam, comprising music genres as diverse as hip hop, funk, reggae, or electronic music. It is frequently hard to determine the exact music genre played by any given DJ. DJ Jase describes his own sets as eclectic, explaining that he combines a wide range of styles from hip hop and funk to reggae. DJ Tri Minh considers himself a musician rather than an electronic music DJ. He uses traditional Vietnamese instruments that he combines with electro beats and the sounds of the city. Moreover, Tri Minh collaborates with the dancer, teacher, and choreographer, LionT, writing the music for his shows. These two examples allude to the diversity and heterogeneity of music genres practiced in the DJing community.

Together with graffiti writing, DJing requires the greatest economic investments. A prerequisite for DJing is access to and the availability of technical infrastructure. This infrastructure is comprised of turntables, mixers, computers, stereos, and so on. Furthermore, Hip Hop DJs need to have access to a large selection of records. Unlike graffiti, where individuals can share the cost of spray cans in order to reduce the economic burden on the individual, the ownership of records is mandatory for DJs. Even if a DJ is able to afford the records, their availability may still remain a challenge. In 2015, there were only two record stores in Hanoi, of which one had a large collection of jazz rather than hip hop music. In Ho Chi Minh City, several shops including The Tea Time LP, diathan, Giadinh Audio, and a coffee music shop sell vinyl records. These record stores offer jazz, pop, and rock, but hardly any hip hop music. In general, Vietnamese produced records, and particularly of contemporary music records, are very rare. The need for technical infrastructure to practice DJing hints at what Star et al. (2003: 244) refer to as the "convergence" of information artefacts and communities of practice. According to Star et al. (2003: 244), communities of practice and information artefacts will converge if "use and practice fit design and access," as both define each other over time. Convergence denotes their mutual constitution. Put differently, the technical infrastructure becomes part of the practice shared in common.

The institutionalization of the community of practice takes place through the organization of events. In 2007, DJ Jase from Saigon founded his own booking company, Beats Saigon, with the aim of organizing his own parties. Likewise, in 2007, DJ Tri Minh founded the Hanoi Sound Stuff Festival, which brings together local artists as well as DJs and musicians from abroad. Both emphasize the need for innovation in Vietnam's DJing scene. DJ Jase calls on local DJs to engage more with urban genres, such as dubstep, Drum'n'Base, and hip hop. In Hanoi, the Hanoi Rock City venue provides room for musical diversity and innovation (Margara, Van Nguyen 2011).

The term breaking, or breakdance, is commonly used as a proxy for hip hop's dance element. Jeff Chang (2005) notes that, while it is true that breaking developed in the 1970s in particular New York neighbourhoods, half of the dance styles associated with hip hop, such as locking, popping, or waacking, evolved on the West Coast of the United States, and were part of a different cultural movement. In the 1980s, media coverage increasingly lumped the New York-based practices of b-girling/-boying and uprocking together with popping and locking, labelling them all "breakdancing." As a result, the West Coast funk movement was overlooked, as hip hop was publicly viewed as the progenitor of funk.

In Vietnam, a variety of dance styles such as hip hop, house, waacking, popping, locking, and breaking is practiced across the country. While members of the community of practice are certainly aware of the specific styles that they each practice, they subsume these different dance styles under the umbrella term "hip hop." Still, each dance style has been subject to different trajectories of uptake. While breaking and hip hop dance were the first styles to be practiced early in the 1990s, waacking, locking, and house dance were practiced much later, beginning in the 2010s.

Yet, this does not mean that the boundaries between dancers and their dance practices are fixed; rather, the boundaries between styles are permeable and constantly crossed, as dancers search for innovations to create their own unique styles. Many dancers reported that some styles have been practiced for quite some time, but that, early on, most practitioners did not know what movements belonged to which styles. For example, before waacking was known in Vietnam, some dancers would already integrate waacking moves into their dance routines, but without knowing what to call them. Waacking seems to appeal to dancers in Hanoi, as it can be easily combined with moves from other dance styles, such as hip hop or house dance. Likewise, the terms of belonging are not exclusive, meaning that a single dancer can be a practitioner of various dance styles, belonging to various crews and thus participate in different dance battle categories. The b-boy LionT, leader of the famous Big Toe Crew, is recognized as an "OG" of Vietnamese hip hop by dancers from diverse styles. He explains that he does not dance a single style, but rather that he likes to combine different styles. Overall, members of the dancing community refer to hip hop as an umbrella term, referring to *văn hoá hip hop*, hip hop culture. In this sense, hip hop becomes a boundary object, translating between the different dance communities. Susan Leigh Star and James Griesemer (1989: 344) define boundary objects as "objects which are both plastic enough to adapt to local needs and the constraints of the several parties employing them, yet robust enough to maintain a common identity across sites." Boundary objects can be abstract or concrete. Although they have differing meanings in different social worlds, their structure remains common enough to make them recognizable to more than one social world. As a result, they can act as a means of translation. Since practitioners of breaking, popping, locking, waacking, house, and hip hop dance all recognize each other as practicing some kind of hip hop dance, and thus belonging and contributing to hip hop culture in Vietnam, they seek opportunities to collaborate and create common platforms, such as dance festivals and battles, where they can share expertise, knowledge, and learn from one another.

Infrastructures and communities of practice

At the nexus of the postindustrial city, hip hop becomes bound up with technological progress and social marginality (Rose 1994). In this ambivalence, infrastructures are incremental to communities of practice, as they contribute to the production of new identities and subject positions. In rap lyrics, MCs talk about urban infrastructures like subways and streets, as well as urban forms of sociality, such as the crew or posse. Graffiti writers spray walls and tag trains, trucks, and playgrounds, whereas breakers perform power moves on sidewalks, improvising outdoors youth centres. Additionally, DJs tap into public electricity infrastructures by connecting their customized turntables to street lights. The practice of tapping into the electric grid can be understood as a "quiet encroachment of the ordinary," a phrase introduced by Asef Bayat (2004) to capture subaltern politics under conditions of globalization. By "quiet encroachment," he refers to mainly individual, and only episodically collective, actions aimed at fulfilling basic needs. Such actions are driven by existential needs, and are not taken at the costs of themselves or the fellow poor, but of the state, the rich, and the powerful (Bayat 2004: 90). An example would be the urban poor's tapping of municipal power lines in order to achieve access to electricity. While members of the hip hop community in 1970s New York were considered marginal urban dwellers, their actions, such as the encroachment on public infrastructures, occurred with a great deal of publicity. Such publicity was exerted with respect to the soundscapes produced by MCs and DJs, as well as the physical assemblage of dancing bodies in public space. Accordingly, infrastructures become part of a community of practice – and even members, from the perspective of actor-network theory. Without the materiality of public space, the technical equipment of turn tables and amplifiers, downloaded beats and microphones, spray paint, walls and public transport, the communities of practice built up around hip hop's four elements would not be able to exist. These infrastructures facilitate the cultural practices of dancing, DJing, MCing, and graffiti writing, while at the same time helping to sustain the community of practice over time. As most of the practices themselves are of an ephemeral character, the infrastructures render them visible, audible, tangible, and durable.

Dance and Gender

In her essay, "Reprise: On Dance Ethnography," Deidre Sklar (2000) reviews the development of dance ethnography since the appearance of her 1991 article, "On Dance Ethnography," in the *Dance Research Journal*. According to Sklar, two new trajectories have evolved in dance research over the last decade. The first trajectory is sociopolitical, building on ideas from cultural studies. Addressing the sociopolitical dimensions of dance means addressing the social construction of human movement (Reed 1998), as well as the bodily theories through which bodies perform, community, gendered, and individual identities (Foster 1995; Sklar 2000; Reed 1998). In *Feminism and Youth Culture*, Angela McRobbie (1998: 195) goes one step further, calling for a sociology of dance "to step outside the field of performance and examine dance as a social activity, a participative form enjoyed by people in leisure, a sexual ritual, a form of self-expression, a kind of exercise and a way of speaking through the body." The second trajectory is kinesthetic as it draws on ideas in the anthropology of the senses and the phenomenology of the body. With a focus on kinesthesia, scholars seek a deeper understanding of movement as a way of knowing, "a medium that carries meaning in an immediately felt, somatic mode" (Sklar 2000: 70).

This book takes up both strands in dance research, but with a wider focus on the sociopolitical. This focus is grounded in my academic background as a Southeast Asianist educated in sociology. While I am not a professional dancer, hip hop music and dance have had and continue to have a deep impact on my personal life. Research on hip hop, gender, and the city thus combines my personal interest and passion for my previous research on the social production of public spaces in Hanoi. Since conducting my first round of field research in Vietnam in 2006, I have been fascinated with young people dancing on the streets. Accordingly, this book is an attempt to make sense of young people's dancing practices, which they variously conduct indoors and outdoors in Vietnam's main urban centres. Delving into the literature on dance, body, and kinesthesia, and attending a hip hop class and breaking workshop to better understand the meaning-making that occurs in and through dance, this book links the street dance practices of young Vietnamese urbanites to the sociopolitical and economic contexts in which they are acted out.

Dance is precious ground to learn about norms and values, ideas of community and hierarchy, and ways the self is constituted, developed, and cultivated. Social and cultural anthropology in the 20th century was already interested in social and political dimension of dance. In *The Kalela dance: Aspects of social relationships among urban Africans in Northern Rhodesia*, J. Clyde Mitchell (1956) studies kalela dance, a form of dance that became popular in the industrial areas of Central Africa's Copperbelt after 1950. The kalela dance was mostly practiced by men, and was comprised of a fixed set of roles and costumes the performers wore. The dance was accompanied by the chanting of joking rhymes. At that time of Mitchell's study, the Copperbelt attracted members of various sociolinguistic groups from across the region to work in the copper mines. Workers often came from rival groups. Thus, the dancers drew on repertoires of joking relationships between different groups, thereby engaging with extant joking rhymes while inventing new ones. Mitchell employs the analysis of the dance as a method to understand contemporary tribalism and social conflicts.

Decades prior to Mitchell's study, Margaret Mead (1928) dedicated a whole chapter to dance in her monograph, *Coming of Age in Samoa*. For Mead, dance is peculiar as it brings together people from all ages, sexes, and genders. She engages with dance in her analysis of child education, outlining the difference between the dancing child and the child in everyday life. Mead outlines two ways in which dance is significant for the education and socialization of Samoan children. First, dance gives room for children to temporarily overcome the social frame of rigorous subordination in which they find themselves in everyday life. Through dance, children move to the centre of the group, whereas they are normally situated at the social margins. Parents and kin praise their children by emphasizing their superiority over the children of their neighbours or visitors. The emphasis on individuality allows for the recognition of each child regardless of age or sex. Second, the dance reduces the threshold of shyness, as even the shiest child dares to enter the limelight to perform at least some motions. Nonetheless, Mead notices a gender component in dance education, suggesting that these early forms of habituation appear to be more beneficial to boys than to girls. Mead argues that while both genders benefit from dance education, as adolescent girls achieve self-possessed persons on the dancefloor, girls are less easily able to transfer such ease and poise to everyday life, as typically happens for boys (Mead 1928: 117-119). Finally, Mead (1928: 121) emphasizes "the function of informal dancing in the development of individuality and the compensation for repression of personality in other spheres of life." Mead's point that dance is a vehicle for developing and performing individuality and personality highlights a crucial dimension of the sociopolitical function of dance that I examine in this book. In addressing the sociopolitical, researchers seek to "specify whether a dance affirms, resists, re-creates, challenges, undermines, or re-enforces the status quo" or whether it does several of these at once since dance can be an ambiguous social action (Sklar 2000: 70). This book is primarily concerned with the renegotiation of age, social hierarchies, moral personhood, and normative categories of gender through dance as social practice.

In her article, "Engendering Dance: Feminist Inquiry and Dance Research," Jane Desmond suggests that the "key challenge for feminist theorists is to link analyses of ideological production (the meanings attached to gender constructions and their representations) with specific social practices, public discourse, institutional structures, and material conditions" (1999: 316). By ideologies, Desmond means the framing of what is perceived as right and good, true and valuable. Feminist inquiries into dance, therefore, ought to consider dance as a social practice related to more general constructions and representations of gender in particular times and places.

Scholars such as Chandra Mohanty, and Raewyn Connell, among many others, have pointed to the necessity of considering the historical, political, and geographical specificity of gender formations. At the same time, Connell (2014b: 522) urges scholars to apply a "mosaic epistemology," by which she refers to separate knowledge systems or projects that occur side-by-side, like tiles of a mosaic. Each of these conceptions is based on a specific culture, language, religion, and so forth, therefore employing particular terminologies and categories. Each tile has its own terms of validity, and none could or should be taken as a master narrative for the whole world. However, this mosaic approach runs the risk of reproducing a colonial view of foreign tribes and other cultures, "with only the colonizing power having the integrating view" (Connell 2014b: 522). That is why Connell calls on feminists around the world to cross-fertilize their work rather than to keep it separate.

Another crucial point raised by Connell is that the historical and sociopolitical contexts under which theories of gender are produced ought to be scrutinized as well. Research in the sociology of gender developed in the Global North throughout the 20th century. Work by Mohanty, for example, her 1991 essay, "Under Western Eyes : Feminist Scholarship and Colonial Discourses," revealed a colonial gaze that constructed a false image of the "third world woman" (Connell 2014a: 553). In fact, the "colonized world provided raw material for metropolitan feminist debates" (Connell 2014a: 553). The harvesting of representations of the Global South for "data" is not confined to analyses of gender, but accounts for much of the development of social theory generally (Comaroff and Comaroff 2012; Connell 2013; Roy 2009; Roy 2014).

Connell suggests a way out of the dilemma of having to choose between Eurocentric or Northern theory and mosaic epistemology: First, we need to recognize the extent to which feminist thought is embedded in a global economy of knowledge that is structured by inequalities between periphery and metropole. Sujata Patel (2014) highlights the power asymmetries that underlie the academic system of knowledge production. For instance, all of the big publishing houses and major social sciences journals are located in North America and Europe – and almost all of them require publication in the English language. With the rise of neoliberalism in the university sector, scholars located anywhere else in the world are required to comply with the competitive logic of benchmarking and citation indexes, especially if they wish to acquire funding. These power asymmetries in academia have so far resulted in the prevalence of Northern theories. In a similar vein, Roy (2014: 16) draws our attention to the "geography of theory," implying the importance of the provenance of theory, the conditions under which theory travels, and the ways that it exceeds and transforms its "geographic origins." Since knowledge production about the Global South is geographically located in the Global North, Roy (2014: 16) proposes that we interrogate and disrupt such "geographies and methodologies of authoritative knowledge."

Second, Connell (2014b: 522) emphasizes the need to overcome the idea of the periphery, namely the Global South, constituted a site for the harvesting of data, the testing of (Northern) theories, and to recognize the periphery as the site for the production of important and in-depth theory. Naturally, Connell (2014a: 560) does not call for a strict separation of Northern from Southern theories. Rather she suggests an advance beyond Northern gender theories, treating them not so much as frameworks but as resources based on Southern experiences. In fact, creative feminist work from the Global South often critically appropriates Northern ideas, combining them with ideas resulting "from radically different experiences" (Connell 2014b: 527). Such Southern experiences include the disruptions and experiences of colonialism. Argentine feminist philosopher Maria Lugones introduces the concept of the "coloniality of gender," drawing on the Peruvian sociologist Aníbal Quijano's concept of the "coloniality of power." According to Quijano, global and Eurocentric capitalist power is organized along two axes, including the coloniality of power and modernity. The coloniality of power denotes the universal social classification of global populations according to the idea of race, "a replacing of relations of superiority and inferiority established through domination with naturalized understandings of inferiority and superiority" (Lugones 2007: 186). In her essay, "Heterosexualism and the Colonial / Modern Gender System," Lugones criticizes her male colleagues' essentialist concepts of gender. For Quijano, for instance, the struggles over the control of "sexual access, its resources and products" define the domain of sex/gender, while the disputes can again be understood as organized around the aforementioned axes of coloniality and modernity. Lugones argues that gender is socially constructed in the process of colonialism. In other words, colonialism introduced gender, both as a colonial concept, and as a mode for organizing relations of production, property, as well as of ways of knowing implied by different cosmologies (Lugones 2007: 186). Lugones is particularly interested in intersections of race, class, gender, and sexuality with respect to the indifference that "men who have been racialized as inferior, exhibit to the systematic violences inflicted upon women of color" (Lugones 2007: 187).

Ultimately, Connell (2014b: 533) suggests that we recognize the resilience of precolonial gender orders, the gendered history of colonization itself, the impact of the colonized on the colonizers, as well as the complex structures of gender relations in the postcolonial era, which have been documented by Southern scholars. Finally, for Connell, the feminist movements' aim to transform unequal gender relations at a global scale, remains intimately linked to theorizing at a global scale: "The goal is not to write a unified theory of gender, even one compiled from Southern sources. It is to create, within the worldwide counterpublic, processes for mutual learning and interactive thinking about theoretical questions" (Connell 2014b: 539). She concludes that one important step in this direction is to pay tribute, and give centrality, to theoretical work from the South.

Gender in Vietnam

Gender studies is not a new academic field in Vietnam, but has been around for quite some time, as shown by the publication of a classic in Vietnamese gender studies, *Phụ nữ Việt Nam qua các thời đại* (Vietnamese women throughout the last era), which was published in 1973 by female Vietnamese scholar, Le Thi Nham Tuyet. Tuyet draws on a rich set of data comprised of myths, narratives, and folk tales, as well as interviews with women. The book offers a history of women in Vietnam, starting with the pre-modern matriarchy that came to an end with Vietnam's occupation by China in the first millennium AD, which was followed by the oppression of women under French colonial rule, and women's liberation by the Communist Party of Vietnam (Fuhrmann o. J.). The reference to Vietnam's matrilineal past is a recurrent theme in gender studies in particular, but also a general theme in Vietnamese history, as Tuyet shows. The two Trung sisters (*Hai bà Trưng*) are reported to have led a mixed-gender army to liberate Vietnam from Chinese occupation in the first century AD, which is why the Trung sisters are part of the Vietnamese pantheon of heroes. Every middle-sized Vietnamese town has a major street named Hai Ba Trung. But even before the Trung Sisters, Vietnam's founding myth of Au Co is cited as further evidence for the strength and (political) power of Vietnamese women. In the myth, Au Co was a mountain fairy who fell in love with Lac Long Quan, the Dragon God, who resided in the sea. A total of 100 children emerged from their union. Longing to return to the Northern mountain range, Au Co took 50 children with her to the mountains, while Lac Long Quan took the remaining 50 children with him into the sea. The 50 children living with Au Co eventually became the ancestors of the Vietnamese people, known as Hung kings. Both the Trung sisters and Au Co are recurrent figures in Vietnam's history books, folk tales, and contemporary popular culture. For instance, the b-boy LionT, whom I will introduce in chapter 4, "BREAKING," choreographed a dance in 2019 that narrated the myth of Au Co and Lac Long Quan.

However, matriarchal rule in Vietnam is represented as a thing of the past, thereby neglecting the plural histories of the diverse sociolinguistic groups that reside within the territory of the Socialist Republic of Vietnam, such as the Ede or Jarai. The Ede or Jarai are two matrilineal sociolinguistic groups that reside in the Central Highlands of Vietnam (Salemink 2003). However, Vietnamese gender studies mostly focus on the Kinh Vietnamese, while research on the 53 or so other ethnic minority groups that are officially recognized by the Vietnamese government is left to social anthropology departments at Vietnamese universities and research institutions. Leading higher education and research institutions, such as the Vietnam National University or Vietnamese Academy of Social Sciences (VASS), include an institute of gender studies. In Hanoi, for example, VASS has an Institute of Family and Gender Studies. According to the Academy's website, the institute's main tasks are:

> "1) to do theoretical and empirical research on family and gender issues, in order to build scientific grounds for the Communist Party and the State strategy-planning and policy-making; and (2) to provide training and consultancy involved with family and gender matters in Vietnam."

The website thus touches on a major goal for research in Vietnam, which is to provide policy advice. In other words, policy formulation and research are closely intertwined in Vietnam. The mutual engagement of both research and state policy also appears in the way that the social sciences, such as sociology and social anthropology, are particularly inspired by Marxist theoretical work (Evans 1985; Soucy 2000). Research on gender or women's studies is no exception, as both fields are similarly influenced by Marxist thinking, as can be seen in the textbook on the *Sociology of Gender* (*Giáo Trình Xã Hội Học Về Giới*), published by Hoang Ba Thinh in 2008 through the Vietnam National University Publishing House. This textbook draws heavily but not solely on historical materialism, as it also draws on the work of Simone de Beauvoir, Talcott Parsons, and Anthony Giddens (Fuhrmann o. J.). Apart from these Vietnamese-language publications, English-language publications on gender by Vietnamese scholars include *Women and Doi Moi in Vietnam*, published by Tran Thi Van Anh and Le Ngoc Hung in 1997, as well as *Ten Years of Progress: Vietnamese Women from 1985-1995*, published by female academics Le Thi and Do Thi Binh in 1997. Both writings were published by the Women's Publishing House (*Nhà Xuất Bản Phụ Nữ*). The fact that a Women's Publishing House exists in Vietnam alludes to the historical and contemporary prominence of women in Vietnam's political sphere. The capital of Hanoi also houses a Women's Museum and the Vietnam Women's Union, one of five mass organizations in Vietnam that operates at all administrative levels, both at the grassroots level and at the national level by giving policy advice.[8]

---

8   Apart from the Women's Union, the Farmers' Association, Youth Union, War Veterans Association, and the Worker's Organization (VGCL) are mass organizations in Vietnam.

One of the scholars mentioned above, Le Thi, also published the English-language monograph, *Single Women in Viet Nam*, in 2004 with *Thế Giới* Publishers, which is Vietnam's publishing house for English-language books. Le Thi is a professor of philosophy and founding director of the Institute of Family and Gender Studies at VASS (formerly the Center for Family and Women Studies), as well as editor-in-chief of the journal *Science on Women* and the monthly periodical, *Family Today*. Le Thi's work comprises several books related to gender equality, women's employment, marriage, and family. Her monograph on single women touches on a sensitive issue in Vietnamese society, as the family is considered the core of society and key to the economic liberalization of the economy. Consequently, recent work by Vietnamese scholars focuses on the transformation of women's livelihoods and changing gender relations in Vietnam. These scholars examine women's mobility concerning their choice of employment, as more and more women leave their home towns to join the large workforces required by the country's industrial centres and export processing zones. Many women also migrate to cities to work as domestic workers in urban middle-class homes or as urban waste traders (Nghiem 2004; Ngo 2004; Nguyen-Vo 2004; Nguyen 2015; Tran 2004). Due to economic stress, female mobility has been increasingly recognized as a necessity, although women's movement between the home and the work place challenges gendered spatial orientations, leading to other social stressors.

In her analysis of gender relations in Vietnam, social anthropologist Minh Nguyen (2019) establishes a parallel between the gendered domains represented in Bourdieu's Kabyle house with the Vietnamese distinction between inside (*nội*) and outside (*ngoại*). While spatially coded, these terms structure relations across kinship, community, and nation (Harms 2011; Luong 1989). Linguistically, both terms are used to mark kinship terms, as in *ông bà ngoại* and *ông bà nội*, translating into "grandparents on the mother's side" and "grandparents on the father's side." For my own children, the former would refer to the maternal grandparents on my side as (in Vietnamese terms) I entered my husband's family from the "outside," while the latter are the paternal grandparents on their father's side, which is considered the origin of the family, and thus the "inside."

This dichotomy is also expressed in the spatial and semantic construction of the city, as the royal capital of Thang Long Hanoi used to be surrounded by a wall. Those living within the walls (*nội thành*) were considered urbanites, while those residing outside the city walls (*ngoại thành*) were considered villagers. Such division between inside and outside the city continues to have implications today (Kurfürst 2012; for Saigon see Harms 2011). While Doreen Massey (1994) convincingly criticizes the drawing of boundaries to distinguish between inside and outside, as yet another way to construct the opposition between "us" and "them," the inside-outside division has been identified as crucial with respect to terms of belonging and local meaning-making in Vietnam (Harms 2011; Nguyen 2019). The inside is considered the male world of the inherited property, as well as the locus of kinship ties, whereas women are situated outside, but allowed to enter the inner family through marriage. Coming from the outside, women are rendered strange or unknown, and thus in need of domestication as they are taught how to nurture the inside. However, a woman can redefine her role, and thus enhance her status in the inside, by reproducing the inside, as indicated by the Vietnamese idiom of *nội tướng*, which means that a woman is "the general of the domestic space." Men, once again, are in charge of the moral order of the inside, while maintaining relations with the outside (Brandtstädter 2008; Nguyen 2019). This latter relationship to the outside is manifest in men's gendered consumption practices, as well. Nguyen (2019: 135) demonstrates how, among rural migrants to the city, men feel entitled to participate in urban consumption, whereas women would abstain from consumption in the city for the greater good of their family. It is socially acceptable for young men to explore themselves, to try something out before they establish their own family. Women's relations to the urban environment, by contrast, are closely monitored by fellow migrants who reside together with them (Nguyen 2015).

Although women are very active in the labour market, sometimes outdoing their husbands in terms of economic performance, a common discourse in media and popular literature relegates women to the domestic sphere (Nguyen 2015: 191). In this discourse, the socialist state takes on an active role in the construction of gender relations and responsibilities, in fact, promoting women's social role as caretakers and providers for their families. Not only in Vietnam, but elsewhere in the world, states are central issues for feminism, as Bina Agarwal (2003) shows in her research on poor women's politics around land and development in India.

In Southeast Asia, post-independence nation-states sought to control women's bodies, particularly in their reproductive functions, as a means of disciplining citizens. Even in the most loosely-structured social systems, such as Thailand (Embree 1950), the modern nation-state intruded on the private sphere, such as through family planning measures. In New Order Indonesia, women and the family became the focus of the nation's agenda of modernization and development. The state promoted images of modern middle-class women as representing the transformation from tradition to modernity, with the family as the functional unit. The family unit was considered the nucleus of society, charged with providing security, morality, and well-being for its members. In other words, the family became a metonym for the nation as a whole. Images of the sexually desirable modern middle-class woman continue to circulate widely across different media. In fact, female sexuality, by contrast with male sexuality, transgresses the boundaries of private and public, becoming a matter of public concern. Reproduction and the family are sensitive political issues as they are taken to have implications for the future development of the entire nation (Berlant 1998; Brenner 1999).

In Vietnam, the state's Cultured Family Program targeted issues such as health, hygiene, and social conduct generally, as well as women's behaviour in particular. Family planning campaigns advised women about when to marry, what kind of partner to choose, and when to bear children. Richard Quang-Anh Tran (2014: 14) explains that the Cultured Family Program fostered a return to traditional gender norms, re-assigning women to the sphere of domesticity, and requiring them to perform "'feminine' attributes." In her research on domestic workers, Nguyen (2015) shows in detail how female migrants' struggles with motherhood and marriage, as they engage with a gender framework produced by various forces, including the state (Pettus 2003; Barbieri and Bélanger 2009). Nguyen writes: "This framework effectively defines as failed femininity when a woman is not married and without a child, rendering them as unworthy individuals" (2015: 190). Harriet Phinney (2008: 348) concludes that the micro-technologies of the family planning program assisted the state in maintaining its authority, while mostly focusing on women's bodies and sexualities.

An intersectional approach to women's livelihoods, moreover, shows an increasing conflation of class and gender. While the socialist state previously considered working-class women as essential to development, and at the same time endangering such development, the state's focus in the post Doi Moi era has shifted toward disciplined middle-class women. In other words, the state turned from emphasizing female diligence and resourcefulness to promoting the well-educated, nurturing middle-class woman as an aspiration to achieve. The middle-class woman, simultaneously cast as desirable wife and caring mother, is central to the state project of building self-reliant, successful families that are able to provide for and protect their members from the uncertainties and ills of the market economy (Leshkowich 2008: 56;

Nghiem 2004; Nguyen 2015: 183). In explaining women's social roles, both past and present, one recurrent theme in gender studies, both in and outside of Vietnam, is the reference to Confucian principles, such as the "Three Submissions" (*tam tòng*) and the "Four Virtues" (*tú đúc*). Such principles almost invariably depict and define women's social roles in relation to men. According to the Three Submissions, women must obey the father until marriage, obey the husband during marriage, and obey the son after the husband's death. The Four Virtues, in turn, define the norms for women's labour (*công*), appearance (*dung*), speech (*ngôn*), and conduct (*hạnh*). Women ought to be skilled at cooking and housekeeping (labour), be physically attractive to one's husband (appearance), use a humble and submissive communicative repertoire and voice (speech), and, finally, embody female integrity by presenting obedience to seniors and the husband (conduct) (Khuat, Le and Nguyen 2009; Ngo 2004). These norms function as a cultural matrix against which the ideal woman is defined and evaluated. While in reality, these ideals have more often than not been and remain undermined, these norms of feminine virtue persist and inform discourses about cultural ideals of femininity (Endres 2008: 48). Yet, rather than applying categories such as the ideal Vietnamese women – which in itself is a construct – Minna Hakkarainen (2018) suggests that analysts trace such notions as socio-historical products of particular social relations at particular times, which serve the interests of those in power. Hakkarainen (2018: 47) considers the narrative of the ideal woman as an attempt to present homogeneity where there is none, and as a means for controlling female behaviour.

In sum, women in late socialist Vietnam must navigate ambivalent roles and pressures placed on them. On the one hand, female bodies are increasingly commodified, creating the "desire to become 'marketable' or 'sexually desirable'" among women, both across classes as well as in both rural and urban areas (Nghiem 2004: 312). On the other hand, women as caretakers and family providers remain doubly responsible for earning an income to support the family while caring for children and the elderly. However, these gendered expectations and responsibilities are differently dealt with, and frequently contested, according to class, ethnic, and spatial imaginations of the rural and the urban, resulting in multiple femininities.

In Vietnam's cities, as is the case in many places elsewhere around the world, women move outwards, appropriating public spaces for social, private, and economic activities. For instance, women open small food and drink stalls on sidewalks, engage in leisure activities like snacking on the streets, meeting friends for coffee, or participating in outdoor aerobics classes, among other things. Liz Bondi (2005: 6) alludes to the potential of the city for the reworking of gender norms, defining cities as "places where embodied meanings and experiences of gender are not necessarily reproduced according to dominant norms, but can be challenged, reworked and reshaped." Female dancers make use of the opportunities offered in urban spaces, dancing along Ly Thai To Garden, the Lenin Monument, or the Soviet Vietnamese Friendship Palace in Hanoi. Unlike the female migrant workers depicted by Nguyen (2019), dancing women's consumption is not directed inward, but rather directed outward, as they participate in urban leisure activities, such as going out eating and drinking, or dancing late at night. What is more, these women perform an elevated status by investing and dressing in hip hop apparel, including branded products. Overall, they constantly permeate and re-work the boundaries between private and public, and femininity and masculinity through bodily performance.

Feminist theorists have shown great interest in the corporeality of the female body and embodiment (Butler 1990; Irigaray 1979). The reading of a person as feminine or masculine often occurs according to gestures and bodily movements. Such gendered assessments are particularly prevalent in dance:

> "Dance, as a discourse of the body, may in fact be especially vulnerable to interpretations in terms of essentialized identities associated with biological difference. These identities include race and gender and the sexualized associations attached to bodies marked in those terms, as well as national or ethnic identities when these are associated with racial notions, as they so often are." (Desmond 2006: 37)

As a result, the sexualized associations attached to bodies are an important point of inquiry when considering the socio-politics and body politics of dance. The aesthetics of different dance styles are most often assigned to binary gender categories. In fact, the aesthetics of many dance styles presented in this book, particularly breaking and popping, are associated with energetic male bodies. One exemption is the style of waacking, whose postures and gestures reference the style's queer history.

Yet, once again, we must recognize the provenance of theory (Roy 2014), acknowledging the Eurocentric discourses represented in many gender theories that are taught at many universities in Europe and North America (Connell 2014a), including my own. Therefore, let me return to an example from elsewhere in Southeast Asia. In her analysis of the theatrical form of *randai* in

Minangkabau culture, Mahjoeddin (2016) likewise attributes gender relations
to bodily aesthetics. In the *ulu'ambek*, which is an esoteric form of the *silek*
martial art, there is a particular preparatory movement repertoire that is associated with the feminine principle of *batino* (Kamal and Mahjoeddin 2016).
In Minangkabau society, batino signals an "equal, but different" relationship
to the male, as Mahjoeddin writes: "This gender attribution is indicative of
the equal value and durational space provided for the feminine, non-potent
aspect of a performance that accommodates receding as well as intensifying
energies" (2016: 364). What is striking about Minangkabau culture, as a matrilineal society, is not only the existence of the term *batino* to describe the
relationship between sexes, but that the aesthetics of a performative form are
ascribed to the sphere of women, rather than men. For the Mother Goddess
religion in Vietnam, ethnomusicologist Barley Norton (2006) has noted the
gendered performance of spirit mediums. In the rituals of the *lên đồng* cult,
the spirit medium adopts different clothing, mannerisms, ways of speaking,
and ways of dancing for each spirit. Such performative vocabulary is highly
informed by the spirit's gender – male or female. Norton points out the particular relevance of dance for gender performativity, since the assessment of
the spiritual medium's dance aesthetic occurs according to the gender of the
embodied spirit. It is evident from the vibrancy of mediums' dances and the
excited reaction they usually receive from ritual participants—especially when
the medium performs a spirit of the opposite gender—that dancing is one of
the main ways that mediums articulate the character and gender of spirits.
Ritual participants consider the music and dances of female spirits to be more
"fun" *(vui)* and "lively" *(linh hoạt/ sôi nổi)* when compared with the "majestic" *(oai
nghiêm)* dances of male spirits (Norton 2006: 65).

In her monograph *Embodying Morality*, Helle Rydstrøm (2003) shows how,
in a rural commune located in Northern Vietnam, femininity and masculinity
are performed through body styles. She describes broad and sweeping movements that take up more physical and social space as bodily manifestations
of masculinity. Girls, in turn, are taught to refrain from broad movements, as
well as from expressing emotions in public. Outbursts of anger – and showing
any emotion generally – are not associated with femininity, and are reserved
for those who orchestrate and thus dominate social interactions. Additionally,
female morality and *tình cảm* "proscribe shouting, swearing loudly, kicking
things, or walking angrily around in the abrupt ways that are connected with
being 'hot-tempered'" (Rydstrøm 2003: 142-143). Spiritual mediums of the *lên
đồng* ritual adhere to those body styles, which are read as masculine or fem-

inine. Nonetheless, the ritual performance opens possibilities for reworking and undermining gendered appraisals of body styles depicted above, and thus for performing gender fluidity.

On writing dance

Both theoretically and methodologically, the issue of writing dance has been a recurrent trope in dance research. Scholars particularly refer to the difficulties to translating somatic knowledge into words, as well as the difficulty of capturing simple dance gestures in critical literary texts (Coros 1982; DeFrantz 2016; Sklar 2000). Fiona Buckland (2002) begins her book, *Impossible Dance*, by pointing to the near impossibility of textually representing improvised social dance, as it defies any discursive description. Historian Susan Leigh Foster (1995) proposes a different relationship between dancing and writing, suggesting that the body is not only capable of producing practices, but also of generating ideas, which she describes with the term "bodily writing." Consequently, Foster calls for verbal discourse to enter into dialogue with bodily discourse, as an "ambulant form of scholarship" (Foster 1995: 9, 16). During my field work, Foster's gesture toward such dialogue came to life when my colleague from the University of Humanities and Social Sciences in Hanoi suggested that we organize a workshop in which both academics and dance groups would participate. On his request to partake in such a workshop, the dancers suggested that they would not know how to present, and instead suggested that we visit their gathering site, watch them dance, and ask questions *in situ*. We followed their suggestion and participated in the popping battle at Ho Thanh Cong, which will be presented in chapter 5, "POPPING." Sklar (2000) also suggests that verbal and somatic experience do not categorically exclude one another, but rather that they are part of the same epistemological process of meaning-making and body-making. Sklar concludes that the transformative effects of movements can be verbally enacted, since words can evoke somatic reverberations.

Besides bodily writing, autoethnographic performance can become a way to communicate bodily texture. Tami Spry (2006: 206) describes autoethnographic performance as "the convergence of the 'autobiographic impulse' and the 'ethnographic moment' represented through movement and language in performance." Autoethnography is informed by research on personal narratives in performance and communication studies, in which the socio-politically inscribed body becomes the central locus of meaning-making (Langellier 1989; Madison 1993; Spry 2006). In *Autoethnography as Method*, Heewon Chang (2016) identifies two academic strands in autoethnography, the analytic, theoretical, and objective approach to autoethnography, on the one hand, and a more emotionally engaging, subjective mode of autoethnography, on the other. Chang refers to autoethnography as the combination of cultural analysis and interpretation with narrative details, considering autoethnography as both a method and literary text woven together out of diverse interdisciplinary praxes (Chang 2016; Reed-Danahay 1997). Spry (2006), for instance, combines qualitative data with personal accounts, while including creative writing in her text, such as poems or prose, thus arriving at a combination of analysis and self-observation. As a consequence, autoethnographic performance can be a means for rhythmically adjusting word play to body movement, and thereby an approach to the somatic and kinesthetic modes of knowledge production in dance. Consequently, this book combines autoethnographic accounts of hip hop dance and sensory ethnography, with narrative and semi-structured interviews as well as digital ethnography.

A sensory approach to dance and martial arts has proven useful in the field of sonic and kinesthetic research. In his research on capoeira, Greg Downey (2005) shows that more than one sense is involved in different ways of learning and knowing, particularly as he learned to listen to the rhythms of capoeira while engaging in its bodily practices. For the Indonesian martial art *pencak silat*, Jean Marc De Grave (2011) shows that learning *pencak silat* rests on the education of the senses. Drawing on the Javanese hierarchy of the senses, De Grave differentiates between four peripheral or external senses, including smell, hearing, sight, and taste, and the central sense, the inner feeling (*rasa*). According to De Grave (2011: 214), *rasa* comprises everything that can be felt and perceived within the body. *Rasa* combines sensations of the skin and proprioception, as well as feelings and emotions. As the work by De Grave (2011), as well as Howes and Classen (1991), has shown, other cultures have sense systems that may result in the emphasis of the senses or on a different number of the senses altogether. In order to overcome the cultural bias in the researcher's sensory perception, Sarah Pink (2015: 60) suggests that it is important to acknowledge one's own "sensory situatedness" before entering the field, starting with an inquiry into one's own personal sensory culture. In a similar vein, Regina Bendix (2006: 8) argues for "sensory reflexivity," meaning that the ethnographer needs to develop a reflexive appreciation of her own sensorium.

Sensory participation goes beyond interviewing and observing, rather entailing co-presence in a shared physical environment, as well as sensory apprenticeship through actual engagement "in the activities and environments we wish to learn about that we come to know them." (Pink 2015: 105). This is why Pink (2015) proposes autoethnography as a way for assessing the ethnographer's own sense system, as well as to be open to other forms of sensations experienced by the participants of our research. Tim Ingold (2000) and Sarah Pink (2015) agree that the sense system in many parts of the Global North is based on the traditional five senses, which largely ignores the importance of kinesthesia. However, kinesthesia is different from the other five senses, since this mode of sense production occurs in movement, and thus differs from the modes of reception associated with the five senses. If we engage in painting kinesthetically but review the product of our efforts visually, or if we produce sounds through the kinesthetic movements of our muscles but hear the outcomes of such movements aurally, these movements are distinct as they are primarily received by the person in movement (Sklar 2000).

Personal experiences of movement, and the analysis thereof, can become an avenue for identifying larger patterns of social meaning embodied in dance, both symbolic and somatic (Ness 1992; Novack 1990; Sklar 2000). According to Sklar (2000), there is no other way to make sense of other actors' somatic knowledge than for the researchers to experience movements through their own bodies. Sklar points to the importance of proprioception, which refers to the awareness of stimuli produced by one's own body. Proprioceptive awareness, then, refers to apprehending "as felt experience, the kinetic dynamics inherent in movements, images, and sounds" (Sklar 2000: 72). These considerations informed my decision to participate in a breaking workshop and hip hop class. By 2016, I had already participated with some of my students in a breaking workshop at a local youth centre in Cologne. I was pregnant with my second child at the time when I learned basic footwork, and I was both surprised and fascinated by the physical exhaustion.

To the extent that it was possible to plan my research in Vietnam ahead of time, I resolved to participate in a hip hop class during my research. As I had been following Vietnamese hip hop for more than 10 years, I was also determined to meet Mai Tinh Vi after I arrived in Hanoi in autumn 2018. I had learned that Mai Tinh Vi was one of the most popular female hip hop dancers in Vietnam, and I hoped to be one of her students. I was lucky when Mai Tinh Vi announced that she would start teaching a hip hop class around the time of my arrival in Hanoi. Over the last decade, dance studios offering hip hop, popping, girl style, waacking, and sexy dance classes have expanded rapidly in Hanoi. I will discuss the inflation of dance classes that cater to growing middle class demand in the chapter "SELF-ENTREPRENEURISM AND SELF-FASHIONING." For now, I would like to share some insights from my own participation in Mai's hip hop class.

Every three months, Mai Tinh Vi starts teaching a new beginner's class. The class that I joined began in the first week of October, just as I arrived in Hanoi. Originally, the class was scheduled to start during the last week of September, but the start was postponed for one week due to *Trung Thu*, the mid-autumn Festival. The class takes place every Tuesday and Friday from 6:30 to 7:30 p.m. The fee for one month is 17 € or 43 € for three months. It is also possible to join a class for a single day for a fee of 4 €. Mai collects the fee in cash after the first lesson, writing down each student's name, phone number, and other contact information in her notebook. The class takes place in Cun Cun Studio on Thai Thinh Street in Hanoi's Dong Da District. Cun Cun is the name of Mai's first dance crew. Together with other crew members, Mai rents a room on the first floor of a residential building.

I had initially chosen the location of my residence due to its proximity to Thai Thinh Street. However, I soon realized that I had underestimated rush hour, although I had been to Hanoi several times. Thus, during my first evening commuting to the dance studio via taxi, I learned that the route from my family's apartment to the studio could take anywhere between 40 minutes to one hour. On the first evening that I attended Mai's class, I got out of the taxi in front of a restaurant to search for the entrance to the studio. To the right of the restaurant entrance, a little alley leads through a garage that opens to a courtyard in the back, where there is a staircase that leads to the studio on the first floor of the apartment building. The garage entrance is monitored by a guard, as is often the case in Hanoi, who sits on a small chair in the front. Loud hip hop beats resonate through the courtyard, as the lesson has already started upstairs.

As I reach the first floor, Mai stands with her back to a large mirror, facing the group of students moving in front of her. I immediately recognize the rose-painted wall from the videos Mai posts on Facebook, with the Cun Cun Logo on the righthand side. On the left side, windows open to the courtyard. A fan pulls fresh air through the open windows into the room. On the opening day, 10 students were present, with a slightly higher number of young women than men, as well as one little girl. The next class on Friday that same week was more crowded with 14 participants, eight of them female. The little girl was joined by a little boy, who wore an XL Jordan jersey as well as an earring. The two children were accompanied by the girl's mother, who sat waiting for them in the back of the room with her tablet. Most of the students are young men and women around the age of 20. Some joined the class as groups of friends, such as one group of three consisting of a boy and two girls, who regularly attend class and always stand next to each other during practice. The boy and one of the girls wear matching t-shirts, which read "dance team." Others join the class individually, including a young 25-year-old woman, who joins the class for the first time. She usually practices the Korean martial art, *taekwondo*, and chose to join Mai's class due to her well-known reputation as a skilled dancer. The young women mainly dress in black tights, sneakers (e.g., white Adidas), and some wear t-shirts tied just above their belly buttons. One of the girls has a navel piercing. Another young woman with short dyed hair always wears wide trousers and long blouses, and hiking boots instead of sneakers. Mai herself always wears wide trousers or sweatpants, sneakers, and a t-shirt. Once she wore a white t-shirt with the Big Toe Crew logo printed on the back, which read "founded in 1992," and sometimes she wears a scarf wrapped around her head or a slider cap.

Mai always takes her spot in the front of the room, in front of the mirror, next to the technical infrastructure. The music is played from a boom box. Mai prepares the music in advance for each lesson, playing a mix tape of U.S. rap music. While I recognize most of the tracks, the track *Hypnotize* by The Notorious B.I.G. (1997) takes me back into my own teenage years. The music is mostly adapted to the dance steps that Mai teaches. On rare occasions, the beats and movements do not quite fit, so Mai fast forwards the music. Verbal interludes are common in rap tracks, making it difficult to dance, particularly for beginners, so Mai also fast forwards the tapes in these cases, too. In general, the class's soundscape consists of hip hop music, the fans circulating the air, occasional street noise, and Mai's verbal instructions, in particular her beat counting. Between teaching particular moves, Mai also talks about the postures particular to hip hop's different dance styles, such as popping, waacking, locking, and breaking. In the first lesson, she introduced students to groove and grooving – using the English term, while spelling it in Vietnamese. She explains that not every groove is the same and everyone can develop their own grooving style. In the first lesson, she also introduces students to the cypher, the circular organization of hip hop dance, supporting her verbal descriptions with hand gestures: With one hand she traces a circle in the air, while pointing with her finger into the middle of the other hand. She then turns to a particular move, introducing us to footwork: She brings her toes together, so that they point at each other. Then, standing on her heels, she moves the toes outwards. Returning her weight to her toes, she brings her toes together once again. In the next step, she shows us how to slide along the floor without entirely lifting our feet from the floor: the right foot turns rightward, while the left foot moves along its tip-toe to the right, in order to shift the left toe that bears our body weight back to the left.[9] She gives us some time to practice on our own. As I have a hard time mimicking her movements, she shows me how to exercise the move properly, standing right beside me. She then turns to the others, moving through the class room, watching the students' foot work, giving them verbal advice, performing the move once again herself, while carefully touching the student's arm or leg. She repeats this procedure throughout all of the classes. First, she performs a move herself, standing in front of the group, supplementing her bodily per-formance with verbal instructions. Second, she gives the students room to practice the new move themselves, while watching them from the front or circulating about the classroom. Third, she resumes her position in front of the mirror, facing the class, and starts counting 4, 5, 6, 7, and then on 8, the whole class collectively performs the newly learned move. Fourth, she turns around to merge with the group, performing the moves with the students from her exposed position in the front, aiming to synchronize the individual bodies into a collective body. Fifth, she turns around to face the class again, explaining with both voice and body what the students are to pay attention to in order to exercise a particular move correctly. For instance, she reminds us to keep our knees together when bowing down, because we would otherwise not be able to get up.

We learned to nod with our head (to the front, right, back and left), and we continued training with our upper body. She let us groove. We had to bring our chests and knees together. She corrects me while I try, because my knees are too high – a habitual movement I learned from aerobics, in which you are supposed to bring your knees as high up as possible. I should bring my upper body lower, to meet the knees in the middle. I am happy that I can do the motion, but I do not always manage to do the steps in sync with the rhythm of the music. She has us practice some steps, back and forth, in the group, as

---

9   I recorded this movement in my notebook immediately after class, and practiced the moves again in front of my desk while writing this book, as I grappled with the difficulty of writing dance.

she counts to eight. We then do these steps in combination with those that we learned the first day, bringing together the toes and heels. I am happy because I can do the movement. I practiced the move two days before when we hung out at Ly Thai To. I was very proud. We then did the next move – something like a moonwalk – comprised of moving to the side (first left, then right), anchoring the big toe of the left foot and the heel of the right foot, while moving to the right and then the other way around.

During the one-hour class, Mai integrates times for relaxation. For example, she calls for a small break, telling everybody to drink some water – all the students bring their own. Moreover, between learning new steps, Mai invites the students to groove. These were my favourite parts of the lessons, as the point was to release anxiety and just relax. This was particularly important during my first lesson, as I felt like a loser, unable to correctly perform the steps. However, I was relieved to find that I was not alone, as other students had trouble, too. During a break in the first lesson, one girl says to another, "so difficult" (khó lắm). After my first beginner's class with Mai, she invited me to stay for her advanced class. I answered that I worried that I would get completely lost, to which she laughed and said, "Just have fun," as fun is what Mai experiences when dancing. Seeing Mai dancing, her face and body express passion and joy.

Mai is very friendly with her students, laughing a lot during class. When teaching, Mai hardly uses any first-person pronouns to address the class. When addressing her students, showing them how to perform particular moves, she uses expressions and terms such as bọn lớp mình (my class), mình (us), bạn (friend). She explains that her class participants usually refer to her as chị (elder sister), and she in return addresses them using the term em (younger sister/brother). Even the mother of the little girl, who is older than Mai, addresses her using the politer term chị, although, according to conventions for age difference, she should address Mai as em. While Mai linguistically constructs a classroom of peers or friends, she nonetheless demonstrates that she is in charge when disciplining the students. For example, when the two children refuse to continue practicing, she scolds them and asks them to sit in the back of the room. If a student arrives extremely late, she comments on their late arrival in front of the class. However, when students need advice concerning a dance move, she encourages them to continue trying, standing by their side to help them.

The beginner's class is followed by an advanced class from 7:30 to 8:30 p.m. on Tuesdays and Fridays. While we are still practicing, the members of the advanced class usually enter, standing or dancing at the periphery of the room while waiting for us to finish. Once again there are usually more young women than men, but they are all similarly dressed, since hip hop apparel is mostly unisex. Thao, a female student with short hair like Mai, also wears a cap. Two other women wear school uniform t-shirts, while a young man wears a bandana around his head. The students all seem to know each other and Mai quite well. The atmosphere is less formal and the class members appear more comfortable with each other while waiting at the margins of the beginner class. Following Mai on social media, I notice that two of them are regular co-performers with Mai, as they take photos and shoot videos together, posting them on Facebook and Instagram.

The idea of "each one teach one" is also embodied by members of the advanced class. As one girl watches me have trouble performing a particular move, she grabs my arm, instructing me to watch her. She performs the steps several times, inviting me to mimic her movement. Each time I perform the move correctly, she signals with a thumbs up. Sharing advice and helping others improve and develop their dance through touch, gesture, and verbal advice or encouragement all demonstrate that dance is not only a physical activity, but relational and affective as well (Hamera 2007).

After attending my first hip hop class with Mai, I wrote into my field diary:

"I really sweat although I felt I did not move too much. I felt uncomfortable as I was not able to follow through the choreography (which I know of former experiences in aerobic classes in my fitness club). But in the end when we just grooved and the music was playing loud and we could practice some of the moves we had learned in the lesson, I felt that it was really great moving with the beat. When I hear the music, I want to move to it, even if it is not within the choreography. When I arrive home, I feel hungry and physically a little bit exhausted."

"In movement one does and feels oneself doing at the same time," thus creating an ultimate intimacy (Sklar 2000: 72). Since it is difficult to record and dance at the same time, I chose to focus on my movements and the music during class, recording recollections of my sensory perceptions with voice recordings immediately after class. The taxi or motorbike ride home to our apartment gave me enough time to record my sensations, emotions, and my physical exhaustion – evident from the shortness of breath in my recordings.

Dance biographies

Much writing in popular music is biographical, whether biographies of others or of the author herself. This seems particularly relevant in accounting for anti-establishment music, such as punk and hardcore, which by its very nature questions the legitimacy of institutions (Attfield 2011). According to Roy Shuker (2005: 22), biographies in the study of popular music tend to be particularly useful for the "construction and maintenance of fandom." In this context, autobiography becomes an important source of data generation and interpretation. For this purpose, I conducted semi-structured and narrative interviews with female dancers. In her research on female spirit mediums, anthropologist Kirsten Endres (2008: 36) considers "narrated life stories are an intriguing resource for the analysis of the dialogic construction of self and the social world." With the practice theoretical turn, anthropology's interest in life history and biography has shifted from uncovering "culturally specific selves," considered stable and enduring, toward understanding how individuals "struggle to constitute themselves as particular kinds of actors and persons vis-à-vis others within and against powerful sociopolitical and cultural worlds," and how these individuals reciprocally shape the social worlds they inhabit (Endres 2008: 35; Skinner et al. 1998: 3, 5).

Mai not only became my teacher, but once she understood my motivation for taking her class, she generously shared her knowledge and experiences as a b-girl, and female hip hop and house dancer in Vietnam. She also introduced me to other female dancers whom she thought could represent a particular style and who were well-known in the community of practice. I accompanied the female dancers to their classes and battles and conducted narrative interviews with them. All the dancers I talked to welcomed and supported my research in every possible way, and I am thankful for their cordial support. Aware of Vietnam's marginal position in the global hip hop industry, they were quite fond of letting the world know that hip hop is alive and well in Vietnam. Consequently, it was quite easy to legitimate my research for those who participated in my research. I borrow the term research "participants" from Sarah Pink (2015), who suggests a collaborative and reflexive approach to sensory ethnography, rather than treating interviewees as objects of research. Moreover, Pink considers a sensory approach to interviews as resonating with feminist methodologies, while Rubin and Rubin (2011: 21) argue that qualitative interviews allow interlocutors to talk back and even contest cultural assumptions that may be implicit in the questions. Such a sensory approach to interviews requires researchers to reflect on their own emotions, as well.

Moreover, Pink conceptualizes the interview as a "multisensory event," referring to the multiple modes and media that are engaged in processes of meaning-making. The multisensoriality of interviews was particularly striking to me when research participants started to make clicking sounds, buzzing a melody, clapping their hands in a particular rhythm, while expressing their emotions with facial gestures. Often while sitting and talking, their affection was accompanied by a clapping hand or a movement of the head or their entire body. In other words, the performing body becomes a part of the interview itself, signifying embodied ways of knowing (Hymes 1957). The use of such non-verbal communication in interviews allows researchers to include socially marginalized forms of knowledge and communication, as called for by feminist research (Pink 2015: 79). However, in dance, research into such non-verbal communication was not limited to female dancers only. The interview with b-boy LionT was a real multi-sensory event, involving listening, watching, and tasting, as we had lunch together. He frequently demonstrated his opinion about, affection for, or refusal of something by making impressive, sometimes theatrical, movements of his facial muscles.

Since dance is so thoroughly embodied, it is difficult to dislocate any discussion of dance from the actual practice of dancing itself. Thus, my research participants would constantly search for photos and videos on their mobile phones to illustrate what they were talking about. Rather than using elicitation techniques in which I might show objects and artefacts to invoke memories, knowledge, and emotions, the research participants themselves referred to information artefacts to help bring me into their social world. When talking about a particular dance event, a battle, choreography, or music and sound, they would frequently pull out their mobile phones, playing a video or mp3 to show me what they meant. Taken together, the multisensoriality of the interview really challenged my method of recording. I soon realized that voice recordings were insufficient to record and archive research data. This is why I chose to take extensive notes during interviews, tried to mimic non-verbal sounds dancers made while transcribing interviews, and spent time doing internet research to find the videos and music they played during interviews.

During the interviews, I could relate to female research participants by sharing my own experiences with the uplifting power of hip hop during my teenage years. Growing up in a middle-sized town in Western Germany during the 1990s, I found hip hop very empowering. At the age of 15 or 16, German hip hop was on the rise, and I either listened with friends or by myself to American and German rap, sometimes starting a cypher ourselves. The 1990s was also the time of great female rappers, such as Queen Latifah, MC Lyte, Laurin Hill, Foxy Brown, or Lil' Kim in the U.S. and Schwester S. or Cora E. in Germany.

Gender politics are essential to the development of hip hop (Rose 1994). In recent years, hip hop feminists have reexamined women's relationships to hip hop culture, seeking to redefine discourses about women in hip hop. Much of the work of hip hop feminism has focused on rap (Johnson 2014). This book departs from the typical focus on verbal expression to highlight the performativity of embodied practices. In fact, the contestation of a male-dominated and defined sphere has taken place on the ground, right from the start. The earliest b-girls in the U.S. included Headspin Janet, Suzy Q, Sista Boo, Chunky, Pappy, Yvette, and Baby Love, along with the Shaka Zulu Queens and the Dynamic Dolls.[10] The well-known Rock Steady Crew always had female breakers. While these b-girls started out dancing in the U.S., roughly between 1974 and 1984, and thus in the early years of breaking, they have not received much attention either in the hip hop community or from scholars. In fact, the smaller number of b-girls compared to b-boys resulted from social constraints, camouflaged as physical constraints, placed on young women (Johnson 2014: 17). In effect, male peers defined movements adequate for women. For instance, girls would often refrain from engaging in power moves, such as the head spin, and instead would partake in popping, locking, or the electric boogie – all styles that are performed while standing, rather than going to the ground. Tricia Rose (1994) notes how girls were discouraged from practicing break moves because some male peers considered them "'unsafe' or 'unfeminine'."Moreover, women who performed such moves, sometimes in conventionally feminine ways, were considered masculine and thus "undesirable," or, on the contrary, sexually "available." This leads Imani Kai Johnson (2014: 18) to conclude: "That b-girls were discouraged from learning these moves speaks to the way in which cultural gender politics shaped the limited ways that b-girls were encouraged to participate."

Interestingly, a discursive shift took place in the 1990s. At least in the U.S., a move away from the focus on gender politics to a focus on training occurred.

---

10   The Shaka Zulu Queens and the Dynamic Dolls are the female counterparts to the well-established all-male crews of the Mighty Zulu Kings and the Dynamic Rockers respectively.

While b-girls did not receive respect equal to their male counterparts, the scope for women's participation in breaking widened. At this time, prominent b-girls such as Rokafella, Honey Rockwell, and Asia One became famous. They eventually became leaders in the breaking community and continue to perform alternative femininities in hip hop in particular, and for broader society in general (Johnson 2014). They are joined by dancers around the globe, reworking gendered expectations about women's bodily movements and postures, and gender norms and expectations toward female bodies.

In this book, I use a multilevel approach that aims to ground the local bodily practices of female Vietnamese hip hop dancers within larger cultural and political movements (Ortner 2006). Such larger movements concern hip hop feminism and the queer movement challenging male dominance and homophobia in hip hop culture on a global scale.

Urbanism and Hip Hop Communities of Practice

The spatiality of hip hop offers interesting insights into the dynamics of the city, as they are closely related to territory. According to Tricia Rose (1994: 25), the development of hip hop is bound up with the postindustrial city of New York. John Mollenkopf and Manuel Castells (1991) adopt the term "postindustrial" to describe transformations occurring with respect to employment away from manufacturing toward corporate, public, or non-profit services, and the concomitant transformation of workers from industrial manual labourers to professionals, service workers, and the like. Under postindustrial conditions, Rose refers to global forces that continue to shape the contemporary urban metropolis. While Rose explicitly refers to the United States, much of those socioeconomic forces restructuring urban America since the 1970s are operative elsewhere in more recent years, including in Vietnam. Progress in telecommunications, the new international division of labour, the increasing power of finance over production, and migration patterns are all forces relevant to the shaping and restructuring of urban space in Vietnam.

After phases of de-urbanization in Hanoi, and zero urban growth in Ho Chi Minh City (Murray and Szelenyi 1984), Vietnam's cities became the primary sites of rural-urban migration. The implementation of the Doi Moi economic reform program by the VI Party Congress in 1986 initiated the development of a private sector economy as well as Vietnam's integration into the world economy. In order to attract foreign direct investment, the government fostered the development of industrial zones on the peripheries of the country's major cities. Vietnam soon replaced China as a production site for labour-intensive export industries due to low wage levels. Today, Vietnam is an important site of production for the international garment, textile, and footwear industry. In recent years, more and more companies specializing in electro-technics moved to Vietnam, with one prominent example being Samsung, which manufactures parts for mobile phones. Of course, the development of an export-oriented economy requires a large work force. The relaxation of the household registration system, which used to regulate access to employment and social services, particularly resulted in the more or less free choice for citizens to choose their employment and residency. Vietnam's capital Hanoi, and the economic hub of Ho Chi Minh City (formerly Saigon) in the south, have become particularly densely populated, as these cities expand into the hinterland due to the high influx of new residents. Additionally, public-private partnerships as well as transnational enterprises participate in the overheated real estate market, shaping and restructuring the urban built environment.

In recent years, an active public sphere has emerged in both cities, negotiating urban redevelopment between the private sector and the state, frequently succeeding in putting contested development projects on hold (Gillespie and Nguyen 2018; Kurfürst 2012; Labbé 2011). The country's rapid economic development resulted in social stratification with an emerging urban middle class. Social security is on the state's agenda, but state measures so far only consist of health insurance, maternity protection, and accident insurance. What is more, a great portion of the population, particularly those working in the informal economy and ethnic minorities living in the highlands, remains excluded from the social security system. In Hanoi and Ho Chi Minh City, growing inequalities materialize in infrastructural development, particularly residential areas. Erik Harms (2016: 5, 21) captures the development trajectory in the idioms of "luxury" and "rubble." Luxury refers to the spaces of exclusive spectacle, where residents claim the importance of "civility" – a form of citizenship that ultimately hinges on the exclusion of others. Rubble, conversely, implies the devastation, displacement, and eviction that accompany urban redevelopment under capitalism, leaving undercompensated those who are dispossessed from development sites for the greater good of capitalist profit maximization. Jenny Mbaye (2014: 402) ultimately links the spatial practices of hip hop to experiences of social and urban marginality, defining hip hop in cities of the Global South as "political action redefining the spatial structure and the social order of the city." In other words, hip hop seeks to reclaim urban terrain, making it work in favour of populations that have been marginalized or dispossessed by substantial urban transformations (Osumare 2001; Rose 1994). In Vietnam, as I will show in this book, the spatial practices of hip hop dance are particularly embraced by members of the middle class, who diverge from conventional life styles, as they frequently seek to make a living from dance, and thence find themselves in precarious working conditions, albeit holding a university degree.

Hip hop's practices related to territory and urban space are diverse. Rap lyrics convey a politics of belonging, when rappers cite land marks, streets, subways, and so on in their neighbourhoods. Soundscapes of neighbourhoods and cities are often recorded and interlooped in rap tracks, creating a signaling effect for those who know the area. Torsten Wissmann (2016) differentiates between three different sounds in urban soundscapes: keynote, signal, and soundmark. The keynote can be understood as the background sound of a society, a sound that is frequently heard, against which other sounds are perceived. An example in rap tracks would be the noise of the ever-running trains and subways across train racks. In the case of Hanoi, the continuous honking of motor scooters could be regarded as a keynote. A signal, by contrast, comprises sounds that are consciously perceived by urbanites. The signal is a sound that carries a specific meaning, like church bells of the Cathedral in my home town of Cologne, or the constant recitation of songs in Cologne's vernacular language (Kölsch) during Carnival celebrations. In Hanoi, the recitation of Buddhist mantras on weekends and the 1st and 15th of the lunar new year are signals. Along more secular lines, the announcement of the latest prices of agricultural products or hygiene measures through public loudspeakers count as signals. Soundmarks, finally, are those sounds unique to a particular community or neighbourhood. Soundmarks are of cultural and historical significance, as they create a sonic sense of place and of belonging. Acoustic ecology, according to Raymond Murray Schafer (1969), further classifies sounds according to their sources, thus distinguishing between human, natural, and mechanical sounds. Breaking and hip hop dancing generally transform sonic experiences into bodily movements, embodying the metaphors induced by the sound.

This is particularly the case with mechanical sounds. Mechanical sounds of drums and beats incite b-boys, b-girls, and poppers to perform robot-like movements or to pantomime gunshots fired from a rifle. As a consequence, hip hop sonically marks and appropriates territory and place. Additionally, dancers convening in the cypher occupy public space, giving it new meanings and introducing new movement repertoires, while often challenging codes of conduct in public space. The most visible and tangible art of hip hop is graffiti writing. Writers create pieces in liminal, often moving spaces such as highways, trains, and public transit, while tagging walls of buildings, monuments, and sculptures. The writers thereby literally mark territory. Accordingly, hip hop is ultimately linked to space and place.

The general idea of space as relational and socially produced, pioneered by Henri Lefebvre (1991), is referenced in diverse discussions of space and place across the social sciences. Acknowledging the relationality and social production of space, Doreen Massey (2005: 140) comprehends places as processes. For Massey, places are articulated moments in social networks, experiences, and understandings. Yet, many of these relations and experiences are constructed at scales larger than what is defined as a place itself in a specific moment, whether a park, street, or entire region. With this understanding, she opens toward an extroverted understanding of sense of place, acknowledging place's interlinkages with the wider world, resulting in an integration of the local with the global. In a similar vein, Edward Casey (1996) emphasizes the gathering power of place, considering places as events, by which he means that places are in a constant process of redefinition. The processuality of place is further outlined by Ingold (2008), who argues that places do not exist so much as they "occur," as they are produced through movement. In the hip hop community of practice, places are constantly created through dance moves and the gathering of members in the cypher. The cypher is a recurrent trope in hip hop vernacular. In academic literature, attention to the cypher focuses on the cultural practice of rap. Cyphers are conceptualized as speech events, demonstrating a vast range of linguistic creativity.

> "The cipher is where all (or some combination) of the Hip Hop cultural modes of discourse and discursive practices—call and response, multi-layered totalizing expression, signifyin, bustin, tonal semantics, poetics, narrative sequencing, flow, metaphoric and hyperbolic language use, image-making, freestylin, battling, word-explosions, word-creations, word-pictures, dialoguing other voices, talk-singing, kinesics—converge into a fluid matrix of linguisticcultural activity." (Alim 2006: 97)

While this reading of the cypher involves a strong sociolinguistic focus, I am particularly interested in the spatial arrangement and materiality of the cypher. For dance, the cypher is a spatial practice and arrangement, medium of communication, mode of cooperation and competition, token of community, and sequence of learning. Dancers convene in a circular formation, taking turns practicing, freestyling, and dancing. The orientation of the cypher is centripetal, with all dancers facing the middle. The circular spatial configuration is not only emblematic of the cypher, but is, in fact, a cross-cultural phenomenon, found in diverse forms of performance. For instance, for many practitioners of the Afro-Brazilian martial art capoeira, the *roda* or "wheel" represents the most traditional form of the practice. The roda is as much a space as an event. The circular space is marked by the bodies of spectators, musicians accompanying the "game," as well as practitioners waiting their turn to enter the game. Like the cypher, the roda is a sonic event, as the music guides actors as to when they should start and stop matches, and informs them how to play (Downey 2002: 491). Likewise, the *randai* of the Minangkabau of West Sumatra is a hybrid theatre form that has been described as "arena theatre" by Minang cultural commentators. Arena theatre denotes the randai's circular staging. The randai is usually performed late in the evening in the village plaza. The circular alignment of bodies, constituting a human border that delineates the stage, is the *lingkaran*. The lingkaran is the ring of eight to twelve players who constitute the circular formation of the randai. Made from human bodies, this circle allows the public to approach the stage from all directions. In sum, the circular assemblage of individual bodies is indexical of martial arts and dance forms in diverse cultures. Such circular formations offer space for social learning and the sharing of knowledge and innovation. Moreover, in an urban context, the spatial practice of the cypher marks the appropriation of public space, rendering otherwise marginalized bodies visible and audible within the city's public spaces.

In fact, hip hop involves multiple senses as it is just as much about visuality as it is about sonic, haptic, kinesthetic, and thus other sensory experiences. More than the senses, it is also about things difficult to express in words, which the dancers I talked to often described as "feeling," "emotion," "love," or *đam mê* in Vietnamese, which refers to indulgence and passion. In this sense, the study of hip hop culture generally, and dance in particular, opens to interesting insights about multisensory perception. Being interested in human perception generally, Ingold (2000: 287) most prominently challenges the assumption that vision constitutes the one dominant and objectifying sense. To the contrary, he suggests that we consider vision in its interrelations to other senses. Indeed, the Western dominance of vision and ocularcentrism has been recently challenged by cross-cultural analyses.

In socio-cultural anthropology, the ethnography of the senses has evolved since the 1980s, researching and acknowledging local senses and sense-making, even questioning the Western five-sense model. In *Doing Sensory Ethnography*, Sarah Pink (2015) calls for the senses to become part of ethnographic practice, rather than being mere objects of ethnographic inquiry. More than a method of data collection, she considers sensory ethnography to be open to and opening toward new ways of knowing and forms of knowledge production. In human geography, the merits of a multisensory approach have been recognized, particularly with respect to studies of place and space. Accordingly, Pink (2015) reconsiders ethnographic practice through phenomenological theories of place and the politics of space, as such an approach "recognises the emplaced ethnographer as her- or himself part of a social, sensory and material environment and acknowledges the political and ideological agendas and power relations integral to the contexts and circumstances of ethnographic processes." (Pink 2015: 25). In other words, as the researcher learns and knows through her experiencing body, ethnographic experiences are embodied. Ethnography, in fact, is a sensuous way of knowing (Conquergood 1991). Drawing on the aforementioned phenomenological approach to place and thus the body, Pink proposes two concepts of sensoriality. The first is "sensory subjectivity," implying that ethnographic research is always subjective, which makes it necessary for the researcher to reflect on her role in the production of ethnographic knowledge. The second concept of "sensory intersubjectivity," referring to the corporeality of sensory experiences and their coming into being in relation to a material environment. Such sensory intersubjectivity is crucial when considering dancers' interactions with the material infrastructures in and upon which they dance.

According to Monica Degen and Gillian Rose (2012), the materiality of the environment together with actors' embodied practices and perceptual memories create particular senses of place. Their reference to materialities and memories indicates that sensory perception is mediated by different and continuously shifting spatial and temporal practices. Memories thus intertwine with sensory experiences. Methodologically, Degen and Rose approach urbanites' sensory perceptions – or intersubjectivity, in Pink's terms – via the walk-along. The walk-along builds on Margarethe Kusenbach's street phenomenology of the go-along, which is a research method for assessing manifold spatial practices, relations, and memories. According to Kusenbach (2003: 463), the go-along stands out from other ethnographic methods, as it enables ethnographers "to observe their informants' spatial practices *in situ* while accessing their experiences and interpretations at the same time."

I first encountered young people dancing in the streets during my research on public space in Hanoi between 2007 and 2008. Since that time, I developed a deep interest in youth activities in public spaces, as I observed transformations affecting major public spaces, such as Ly Thai To Garden, the Lenin

Monument, and more recently the Soviet Vietnamese Friendship Palace. All of these spaces were either planned and built during the French colonial period or in the period of socialist urban planning. When Hanoi was founded in 1010 as a political and sacred centre of the first centralized Vietnamese state, Dai Viet, urban spaces were created and coded according to their functionality and exclusivity. For instance, the rectangular walled compound of the royal citadel was only accessible to the king, members of his family, as well as high-ranking mandarins. With the construction of the commoner's city along the banks of the Red River in the 15th century, markets formed outside the citadel's main walls. Other than these markets, geographic and symbolic centres where strangers could meet remained absent from the urban landscape. Places for social interaction, such as Buddhist pagoda, Confucianist temples, or communal houses only existed at the communal or neighbourhood level. However, these were primarily sacred spaces, and access to them was granted on the basis of age, gender, and social status (Drummond 2000). As a consequence, the construction of squares and parks, such as the contemporary Ly Thai To Garden or the Lenin Monument, introduced new categories of urban space to Hanoi.

The introduction of public spaces went hand-in-hand with the overall transformation of the indigenous urban landscape, thereby demonstrating the power of the French colonizers over the local population. After declaring independence from France in 1945, the colonial regime was replaced by the one-party rule of the Communist Party. With this change among the political elite, the urban planning regime also changed. After periods of de-urbanization and zero urban growth during the two Indochina Wars (1946–1954 and 1968–1975), the party-state remained dominant in defining Hanoi's urban landscape until the 1990s. The primary function of public space in socialist Hanoi was to demonstrate and symbolize the state's power. Public spaces served as stages on which to assemble and control the masses. However, since the introduction of the Doi Moi economic reform program in 1986, which initiated private sector developments and began integrating the country into the world economy, citizens have come to challenge the state's predominant power to shape the urban landscape. As Li Zhang (2012) notes of post- or late-socialist countries, urban space in such contexts becomes a prominent arena for the articulation and negotiation of social aspirations, lifestyles, and class identities. In Hanoi, urbanites contest the state's power by appropriating former spaces of officialdom. In fact, they make these official spaces public by conducting their everyday routines within them, using these spaces for private activities such as walking, exercising, cooking, eating, and drinking, nurturing children, and so forth. Moreover, public spaces, such as streets and sidewalks, are often appropriated for private economic activities like petty trade (Drummond 2000; Kurfürst 2012; Kurfürst 2019; Kim 2015; Thomas 2002).

According to Michel de Certeau (1984: xiv), everyday practices are spatial practices that lie beyond the control of the state. They are sometimes modes of resistance that are able to evade discipline from within the sphere of their exercise. Peter Goheen (1998: 489) emphasizes the "unreadibility" of everyday practices by the state, highlighting their subversive potential. Such unread-ability recalls DeFrantz's arguments about the public and private transcript of dance. Likewise, the meanings of hip hop's diverse dance styles are not eas-ily decipherable by the state, or even by passers-by assembling and watching such dance performances in public space. What is more, the appropriation of public city space does not only depend on the (un)readability of the practices themselves, but it is also dependent on more general forms of control exer-cised over urban public space by authorities. In fact, public spaces are marked by a continuum of state control and surveillance, with some public spaces of-fering more freedom to perform recreational and social activities than oth-ers. In their analysis of "Youth-driven tactics of public space appropriation in Hanoi," Stephanie Geertman et al. (2016) explain that the municipality of Hanoi assigns different categories to public space, which define or delimit the activities that can be carried within them. In most cases, the category of public space is deducible from the Vietnamese term for public space. For ex-ample, the full Vietnamese name for Ly Thai To would be *vườn hoa Lý Thái Tổ*, translated as Ly Thai To Garden. The Urban Planning Law of 2009 attaches particular relevance to open green spaces, and includes public gardens to-gether with large squares, green spaces, water surfaces, and open space areas in its list of urban design objects required in the city. The *Public-Use Greenery Planning in Urban Areas: Design Standards* (Article 3.1) define public gardens as "green areas [of a few hectares or less] mainly for pedestrians to stroll and relax during short periods of use" (Pham and Labbé 2018: 174). A further cate-gory of public space is parks. The *Design Standards* define parks as "large green areas serving the goals of outdoor activities for the entertainment of urban residents, for mass cultural activities, contact with nature, and improvement of material and spiritual life;" (Pham and Labbé 2018: 174). An example of such a park would be Thong Nhat Park (*công viên Thống Nhất*), located south of Hoan Kiem Lake.

However, the municipality identifies a further category of park, namely, cultural parks (*công viên văn hoá*). Formally, recreational activities are prohibited within cultural parks. An example of such a cultural park would be the Lenin Monument located at Dien Bien Phu Street, opposite the UNESCO heritage site of the royal citadel. The overall outline of the public space is triangular. The area is comprised of a wide-open space made from stone, housing a statue of Lenin, as well as a wooden pavilion in the park behind the monument. Originally built during colonial times, as a memorial to those who had fought for France, the party-state chose to replace it with a statue of Lenin in 1985, thereby following the model of many other socialist countries at that time (Logan 2000: 198). The Lenin Monument, consisting of a 5.2 metre high effigy of the founding father of the Soviet Union, stands on a 2.7 metre high stone pedestal that was erected in the park. In theory, youth should not be allowed to practice around the Lenin statue (Geertman et al. 2016). In practice, however, the Lenin Monument is used for diverse activities, such as badminton, skateboarding, ballroom dance, economic activities, and so forth (Kurfürst 2012; Thomas 2002). Acknowledging that space for youth activities is limited in the densely settled city of Hanoi, municipal authorities tolerate use of the Lenin Monument for diverse youth activities, while maintaining that this arrangement is only temporary. What is more, these activities are easily forbidden when state festivities occur, or when considered inappropriate by the authorities (Geertman et al. 2016). Against this background, the persistence and gradual growth of dancers occupying these official spaces is all the more astonishing.

Ly Thai To Garden is located right in Hanoi's historical centre on the banks of Hoan Kiem Lake. Built by the French in the 19th century, it was one of the first Western public spaces introduced to a society in which only exclusive spaces previously existed, access to which was granted on the basis of social rank and gender (Drummond 2000: 2381). The city's precolonial urbanism was defined by the triple structure of the royal citadel, the commoner's city on the banks of the Red River, and an agglomeration of villages located west of the royal citadel. As I have argued elsewhere, Hanoi's urbanism was characterized by the tripolarity of the sacred, official, and profane. While the royal citadel constituted the sacred and political centre of the city and the country, manifest in the rectangular outline of the royal city, the commoner's city was a sphere of profane production and reproduction. In the precolonial city, public spaces, as spots for strangers to mingle, hardly existed (Kurfürst 2012: 35; Nguyen 2002: 280).

French colonial urbanism with its Hausmann-style, tree-lined boulevards, parks, and public spaces completely transformed the indigenous urban landscape. Consequently, Paul Bert Square developed in 1890 and named after the recently deceased Résident Général Paul Bert, provided a new category of space in the colonial city, which invited encounters among individuals from different social strata, ages, and genders. The physical structure of Paul Bert Square linked the main institutions of colonial power, including the town hall, the treasury, and the post office, as well as the *Résidence Supérieur* (Bourrin 1941: 50; Service Géographique de l'Indochine 1902). The square consisted of a wide space with a statue of Paul Bert facing Hoan Kiem Lake, and a pavilion where, between 1897 to 1934, military concerts of the *Garde Indigène* were held on Sundays (National Archive Nr. 1, Toa Doc Ly Ha Noi, No. 2940 and Series G-X, No. 005015). The statue of Paul Bert was erected on July 4, 1890 at the exact same site where the statue of liberty had stood before. The statue of liberty was again moved to the pagoda in Hoan Kiem Lake (Bourrin 1941: 48). In other words, the colonial power took a religious symbol and superimposed a profane icon on it, thereby demonstrating its overall domination over the indigenous population. After the country gained independence from France, the square was named Ghandi Park to honour the good relations with India at that time. However, after a public debate about the park's name among Hanoians and intellectuals, the municipality changed the name and erected a statue of King Ly Thai To, the first king of a centralized Vietnamese empire following 1,000 years of Chinese domination, and the founder of Hanoi in 1010, at the site where the 19th-century statue of Paul Bert once stood.

Today, the public space is made up of two different kind of materialities. First, the square housing the king's statue is made from stone, offering a flat surface for dancing. Second, located behind the statue, there is another small square made from stone, housing the ancient pavilion with a wooden roof. From there, a concrete path leads into a small park with benches for recreation. In 2007 and 2008, when I first encountered hip hop dance practices in Hanoi's public spaces, b-boys mostly gathered in front of the statue. At the time when I conducted my field work, members of the MiNi Shock and FIT Crews were regularly practicing on the platform, starting late in the afternoon. They got to know each other from practicing in this shared space and were very open to newcomers. According to crew members, the site became more crowded each day.

At the same time, female dancers who were members of Big Toe Crew regularly gathered in the ancient pavilion behind the statue. Upon their arrival at the park, they swapped their school uniforms for sweatpants and tummy tops. Ten years later, when I returned for my fieldwork on hip hop in Vietnam, I recognized Mai Tinh Vi from a photo that I had taken in 2008. In the meantime, she had become one of Vietnam's most renowned hip hop dancers and b-girls. In 2007 and 2008, a gendered division of spatial practices at Ly Thai To Garden could be observed. At that time, mixed-gendered groups were almost entirely absent. Instead, groups consisted of either young men or young women. While the b-boys mainly gathered in front of the statue, the b-girls occupied the pavilion to practice. Since the girls often assembled right after school, the wooden pavilion provided some shade, especially in the hot and humid summer months. Neither space was exclusively used by either male or female dancers, but if both groups were present, they would usually retreat to their regular spot.

By 2018, the situation had slightly changed. First of all, dancers would start mingling much later, starting around 8 or 9 p.m. Second, both b-boys and b-girls – although the majority was still male – jointly occupied the flat, smooth surface directly in front of the statue. This part of the square is slightly elevated from the main square with a staircase leading toward the statue. By contrast, the park behind the statue was frequented by different aerobics, dance, and sports groups, mainly consisting of middle-aged women except for a small group of girls who practice K-Pop dance. Considering these locally concerted actions, it becomes obvious that each activity group, whether aerobics, gymnastics, K-Pop, and so on, occupies their own spatial niche, practicing separated from the other groups. Sonically, the non-routine visitor to these public spaces will be overwhelmed by the cacophony produced by competing amplifiers. However, for the everyday users of these spaces, it is far from a competition over whose amplifier is the loudest, as they are capable of focusing on their immediate sonic environment, produced by their own music and their own bodies. The soundscape becomes even denser when different groups that frequent the square need to withdraw from their particular spot and rearrange, as occurs when their activity spaces are cordoned-off or occupied by an official stage. Such interruptions of urban routines occur frequently around Ly Thai To Garden, as it is a common stage for official celebrations such as the Liberation Day of Hanoi, celebrated annually on the 10th of October.

Compared to 2007 to 2008, not only has the gendered appropriation of particular spots of the square changed, but so too has the time for the main activities. While previously, practice would often start at daylight, now the

practice period has shifted to later evening hours after school. Starting at
8 p.m., dancers with different levels of skill and experience come together
to practice, carrying a portable music player with them. Breakbeats play the
entire time. Although the music is quite loud, and the usual curfew in Hanoi
for bars and coffee shops is around 10 p.m., breaking after 10 p.m. is not
prohibited. In 2018, like to 10 years prior, the two official guards monitoring
the space showed more interest in the dancers' bodily contortions than in
preventing them from dancing. One of the guards in charge of Ly Thai To
Garden regularly works from 5 to 11 p.m. between October until December.[11]
His working hours indicate that the park patrol time has been adjusted to
accommodate dance practices taking place there, as breakers would usually
go home around 11 p.m. In contrast to members of other "street disciplines"
(bộ môn đường phố), such as traceurs or skateboarders, who are perceived as
disturbing or even damaging the urban environment (Geertman et al. 2016),
dancers are not perceived as such. In the past decade, on the contrary, they
have assembled a growing public with more and more passers-by interrupting
their daily routines to watch them dance, and more young people joining in
to practice themselves. In contrast to the early years, when breaking used to
be prohibited in public spaces, the number of dancers mingling around the
Lenin Monument and Ly Thai To Garden has increased since the 2000s. The
only space dancing has been banned from is the Soviet Vietnamese Friendship
Palace, although it is one of those spaces where hip hop dancing in Hanoi
began.

The Soviet Vietnamese Friendship Palace is located at Tran Hung Dao St.
91, close to the central train station. It is situated at the former site of the colonial exhibition and market centre (Nha Đấu Xảo), which would later become
the Maurice Long Museum of Indochina. Built by French architect Adolphe
Bussy, the colonial exhibition hall housed the L' Exposition de Hanoi from 1902
to 1903. During the Japanese occupation of Hanoi in the 1940s, the occupying forces placed military personnel and supplies there. The edifice was completely destroyed at the end of World War II. Palace construction started in
1978, the same year the Socialist Republic of Vietnam signed the Treaty of
Friendship and Cooperation with the Soviet Union in order to guarantee bi-
lateral economic cooperation. The edifice is located close to the office of the
central party committee of Hanoi, and was a gift of the central committee of

---

11   In our conversations he did not mention the dancers, practicing right next to us, at all,
      but rather talked about his family, while showing an interest in Germany.

Soviet trade unions to the socialist state. The construction projects were part of the city's overall transformation to socialism. With assistance from Soviet architects, particularly Gragold Grigorievich Isakovich, the urban landscape was to represent the ideological and economic vision of the Socialist Republic (Anon. 1962; Logan 2000: 186, 194). The palace architecture followed the model of the Moscow Palace of Labour in modern constructivist style, offering lecture halls, theatres, and meeting rooms (Logan 2000: 183). Large official celebrations take place there, such as National Independence Day on September 2nd. As such, it symbolizes the socialist state's power. However, this icon of officialdom is, or at least used to be, contested by young dancers who practice alongside the palace's outer walls. On the front, stone pillars line the left and right corners of the rectangular palace structure. The colonnades along the palace's outer walls offer a dry, open space for practice during the monsoon season, while offering shade from the sun in the dry season. The flood lights on the corner of the building, and the lamps in the colonnade ceiling, offer enough light in a city where the sun regularly sets around 6 p.m. Since dancers usually gather in the evening, the flat, cold, stone palace floor provides ideal infrastructure for dancers. The materiality of the palace, together with the embodied practices and perceptual memories of the dancers, create a particular sense of place. Hoang Phuong, a female hip hop dancer, explains that she liked to dance here because the place had a good "spirit." It reminded her of the first dancers who practiced in this very space, creating a place for hip hop in Vietnam.

The *cung* (palace) or *cung xô* (Soviet palace) – as it is colloquially referred to – used to be a popular space for young people to mingle in the evening. The first hip hop dancers, such as Phuong Silver Monkey and Thanh C.O., practiced there regularly. Thanh C.O. is the leader of C.O. Crew, which was founded in 2001, originally under the name C.O.L.D Crew. However, they changed the crew's name to C.O. in 2007 as other dancers found the name too long, and often called them "C.O." The C.O. Crew regularly practiced in the house of culture (*nhà văn hoá*) at the palace. While most of the dancers assembled in the gallery in front of the palace, the C.O. Crew had a small studio in the back of the edifice. As more dancers from different dance styles joined, it became very crowded and some groups did not clean up after practice. Therefore, the state seized control of the place again. For several years now, dancing has been prohibited in the colonnades. A sign reads that all "activities of freedom" (*hạnh động tự do*) are prohibited. The sign implies that all self-organized rather than formally sanctioned activities are prohibited in

Colonnades along the Soviet Vietnamese Friendship Palace

Source: Nils Kurfürst (2018)

the space. The assembly of young dancing bodies in front of the socialist icon is apparently considered a thread to the urban order. Nonetheless, hip hop's past and present remain inscribed into the space via graffiti.

The right outer wall is an evolving palimpsest of tags from various writers. The tags display quotes from hip hop vernacular, such as 'CYPHER,' 'CREW,' 'HIP HOP DONT STOP...'. While cypher and crew refer to the spatial practice of dance, and the social organization among hip hop practitioners, "HIP HOP DONT STOP..." is a common rap lyric line and the title of a CD compilation of

Graffiti along the palace's outer walls

Source: Sandra Kurfürst (2018)

hip hop classics published in 1997. Consequently, while ephemeral embodied practices have been banned from the palace, the tags invoke dancers' perceptual memories. Furthermore, the tags and graffiti that cite hip hop vernacular link the particular place of the palace to places beyond, as suggested by Massey (1994). In other words, the palace constitutes a node within a wider network of local and global places, which are frequented, and in the process created, by hip hop dancers. As shown in subsequent chapters on particular dance styles, local practitioners who started out dancing at the palace also gathered and practiced around the Lenin Monument and Ly Thai To Garden. At the same time, international hip hop dancers, such as from Germany, come to these places to exchange movement vocabulary with Hanoian dancers.

Moving from one public space to another, dancers in Hanoi create intimate, affective spaces in what is otherwise the anonymous environment of the late socialist city.

"Over time, technique creates 'vernacular landscapes' within urban environments. (…) It organizes relationships across culture and class to form affective environments, geographies of the heart. The vernacular landscapes constructed through dance technique are literal and psychic spaces for the daily, routine time and talk that bind practitioners to one another." (Hamera 2007: 60-61)

In other words, the publicity of performance is crucial to sharing and exchanging bodily knowledge, and to creating and maintaining social relationships.

Social learning

In this book, I argue that distinct communities of practice have evolved in Vietnam since the 1990s in relation to hip hop's four cultural practices, with a focus on the community of hip hop dancing. Originally, the communities of practice concept developed as a theory of learning from the collaboration between sociocultural anthropology, namely, anthropologist Jean Lave, and educational theorist and practitioner, Etienne Wenger, at the Institute for Research on Learning in Palo Alto (Duguid 2008). In their 1991 book, *Situated Learning: Legitimate Peripheral Participation*, Lave and Wenger identify "legitimate peripheral participation" as determining membership in a particular community of practice. Through participation, newcomers are integrated into social relationships, learning as much about the social relations they become a part of as they learn about a particular craft or practice. As a result, learning takes place in "real-life settings, under real performance requirements on actual individuals" (Fuhrer 1993: 179).

Crucial to such an understanding of learning is the concept of apprenticeship, introduced by Lave in the 1970s to overcome the formal-informal divide in educational and learning theory (Lave 2011: 21). Decades later, in her 2011 monograph, *Apprenticeship in Critical Ethnographic Practice*, Lave elaborates on apprenticeship as both a research method and object of study, drawing on her research on apprenticeship among Vai and Gola tailors of Liberia. At the time when she began this research, there was a rigid dividing line between what was called "formal" and "informal" education. In the 1970s, cross-cultural psychologists assumed that only formal education and schooling could result in generalizable knowledge that could be transferred to new domains. By contrast, informal education was considered to be based on everyday life experiences, and thus bound to merely reproduce traditional, allegedly context-bound knowledge (Lave 2011: 19). Against these ideas, Lave offers a complex account of local educational practices to question what at the time was the mainstream account of "non-schooled" and informal education (Gibson 2011: X, foreword in Lave 2011). Starting from practice theory as a theory of relations, Lave (2011: 3) "began to consider seriously the possibility that learning, knowledgeability, skillfulness, whatever else they might be, are always only part of ongoing social arrangements and relations."

While many dance students engage in self-learning through online tutorials, the sharing of bodily knowledge primarily occurs within master-student relationships as well as among peers within crews. Newcomers learn basic dance techniques through legitimate peripheral participation, by copying and mimicking the so-called "old timers" (Lave and Wenger 1991). According to Hamera (2007: 6), techniques are "codes of governing and standardizing dance practice," rendering performing bodies legible. Newcomers who have been initiated in movement vocabulary eventually become advanced students, who are then able to develop their individual styles. The final stage of initiation is crew membership, which is crucial to identity construction. In this regard, Wenger emphasizes trajectories through different levels of participation in the community, as well as the existence of internal structures, such as periphery and centre (Cox 2005: 531-532). In the hip hop dance community, I have identified three different relationships or trajectories through which newcomers move from the periphery to the centre, with the centre defined by membership in the dance crew:

a) Master-student relationship
b) Appointment by the crew leader
c) Formal recruitment process

These categories are not exhaustive, but rather dynamic. Sometimes these forms of recruitment are combined or overlap with respect to individual dancers, since an individual can be a member of multiple crews.

Master-student relationship

Newcomer to the hip hop dance community in Vietnam explained that they first participated in dance classes in dance studios or in public spaces. Many explained that they chose their teacher themselves. Some personally approached a well-known dancer, or someone they had seen performing in public space, either by directly asking them to be their teacher, or by signing up for their dance class. Hoang Phuong, a female hip hop dancer and co-owner of the Wonder Dance Studio in Hanoi, recalls how Phuong Silver Monkey used to dance to music from big loud speakers in the lobby of the Soviet Vietnamese Friendship Palace. Training in public, he made his actions "visibly-rational-and-reportable-for-all-practical-purposes," and thus accountable to others (Garfinkel 1967: vii). Phuong Silver Monkey introduced a new bodily practice to the city, thereby unsettling extant movement repertoires within public space. Furthermore, he made his bodily practices reproducible to others, enabling them to engage in a mimetic process that Marcel Mauss (1973: 73) referred to as "prestigious imitation." As they admired his bodily movements, Hoang Phuong and a friend approached him, asking him to be their teacher. In the context of capoeira, Downey (2002) makes similar observations, noting that beginners imitate those players whose movements they admire most. However, students of hip hop are merely able to choose their own teacher, as the master-student relationship requires mutual agreement. Thus, Phuong Silver Monkey, in turn, asked the two girls to perform for him, before accepting them as students. As the master-student relationship was agreed to, they started practicing indoors in a rented room. Then, after a year of practice, the group moved outdoors to the Lenin Monument. As more people joined the class in public space, they finally founded New York Style Crew. Initiated into the practice, and practicing ever since, Hoang Phuong was able to develop her own style, eventually becoming a renowned hip hop dancer, as will be seen in more detail in the chapter on hip hop dance. Today, Hoang Phuong has students of her own, a group of girls who have been following her for almost three years. Together with these students, she founded the hip hop crew Wonder Sisters, which is the counterpart to the popping crew, Wonder Brothers, headed by the co-founder of the Wonder Dance Studio, CK Animation. Despite her personal success and reputation in the hip hop dance community, she still refers to Phuong Silver Monkey as her teacher, addressing him with the proper honorific Vietnamese term, *thầy*.

This lifelong master-student relationship is idiosyncratic to the hip hop community of practice, as even famous dancers still refer to themselves as students of their teachers. However, this relationship is also related to the particular status of teachers in Vietnamese society. Since education is highly valued among other status markers, teachers enjoy elevated social reputations in Vietnam. Even if students become more successful than their teachers, they would still refer to the teacher as "master" (*thầy/cô*), and to themselves as "student" (*em*), maintaining and reproducing the asymmetrical relationship between master and student. The special role of the teacher is also manifest in the annual Teacher's Day. On November 20, students throughout the country pay tribute to their teachers, visiting them at home, writing them letters and greetings cards, and presenting them with flowers. Such tributes are also paid to dance instructors on Teacher's Day, as dance teachers post photos of the greetings they received from students on Facebook and Instagram, while students wish them well online.

Like Hoang Phuong, Nguyet (aka Waacking Howl or WHowl), and her husband Bi Max chose Phuong Silver Monkey as their teacher. Having previously engaged in other dance styles such as waacking and breaking, they set out to learn hip hop. Nguyet remembers how, in the beginning, she thought her teacher was too "cool" to talk to. It was after when she joined his class that she noticed that he was not as aloof and distant as she had expected. What began as a master-student relationship for Nguyet and Bi Max soon turned into crew memberships. Today, hopes for continuity in the crew rest with Nguyet and Bi Max, who recruit new and younger members. However, Nguyet is not only a member of New York Style Crew, but also of Soul Waackers, a waacking crew founded by C2Low. What is more, Nguyet teaches her own class comprised of six female students twice a week in the evening. Thus, students become teachers and thus multiply the training of other dance students.

Mai, like Hoang Phuong, was just 12 years old when she decided to learn hip hop dance. She accompanied a friend to the Soviet Vietnamese Friendship Palace in search of a teacher. She first approached the ZickZack Crew that was practicing there. However, as she explains, they were too "cool" to let her join and just ignored her. Mai then approached another crew, the N-least Crew, but they also did not welcome her. In 2004, finally, Mai went to Big Toe Crew, which let her join their dance exercises. The leader of Big Toe, Thanh (aka LionT), trained her together with another girl. After training, Mai watched members of the Big Toe 3 Team practice together, hoping that one day she would become a member of the team.[12] Overall, Mai identifies the master-student relationship as the best way to learn dancing, especially compared to a dancing class. As a newcomer to the hip hop dance community, she suggests, it is best to choose one or two teachers and to practice regularly with them over long periods of time. Interestingly, she does not refer to Thanh as her teacher, but rather sees him as a "leader" since she identifies as a member of Big Toe Crew.

In summary, the examples discussed above illustrate elected master-student relationships. With the increasing commodification of dance practices, however, master-student relationships are increasingly being mediated as economic relationships. In other words, master-student relationships are increasingly structured by economic exchanges, especially as manifest in commercialized dancing classes.

Many of the dancers I talked with were either full- or part-time dance instructors. Mai regularly offers a beginner hip hop class at the Cun Cun Studio on Thai Thinh Street. Every three months, she starts a new beginner's class, while also teaching an advanced class. In autumn 2018, when I was studying with her, she led a beginner's class on Tuesday and Friday evenings from 6:30 to 7:30 p.m. Overall, the class lasts three months. The fee for one month is 500,000 VND, 1,200,000 VND for three months, and a single class for 100,000 VND. After the first lesson, she asked people to sign up and to pay the fee in cash. Mai's class had 11 members on the first day, seven of whom were female including a girl who was 7 or 8 years old, and four male, all of whom were around 20 years old. While we were practicing the final moves, members of the advanced class often arrived early. Mai explains that, in the last two years, many students sought her out as their teacher. She is aware, however, that those joining her evening classes have little spare time for dancing, especially for the beginner's class. By contrast, those joining the advanced class that starts at 8 p.m. are regular students, who regularly hang out with Mai and also practice together outside the formal class setting.

In sum, the master-student relationship also lays the groundwork for crew membership. In many cases, crew members were initially students of more advanced dancers, oftentimes crew leaders, and would later join the crew after practicing together for a couple of years.

---

12   At that time Big Toe had three sub-groups, divided into Big Toe 1, Big Toe 2, Big Toe 3, according to the level of practitioners. Big Toe 1 comprised the old timers or "big ones" as Mai puts it.

Appointment by the leader

The second process for integrating newcomers is by invitation from a crew leader, which often depends on long-term personal relationships. Renowned practitioners of particular dance styles approach individual students, or a group of students, to invite them to join their crew. C2Low, one of the first waackers in Vietnam, started a free waacking class at the Lenin Monument, in order to motivate others to learn waacking. By teaching and practicing with others in public, he made his actions accountable to and repeatable by interested others. Nguyet was first invited by C2Low to join his Soul Waackers Crew. As she and her husband were seeking to learn another dance style, they joined Phuong Silver Monkey's hip hop class. After practicing with him for some time, Phuong Silver Monkey finally asked her and Bi Max to join his crew, New York Style Crew. While her crew membership appears to have been a long process involving regular practice, Nguyet recalls the moment she "officially" joined the crew. This moment was defined by the collective decision to join a showcase battle in Singapore, for which Phuong Silver Monkey, Bi Max, Nguyet, Thanh Phuong, and a few others recorded a video to submit to the organizers. This joint enterprise gave them a sense of mutual belonging, which finally established the crew.

Nam, the leader of the popping Funky Style Crew, started practicing in a dance studio before joining the Wonder Dance and Milky Way Crew. His own crew practices every Monday, Wednesday, and Friday evening at 7 p.m. in Nghia Do Park located along Cau Giay and Nguyen Van Khuyen Streets. Like Phuong Silver Monkey and C2Low, Nam makes his practice visible and accountable to others in public space, which is how he was approached by a young woman named Phuong. When I met Phuong at the Ho Thanh Cong popping battle for the first time, she had only been practicing popping for two months. She asked Nam if she could join his crew, so he invited her to practice with them. Nam himself does not see himself as much as a teacher, but rather as the crew leader (*nhóm trưởng*).

CK Animation also integrates former students into his Wonder Brothers Crew. Nonetheless, he differentiates between the process of becoming a member of Wonder Dance Studio and the process of becoming a member of his crew. To participate in a dance class, it is sufficient to sign up at the studio and pay for classes. To become a crew member, by contrast, requires a longer period of apprenticeship, practice, and hanging out. In fact, CK Animation identifies the following as requirements for a new crew member: regularly hanging out together, "playing" (*chơi*) or dancing with each other, and being really good at training.

Tien, a young dancer from Ninh Binh, practices with a member of the Ti-Tan Crew, one of three local hip hop dance crews in Ninh Binh Province, north of Hanoi. TiTan Crew is from the province's capital city, Ninh Binh, wheareas WinDy Crew is located in the provincial city of Tam Diep, and yet another crew in Hoa Lu. By 2018, TiTan Crew had already been around for 11 years. The crew features two dance categories, breaking and freestyle. Hip hop, waacking, and popping dancers come together in the freestyle category. Tien explains that, since the crew specializes in breaking, there are only a few female members, including two b-girls, two female hip hop dancers, and one female waacker. Apart from the members, the crew has more than 50 students. Before becoming a student to one of the crew members, Tien already had dance experience, as he is also a member of his high school's dance club. However, in the school's dance club, they mostly did choreographies for graduation or Teacher's Day.

In September 2018, Tien responded to a post that the crew left on Facebook, seeking to recruit new students (rather than members) to train, since the crew wanted to push hip hop in Ninh Binh City. While he studies with a crew member, this does not automatically imply crew membership, which is why Tien carefully distinguishes between the crew's students and members. For instance, as a newcomer, he became the student of a female crew member who specializes in waacking. In order to become a crew member, he first needs to become a good dancer, and then be accepted by the rest of the crew as a whole. When asked about the recruitment process, his teacher explains that hip hop is as much a profession as it is a lifestyle. Therefore, it is important that community (*cộng đồng*) builds around the dance style. She affirms that all crew members jointly decide who to accept into the crew.

Consequently, the selection and integration of new crew members is a collective process. Formally, the leader appoints new members, but eventually the crew decides as a collective. In the Soul Waackers Crew, the leader calls on his students to join the crew, but the other crew members have a say in the decision, as well. Crew members primarily evaluate proposed newcomers on the basis of skills and social factors. For example, one indicator is if the newcomers "play" well with other crew members, and whether it feels good playing together. Other factors are whether newcomers appear to be hard working and take crew practice seriously. The examples of the Wonder Brothers, Soul Waackers, and TiTan Crews demonstrate that the integration of newcomers into a crew does not solely depend on skills and techniques, but also on social fit.

Formal recruitment process

Some crews initiate formal recruitment processes, organizing casting events. Usually, such casting events are advertised on the crew's Facebook page. The crew will set a date, inviting all interested dancers to participate in the casting process at the crew's training facility. During the audition, newcomers are asked to perform while the crew members judge them according to their dance technique and performance. Such recruitment processes mostly seem to be initiated by crews that have been in existence for quite some time, and have received a certain reputation within the community of practice. These crews frequently participate in dance battles.

The Milky Way Crew, one of Vietnam's oldest popping crews, initiated such a recruitment process in March 2019. For this purpose, Mai Tinh Vi, who is not a member of the crew herself, together with the crew leader TF Star, and two other dancers, produced a live video on Facebook, inviting interested dancers to participate in the casting. The live video lasted 77 minutes, and they took questions from dancers interested in crew memberships. Interested dancers were able to post questions in the live chat, while the crew members responded as music played in the background. They repeatedly mentioned that a crucial condition for crew membership is fitting in socially with the crew. These social aspects of membership were explained by other crew members as the willingness to hang out with each other, including beyond crew practice meetings. In fact, crews often post photos on social media of their get-togethers for dinners, lunches, or weekend trips. While there are no financial requirements explicit in crew membership, the visual markers of hip hop apparel, such as sneakers, baseball caps, t-shirts, and the like, imply a requirement to make financial investments necessary to be visually recognized by peers. What is more, except for the first generation of dancers, such as Thanh, Phuong Silver Monkey, and later Mai or Hoang Phuong, who learned to dance in public space, the recruitment of new dancers often occurs in dance studios, access to which requires financial resources. Accordingly, while crews appear to be open to newcomers, and the community of practice is rather inclusive, certain financial investments and resources are implicitly required for participation, beyond skills and technique.

Social learning, social responsibilities

Overall, the master-student relation appears to be key to integrating new-comers into the community of practice. As indicated by the concept of social learning, the role of master is not reduced to the sharing of knowledge and training of skills, but also involves social responsibility. Masters teach their students bodily skills, techniques, and kinesthesia, while sharing their knowledge of the history of a particular dance style with their students. But more than that, teachers also provide mental and emotional support to students, for instance, when they join a battle for the first time. When I first met CK Animation at the Ho Thanh Cong popping battle in October 2018, he had not come to participate in the battle himself, but to watch and support his students. As we talk, two male students approach him, and say, "Chào anh." Their greeting indicates a hierarchical relationship, as they use the honorific second person address, *anh*, which signals the higher status of the addressee over the speaker. This honorific address is further supported in the gesture of shaking hands, as students hold their right arm with their left hand, while shaking their teacher's hand. One of the students tells CK Animation that he is scared. CK Animation answers in a very friendly and calm manner, suggesting that there is no need to worry. Accordingly, teachers support their students emotionally and celebrate their success. Several teachers celebrated students' regional, national, and international successes on Facebook, posting photos of master and student together during award ceremonies or right after battles.

Apart from offering mental and emotional support, teachers also feel social responsibility with respect to their students' livelihoods. Thanh reports how proud he was when Big Toe Crew won a lot of competitions, becoming top 5 in the world. Yet, at the same time, he felt bad because he was not able to provide stable income for his crew members and fellow dancers. At the height of success, the crew finally broke up in 2011. Afterward, many former members stopped dancing altogether, looking for other jobs to make a living. Reflecting on this time, Thanh locates the reason for the crew's disbanding in the inability to make a living from dancing. This is why he decided to open a dance studio, inviting former crew members to become teachers in his studio. Some of the old members still work in his studio, teaching and practicing, but no longer participating in battles. He wants to make a difference for the "new generation," as he calls it, giving them the opportunity to dance and generate an income while still going to school. Some of his current students are still in school at only 16 years old. In the evening, they teach a class at his studio, then practicing themselves after class, before returning to school the next morning. For Thanh, it is important that they are independent, not needing to ask anyone for money to support their ability to dance and travel abroad to participate in battles.

Students, in turn, look up to their teachers as role models. One locking student considers her teacher both an inspiration as well as her caretaker, saying that he "not only teaches us how to dance, he also teaches us how to live." Her statement hints at how hip hop is not only a bodily practice, but a way of life shared by the members of the community of practice. Furthermore, her statement points to the importance of trust in the master-student relationship. Of course, trust must be established and maintained among master and apprentice. But with more children and teenagers attending dance classes, the building of trust among teachers and parents likewise grows in importance, as well. A young girl and sometimes a small boy participated in Mai's class, and both were always accompanied by their mother. Thanh likewise explains that some parents bring their children to his dance academy, as they used to dance with him in the past. Other parents bring their children because they want them to become professional dancers, while others know that Thanh can provide them with a job. He narrates the story of a former student who wants her daughter to become an internationally successful dancer. At ten years old, her daughter had already won a major freestyle and waacking event in China. In other words, Thanh's reputation as a skilled dancer, as well as provider for his students, facilitated parents' trust in his ability to take good care of their children.

In sum, as indicated by Lave and Wenger, the master-student relationship is as much about learning a particular practice – in this case, hip hop, waacking, popping, locking, or breaking – as it is about learning and being integrated into social relationships. Teachers like Thanh, CK Animation, or C2Low not only see their role in mediating bodily skills, and conveying particular movement vocabularies, but also in providing emotional and mental support to their students, and potentially even financial autonomy, as in the case of Thanh.

Social learning and material infrastructures

Social learning in the form of peripheral legitimate participation mainly occurs in public spaces. Public dancing attracts others interested in the bodily practice, thus facilitating social interaction. Ethnomethodology has been influential in studies of situated social practice, and aiming to understand ongoing local productions of social order and meaning. Ethnomethodology assists in understanding orders and rules, and how to deploy them toward one's own ends. For instance, in his account of how to cross an underregulated crossroad "Kincaid" in Oregon, Kenneth Liberman (2013) studies the methods actors adopt to make their way through such complexity and crowd. According to Harold Garfinkel, one of the founders of ethnomethodology, interaction requires work or effort in order for actors to produce a mutually intelligible social world. Such work encompasses "a public, visible, and orderly passing back and forth of recognizable sounds and movements," and, as such, it can be studied in empirical detail (Garfinkel and Rawls 2005: 7). Actors working together within a shared field of practice assign public and mutual meaning to actions in order to produce witnessable orders.

In the communities of hip hop dancing, the production of such public, visible, and witnessable orders frequently occurs through interactions in public space. As I show throughout this book, most of the dancers that are well-known today started out practicing in public. More precisely, they participated legitimately in peripheral public space. Both Mai Tinh Vi and Hoang Phuong first came in touch with the embodied practices of hip hop when they watched the 1st generation of hip hop dancers' practice outside the Soviet Vietnamese Friendship Palace. Likewise, Nguyet participated in her first waacking class at the Lenin Monument. Although Mai's first attempts at legitimate peripheral participation with the first two breaking crews she approached were unsuccessful, she nonetheless got a glimpse of what was going on. In contrast, Hoang Phuong was able to watch Phuong Silver Monkey, who is said to be the first hip hop dancer in Hanoi, as he practiced outside the palace and eventually asked him to be her teacher. Training in public, Phuong Silver Monkey made his bodily practices observable by and reproducible for others, enabling them to engage in a mimetic process. Having learned from him, today Hoang Phuong owns her own dance studio and is the leader of an all-female hip hop crew. Accordingly, social learning within the community of practice takes place through publicly situated and shared practices. Apart from the accountability and reproducibility created by dancing in public, a further quality assigned to public space is kinesthesia. As stated earlier, WHowl's class takes place once a week outdoors at the Lenin Monument. In her choice of location, she pays attention to the sensory experience of public space, stating that the kinesthesia experienced by practitioners differs from the dance studio, as no mirror is available to control the movement. Yet, apart from this learning process in which the situatedness of action becomes tangible, her explanation about the differences between spaces also involves processes of place-making. Similar to how Mai and Hoang Phuong recall their experiences at the palace, Nguyet likewise remembers how she first got in touch with waacking in this same space. To Nguyet, the Lenin Monument is emblematic of waacking. Therefore, she is eager to maintain Lenin Monument as a "traditional space of hip hop" in Vietnam. Similarly, Hoang Phuong used to take her students to either the monument or the pavilion at Ly Thai To to practice hip hop dance. That was before she owned her own studio and was able to teach her students indoors. Yet, she explains, she sometimes still takes her students to practice in public at Lenin.

The Halley Crew, a renowned Hanoian breaking crew, likewise started out training at the Soviet Vietnamese Friendship Palace. After watching the b-boys from Zic Zac Crew train at the palace, Hoang C-Floor decided to found the Halley Crew. The crew founder is very fond of the crew's diversity, stressing that no one is alike. That is why they are a very "colorful" group (*có nhiều màu sắc*) that harmonizes well with each other. In 2015, Halley Crew regularly gathered in front of the palace in the evening. The dancers assembled on the rectangular square in front of the Soviet-style building, which offers an open space for the b-boys and b-girls to practice. The social community and space mutually constituted each other through this very practice. Breakers usually convene to practice in a circular cypher where individual dancers exchange their latest moves. Yet, given the architecture and morphology of the space, they did not create circular formations but rather rectangular assemblages. Three different socio-spatial formations emerged, which differed according to the performative vocabulary and physical skills of the practitioners. The beginners and newcomers practice together, as do intermediate dancers, as well as the advanced or old timers. The result is three different spatial configurations in which dancers exchange dance moves according to their skill levels.

Only those with advanced techniques and styles are able to join the Halley Crew. In other words, dancers move from the periphery to the centre, as they become old timers over time.

In conclusion, dancing in public is as just much about a specific sensory experience and thus a sensory mode of learning as it is about social learning. Training in public, dancers make their actions visible, accountable, and thus reproducible. This is not only the case in Hanoi, but also in provincial cities like Ninh Binh. A female waacking dancer from Ninh Binh City recalls when she encountered hip hop's corporeal vocabulary for the first time as a little girl, when her father took her out for a stroll in the park. What is more, while practicing in public space, members of the dancing community signal that they are open to newcomers. Several dancers explained that everyone interested in dancing is welcome to join. This was already the case 10 years ago when I interviewed the b-boys who regularly hung out around the Ly Thai To statue. In fact, the integration of newcomers frequently occurs through legitimate peripheral participation in such public spaces. This openness and inclusiveness are essential features of the community of practice. However, in order to enhance their bodily skills, most people agreed that it was important for them to identify one crew member to serve as their teacher. By learning from this teacher, they might one day gain access to the crew. Thanh explains that, within Vietnamese breaking crews, respect is paid to the older crew members and that many crews are hierarchically organized (Margara, Van Nguyen 2011). Such social hierarchies in dance are expressed in the sociospatial configurations of dance communities. Moreover, hierarchy within the crew and their collective practice become tangible through students' and newcomers' demeanor toward the elders. Hierarchy manifests itself in what Erving Goffman (1986: 4) refers to as "supportive interchanges," such as greeting ceremonies. Before joining dance practice or a battle, students approach their teacher, shaking their hands with their right hand, while bowing slightly before the elder. Accordingly, hierarchy is expressed both in terms of demeanour and body postures, as well as in spatial orientation. The deferential behaviour to dance elders, and the movement from the outer circle to the inner circle of the Halley Crew, recalls Deborah Durham's depiction of the circle of men in Botswana. Durham (2004: 593) demonstrates the operation of hierarchy and generation in the context of the circle, in which men convene on the occasions of funerals and weddings. First of all, younger men who want to pay respect to their seniors would approach them in a deferential manner, allowing the seniors to lead in conversation and greeting. Second, young men will start by sitting outside the inner circle of elderly men, and then, by the age of 30 – sometimes earlier, sometimes later – move into the inner circle, not as deferential as they used to be. Consequently, the achievement of seniority through age, accolades, or performance becomes manifest in space. Additionally, hier-archies are enacted verbally, through the use of honorific forms of first- and second-person address in Vietnamese, which indicate status differentials be-tween teacher or crew leader and their students and other crew members.

Overall, crew membership is not always performed verbally. One exam-ple can be drawn from the B Nashor Crew, which is one of the most recent open style hip hop crews in Hanoi. All the crew members have a dance name, including Nashor, as a suffix or prefix. Main protagonists are Mia Nashor and Mai Tinh Vi. In fact, Mai Tinh Vi is the only dancer who does not use the Nashor particle, possibly because she has already been known under her dance name for several years. Whenever they recruit new members, they will be assigned the family name Nashor. What is more, the B Nashor crew makes extensive use of the hashtag #family. The family metaphor appears to be a cross-cultural practice in the social organization of hip hop. For instance, Ian Condry (2001: 237) characterizes the organization of Japanese hip hop as "loose groups of 'families' (*famirii*)." In Japanese rap, a family consists of a col-lection of rap groups headed by a famous rapper with a number of protégés. One of the first popping crews in Hanoi, the Milky Way Crew, likewise fash-ions itself as a family, including when recruiting new members in the process described above. Since its beginning, diverse subgroups with different dance styles have flourished under the umbrella of the Milky Way Family.

Power and language in communities of practice

Similar to its implications for the field of social learning, the introduction of the concept of communities of practice to linguistics likewise challenged long-established ideas, concepts, and ideologies of language. Language was long thought of as a bounded system consisting of grammar, vocabulary, and structured sounds, which were distributed across spatially discreet entities, as represented in the concept of a "speech community." According to Duranti (2001: 18), a speech community denotes the boundaries of what should be studied as a unit, while Hymes (1972: 54) defines a speech community as "a community sharing rules for the conduct and interpretation of speech, and rules for the interpretation of at least one linguistic variety." What Hymes calls linguistic variety is embedded in knowledge of how to engage in communica-tive practice (Eckert and McConnel-Ginet 2003: 56). The conceptualization of language as a speech community is best exemplified in the linking of a particular language to a nation-state. With the rise of the nation-state in the 19th century, language was apprehended as spatially fixed to a particular territory (Gal and Irvine 1995; Taylor 1990 cited in Blommaert and Rampton 2011). Jan Blommaert and Ben Rampton (2011: 4) refer to this idea of language as an "ideological artefact" operating in the "apparatus of modern governmentality." In fact, a vast amount of literature has been produced on language ideologies deconstructing the idea of such distinct languages. Against this background Penelope Eckert and Sally McConnell-Ginet (2003: 57) comprehend of speech communities as shared practices within socially and geographically defined communities, yet instead of considering these practices to be spatially fixed to particular territories, they suggest that the boundaries of such communities are fluid, depending on the level of specificity one is looking for. Turning to more concrete social collectivities based in everyday practice, they call for attention to communities of practice. Already in their 1992 article, "Think practically and look locally: Language and gender as community-based practice," Eckert and McConnell-Ginet discuss communities of practice with respect to language, gender, and power, defining a community of practice as:

> "(...) an aggregate of people who come together around some enterprise. United by this common enterprise, people come to develop and share ways of doing things, ways of talking, beliefs, values – in short, practices – as a function of their joint engagement in activity. Simultaneously, social relations form around the activities and activities form around relationships. Particular kinds of knowledge, expertise, and forms of participation become part of individuals' identities and places in the community." (Eckert and Mc Connell-Ginet 1992: 464)

Instead of replacing the concept of speech community with community of practice (Blommaert and Rampton 2011), they draw our attention to the interconnections between the two. The authors argue that ways of speaking are most closely coordinated at the level of the community of practice, while drawing on repertoires from broader and more diffuse speech communities. At this interface, communities of practice refine the practices of speech communities for their own purposes. In this sense, communities of practice assist scholars in rethinking traditional notions of community and identities, such as gender, since the boundaries of such communities of practice are determined internally, "through ethnographically specific social meanings of language use" (Bucholtz 1999: 214; Eckert and McConell-Ginet 1992). Combined with ethnographic research, the community of practice approach allows scholars to examine both the actions of individuals, and the structures that are thereby (re)produced as well as resisted and subverted.

Mary Bucholtz (1999: 221) suggests that the community of practice concept is valuable as it enables "researchers of socially situated language use to view language within the context of social practice." Accordingly, communities of practice develop among groups of people responding to a shared situation. People engage in practice together because they share an interest in a particular place at a particular time. Through such mutual engagement, communities of practice can produce certain ways of pronouncing things, nicknames, or specific forms of greetings (Eckert and McConnell-Ginet 2003). In the Vietnamese hip hop dancing community, such specific ways of talking evolve at the interface of the Vietnamese speech community, and the transnational hip hop community of practice.

While sociolinguists have shown great interest in hip hop, and particularly rap, they have seldom included the community of practice concept in its analysis. In *Roc the Mic Right! Language of Hip Hop*, H. Samy Alim (2006) conceptualizes the Hip Hop Nation as a speech community, examining how Hip Hop Nation language builds on and simultaneously expands African American oral traditions. The term Hip Hop Nation recalls the aforementioned discussion by Blommaert and Rampton on the pairing of a particular language with a particular nation-state. However, here nation refers to a self-chosen and appropriated term. That the Hip Hop Nation exists well beyond the boundaries of a nation-state is exemplified by the idiom "Global Hip Hop Nation." While drawing on linguistic anthropology, and understanding language as social practice, Alim stresses that Hip Hop Nation Language is rooted in Black Language (BL) and communicative practices (Spady and Eure 1991; Smitherman 1997; Yasin 1999). However, taking a Global South perspective to hip hop reveals an interesting symbiosis. While the uptake of English terms such as beat, flow, or battle, and particular phrases such as "yo yo yo!," is a common practice among members of the Vietnamese hip hop community, Vietnamese practitioners still adhere to the hierarchically structured linguistic system of Vietnamese, particularly when it comes to first and second person address.

This is particularly interesting since the community of practice approach has been criticized for its failure to allude to power differentials, especially in the field of sociolinguistics. The volume, *Beyond Communities of Practice: Language, Power and Social Context*, edited by David Barton and Karin Tusting (2005), contributes to this discussion by embedding the communities of practice concept in theories of language use, literacy practices, and discourse.

Drawn from disciplines such as linguistics and educational research, the authors allude to conflicts and questions of power arising in communities of practice as well as to the significance of the broader social context.

Understanding language as social practice, linguistic markers such as the use of honorific forms of first and second person address helps to identify power asymmetries within the Vietnamese community of hip hop. In general, the concept of communities of practice has been criticized for suggesting a romantic assemblage among equal peers (Cox 2005). This idea of peer interaction is emphasized when looking at forms of second person address frequently used in the English or German community of hip hop, since both languages employ kin terms such as "bro" or "sis" or the German terms *Bruder* or *Schwester*, that imply parity of status. However, the use of such kin terms in peer interaction does not work well in Vietnamese. On the contrary, Vietnamese kin terms are deployed to convey status asymmetry (Sidnell and Shohet 2013).

In the hierarchically ordered social system, self-reference and second-person address are always produced relationally within the speech event. As a result, the terms deployed to speak of oneself and to address the other shift according to who participates in the conversation, according to respective ages, genders, and other markers of social status. Before a conversation in Vietnamese actually begins, interlocutors who meet for the first time would frequently ask "How old are you?" in order to establish age-appropriate forms of address. These forms of address representing status are also held up in Vietnam's hip hop community. However, these forms of address are gradually refined, as the following cases illustrate.

In the master-student relationship, the proper way for a student to address the master in Vietnamese would be *thầy* for male and *cô* for female teachers. By contrast, the teacher (whether female and male) would address students using the term *em*, which literally translates as "younger brother" or "younger sister," and is the proper address for pupils at a certain age. In the Vietnamese hip hop community, these formal forms of address can be used, as well. However, as they signal some form of social distance, they appear to primarily apply in social situations where the age difference between master and apprentice is quite high (as among adults and children), or when the relationship between master and apprentice remains more technical, lacking a social dimension.

In what follows, I present some examples to illustrate two different situations. First, a higher age difference exists between teachers and students in the New York Style Crew. In an effort to recruit younger dancers, the crew has invited children to practice together with them during practice. When Nguyet and Bi Max practice with them, the children call them *cô* and *thầy*, while they address the children in turn using the kin term *con*. *Con* literally means child and is used by parents to address their children, whereas children would refer to themselves as *con* when talking to their parents. The reason that they do not refer to students as *em*, as Nguyet explains, is that they are only ten or eleven years old. In a conversation with Nguyen Ngoc Binh, a linguist at the University of Social Sciences and Humanities in Hanoi, he explains that *con* is used as a second-person address for children in kindergarten, whereas students are called *em* at school. In the southern Vietnamese dialect, *con* is also used to refer to students in school, then the proper relations of address would be *cô-con*.

Second, the pronouns *cô* and *thầy*, as well as *em*, are used in situations where the social connection between teacher and student appears to be lacking. CK Animation, who teaches popping classes to both children and adults, differentiates between students he is close to and students that are not close to him. While the first category of student calls him *anh*, or "elder brother," students who are more socially distant address him with *thầy*, "teacher." But what happens when the teacher is younger than the student? This scenario is exemplified in the relationship between Nguyet and her teacher C2Low. In a Facebook post, she reacts to a photo that he has posted by using the term "teacher" to address him. In his response, C2Low, who is roughly four years younger, addresses her with the term *chị ạ*, or "elder sister." The emphasis on age is conveyed by his amendment of the second person address *chị* with the term *ạ*, which in Northern Vietnamese, is a polite form of addressing interlocutors of higher status, such as those older in age.

Thanh, recognized as one of the founders of hip hop dance in Vietnam, is referred to by members of the community as *Đại*, which translates as "grand." In conversations where he was not present, my interlocutors would also refer to him as OG, which is an American English term that stands for "original gangster," indicating a classic or old-school style. But nowadays, OG can simply be used as an abbreviation for "original" (Urban Dictionary 2019).

While the above analysis of pronoun use in the hip hop community alludes to existing status asymmetries, and variously indexes social proximity or distance among members of the community, I will now turn to the linkage between language and gender.

Several sociolinguists have deployed the community of practice concept in their analysis of language and gender (Eckert and McConnell-Ginet 1992, 2003; Bucholtz 1999). Locating language within embodied selves, the community of practice concept presents a theoretical entry point for feminist researchers interested in the gendered body. Furthermore, the community of practice approach focuses on identity, allowing researchers to ask how speakers use language to project identities, for example, as gendered beings. As a consequence, the community of practice can be constituted around a social practice, no matter how marginal it may be from the perspective of the traditional speech community. This is especially important for inquiries into gender, since women and other groups that do not conform to dominant gender identities have frequently been defined as marginal to vernacular speech communities (Bucholtz 1999: 204, 208).

Such a marginal position of women is represented in the Vietnamese speech community, where young women and girls occupy the lowest positions within the sociolinguistic hierarchy, as they are mostly addressed as *em*. For this category of young people, no gendered identity exists at all. Young males and females are likewise addressed as *em*. Only if a woman is older than her interlocutor, the terms of address change to value her older age, as in *chị* (elder sister), *cô* (aunt, young lady), or *bà* (grandmother, lady). When a man and a woman are of the same age, and in a (conjugal) relationship, gender outweighs age. Shohet and Sidnell (2013: 622) describe the sociolinguistic framework for Vietnamese "in which neither age nor generation matters so much as does the (conjugal) gender hierarchy in which a man is traditionally the master of his wife and superior to other women of a similar age." Even if the woman in a relationship is older than her husband or boyfriend, the man is addressed with the senior pronoun *anh*, while the woman remains his inferior as *em*, thus maintaining the gender hierarchy.

This gender hierarchy appears to be maintained in Vietnam's hip hop community. This becomes particularly evident when considering social media, where a common form of addressing community members is *anh chị em*, abbreviated *ace*. In Vietnam, *anh chị em* is an inclusive term for addressing members of different genders and age cohorts. However, in the community of practice under consideration, while *anh chị em* is similarly abbreviated as *ace*, it is even further abbreviated as *ae*, omitting the *c* that stands for *chị*, which is the proper form of address for females of higher age or status. This change suggests that men still constitute the majority in the community of hip hop dancing, and that women continue to occupy an inferior position in the Vietnamese speech community.

However, while there appears to be considerable overlap between the wider speech community and community of practice under consideration, the community of practice simultaneously offers novel possibilities to address other dancers as peers, thereby reworking linguistic hierarchies in the speech community. One possibility to overcome the dilemma of peer address in Vietnamese is the use of first names, which can replace first and second person pronouns and thereby circumvent pitfalls of status, gender, and age difference. As I show in the chapter "BREAKING," male community members applied this strategy to express their respect for a renowned female dancer who was younger than them. Consequently, the Vietnamese speech community and hip hop dance community frequently overlap, particularly with respect to the maintenance of the hierarchical social order. Nonetheless, power asymmetries can be overcome in the community of practice, for instance, through self-reference and second person address, as I show throughout this book.

Breaking

Breaking constitutes one of hip hop's four elements. Whereas the other dance styles discussed in this book are not explicitly mentioned in the canon of hip hop, breaking is one of hip hop's four cultural practices, apart from DJing, MCing and graffiti writing. Breaking is a transnational, eclectic, and referential bodily practice. The style integrates black dance with Russian footwork, gymnastics moves, pantomime, martial arts, among other disciplines (Holman 1984). While the date and location of breaking's origin typically refers to 1970s New York City, the historical roots of the dance style have been traced to parts of Africa, feudal China, tribal Eurasia, as well as to Caribbean and South American dance styles (Banes 2004; Holman 1984). Notwithstanding such multi-referentiality, scholars agree that the main source of breaking's movement repertoire is black dance. Accordingly, breaking, like the cultural practice of MCing, is closely linked with regimes and experiences of suppression and subordination, in particular to slavery in the United States in the 18th and 19th centuries, where European and African dance styles began to mesh. Whereas Europeans introduced the minuet, the waltz, and the quadrille, enslaved Africans introduced a shuffle step dance, called the juba. Slaves mimicked while simultaneously mocking the masters' dance (Holman 1984). As such, the juba dance is a perfect example of mimicry identified in postcolonial theory, in which mimicry has a double meaning. While the imitation of colonizers by the colonized is often a means for establishing domination and suppression, mimicry may also serve as a powerful medium for mocking colonizers and undermining the sociopolitical status quo. Accordingly, Homi Bhabha (1984: 127) refers to mimicry as both a resemblance and menace. In fact, as a rather recent discourse and sensation, hip hop embodies subversive meanings of mimicry. For example, hip hop scholar Tricia Rose (1994: 99) suggests that the oppressed make use of language, dance, and music to mock those in power and produce subversive imaginaries. Drawing on frameworks developed by James C. Scott (1990), DeFrantz (2004) similarly draws attention to public and private transcripts latent in black social dance, arguing that dancers perform for two communities, their black community and white spectators, with the latter largely unaware of submerged and subversive layers of communication involved in the performance. Accordingly, the element of protest remains part of the private script, only legible to those who are initiated in black social dance styles. Scott considers the open interaction between subordinates and those in power as part of a public transcript, which serves as a self-portrait for the ruling elite, evolving around discourses represented by those in power. By contrast, the hidden transcript can be expressed through rumours, folk stories, narratives, gestures, and theatrical performance. Hidden transcripts formulate a discourse that takes place outside the public stage and withdraws itself from observation by those in power. Hidden transcripts are specific to the localities and actors they are performed in and by. Dance as a hidden or private transcript thus conveys meanings beyond its formal qualities, as it is performative in the sense that dance can incite action. DeFrantz (2004: 4) captures the performativity of dance with the term "corporeal orature": "Corporeal Orature aligns movement with speech to describe the ability of black social dance to incite action." Corporeal orature is linked to the linguistic practice of call and response. In many African diasporic dances, call and response occurs when the body responds to the call of the drum (DeFrantz 2004; Thompson 1966). Furthermore, the differentiation between public and private/hidden transcripts in hip hop dance becomes important when considering the separation between audience and performer. DeFrantz (2004: 10) notes how separation across cultural and racial lines affects the power of hip hop as an instrument of struggle, preparing the dancers to oppose oppressive societal forces.

In this context, we need to ask how public and hidden transcript are altered when hip hop travels beyond the African diaspora, for example, to Vietnam. First of all, it should be noted that within the Asian American community, and particularly the Vietnamese diaspora, hip hop has been embraced as a tool for combatting oppressive societal forces. The first Vietnamese rap track, published in 1997, was produced by a young man named Khanh Nho from Oregon in the United States. Khanh Nho rapped about his family's flight from Vietnam to the U.S. Today, rappers like Lee 7, who migrated from Vietnam to Germany, can relate to and identify with Khanh Nho's story. Likewise, contemporary Viet rap—frequently performed in Vietnamese language—addresses social, political, and economic inequalities. In other words, the diasporic experience and marginal positionality of individuals who have migrated to the U.S., such as Khanh Nho, is negotiated in the social world of hip hop.

Second, the multiple layers of communication embodied in hip hop can be found in other communities, as well. Yet, these layers change according to locality, sociopolitical context, and history. The legibility of embodied practices employed by those initiated into the dance style is crucial, as the following anecdote suggests: A well-known b-boy in Vietnam was asked to curate dance choreography for a national television program. He suggested choreography that depicted a prison brawl. Of course, the authorities did not welcome the theme, asking him to rewrite the show. In response, he altered the choreography and submitted a second draft, whose hidden transcript was still about an imprisoned man. For the public transcript, he altered the narration: "There is no need to tell what hip hop is about. Now we can do what we like." Again, the separation between performers and audiences opens opportunities to confer diverse meanings through bodily practices. What is more, the hidden transcript in this anecdote alludes to the political and social marginalization embodied in hip hop.

Origins of breaking

Etymologically, the term break was used as a signifier for diverse practices in the 1970s. Break was often used as a reaction to an insult, for example, "Why are you breaking on me?" According to Israel (2002), the 'b' in b-girl/b-boy may also connote being "broke," which means financially strapped or being at one's emotional, psychological, and financial "breaking point." Moreover, break also denoted the percussive rhythms of musical recordings that were most aggressive. Breaking as dancing, in fact, evolved from the dancers' reactions to such musical breaks, as freestylists danced in the breaks of funk and disco records. With the improvement of technical infrastructure, DJs such as DJ Kool Herc were able to prolong the breaks by using two turntables, a mixer, and two of the same records. DJ Kool Herc also coined the terms b-boys and b-girls, or "break boys" and "break girls," respectively (Chang 2006). The simultaneous evolution of the terms b-boys and b-girls also points towards females' early involvement in the bodily techniques of hip hop. This is further indicated by the co-presence of the breaking crews, Zulu kings and Zulu queens, which were both part of the Zulu nation that was founded by Afrika Bambaataa.

Original breakers were black and Hispanic teenagers, most of them male. The fact that teenagers practiced breaking highlights the close connection between breaking and adolescence, since breaking embodies the anxieties and aspirations of adolescence. Breaking was first performed indoors at parties during school breaks or in the cafeteria, as well as outdoors in parks and the subways, only visible and recognizable to those who knew (Banes 2004; Holman 1984). Just like graffiti writing, breaking is about marking territory. Graffiti writers claim public space by spraying tags and pieces on walls, public transport vehicles, and the like, while b-boys and b-girls appropriate public space with their bodily postures and ghetto blasters (Banes 2004). Accordingly, dancing oscillates between visibility and invisibility. Drawing on a sensory code, which among other senses, relates to vision, breaking can be seen by passers-by, yet the meaning conferred through the bodily practices remains exclusive to those initiated in the dance style, as demonstrated in the prison choreography mentioned above.

The aesthetics of breaking are commonly associated with powerful, energetic male bodies, at least in Western culture (Bragin 2014). As Imani Kai Johnson writes:

> "The aesthetics of breaking are steeped in performances of clichéd masculinity. The dance is a clash of big acrobatics, a steady rhythmic flow, small gestures of humorous or violent retribution, and an aggressive, threatening attitude, especially in battles. Gestures of sexual domination, shooting, chopping off heads, or breaking backs all remind us that key aspects of breaking aestheticizes violence. The confrontational and aggressive qualities of breaking are more aligned with conventional notions of masculinity than femininity in Western culture." (Johnson 2014: 15)

The term "Western" can be contested, since breaking is practiced around the world, and in many cultures is associated with masculinity. The term culture, likewise, requires further explanation. In the case of breaking in the U.S., Bragin and Johnson both point to the aesthetics of embodied practices linked to masculinity. Likewise, Matthew Ming-tak Chew and Sophie Pui Sim Mo (2019) point out the relevance of "cultural issues" in their assessment of Chinese b-girls' hip hop-based gender politics. One of these cultural issues is linked to dress, women's bodies, and fear of indecent exposure. Many of the movements performed in breaking, particularly power moves, may lead b-girls to accidentally reveal their bodies or underwear.

Vocabulary for breaking movements is quite diverse, comprising foot-work, rocking, power moves, freeze, and thus targeting diverse lower and up-per body parts, including facial gestures. Sally Banes (2004) describes a rather fixed format for the dance in its inception. Dancers and onlookers formed an *ad hoc* circle, also referred to as a cypher, taking turns performing. Each dancer received a time slot of only 10 to 30 seconds. A single dancer's routine was comprised of three sequences referred to as entry, footwork, and exit.

> "It began with an entry, a hesitating walk that allowed him time to get in step with the music for several beats and take his place 'onstage.' Next the dancer 'got down' to the floor to do the footwork, a rapid, slashing, circular scan of the floor by sneakered feet, in which the hands support the body's weight while the head and torso revolve at a slower speed, a kind of syncopated, sunken pirouette, also known as the helicopter. Acrobatic transitions such as head spins, hand spins, shoulder spins, flips, and the swipe – a flip of the weight from hands to feet that also involves a twist in the body's direction-served as bridges between the footwork and the freeze. The final element was the exit, a spring back to verticality or a special movement that returned the dancer to the outside of the circle." (Banes 2004: 15)

In fact, these sequences were so standardized that there was little room for the development of "personal" style. The only sequence that allowed for the expression of individual style was the freeze, an improvised pose or move-ment that broke the beat. In a dance battle, the freeze was meant to be as insulting and obscene as possible. The freeze sequence is often comprised through pantomime, which graphically emphasized the insult (Banes 2004: 16). Dance sequences, such as the freeze, frequently involve explicitly sexual and militaristic gestures. The freeze's primary function is to provoke and chal-lenge an opponent in a dance battle. As such, it celebrates the physical fitness, flexibility, and sexuality of the adolescent male body. Pantomimes of gun im-agery combine both militaristic and sexual gestures, simultaneously symbol-izing a physical as well as phallic assault against the challenger (Banes 2004; DeFrantz 2016). However, such referentiality also occasions citation of sym-bolic materials outside the standardized dance themes, often resulting in the queering of movements and bodies. Such quotations may involve historical or contemporary events, past and present popular culture, as well as family affiliations, thus demonstrating personal style while resulting in admiration from the group. An example common from the 1980s includes the incorpo-ration of a feminine posture by b-boys and b-girls alike at the end of their floorwork, when many ended their dance with a female fashion model pose. According to DeFrantz (2016: 67), such feminine expressivity was accepted due to its exhibition of physical agility, while also demonstrating "fleeting connotations of queer sexual identity." In other words, queer postures are accepted and even celebrated in breaking, since they index a dancer's virtuosity, in part through their ability to quote symbolic materials beyond routinized dance vocabularies (DeFrantz 2016).[13] These improvisational practices lead Johnson to redefine the term breaking in relation to dance and gender, as "playing with and breaking through social conventions in life to expand the terms by which bodies are able to move through the world" (Johnson 2014: 17).

Social learning in breaking mainly occurs in the master-apprentice relationship. The relationship is rendered equivalent to kinship ties, as master and apprentice refer to one another as father and son (Banes 2004), at least in the U.S. context. For Vietnam, teacher and student(s) frequently refer to each other as elder brother or sister and younger brother or sister. However, as the use of kin pronouns is quite common in the Vietnamese speech community, the use of such terms in the master-apprentice relationship deserves closer examination. In chapter 3, I examined the use of kin terms in the hip hop dancing community. In American breaking, the relationship between master and apprentice is also linguistically marked by the choice of dance names. Dance names index intimate relationships, as seen in the example of master Ty Fly and his apprentice, Kid Ty Fly (Banes 2004). In Vietnam, interestingly, there is no indication that master-teacher relationships are established via dance names. While it is a common practice to register for a battle, using one's dance name and the crew name to which one is a member, I have not found any relationship between dance names of teachers and students. On the contrary, most dancers explained that they came up with their dance name themselves, suggesting that the initiation of a master-apprentice relationship is not marked by any baptismal moment of bestowing a dance name.

Breaking in Vietnam

Nguyen Viet Thanh, also known as b-boy LionT, recalls the first years of breaking in Vietnam: "In the beginning no one really knew which dance style they were practicing" (Margara 2011). Basically, people just mimicked what

---

13   See Schumacher (2004) for referentiality and intertextuality in hip hop music.

they had seen from foreigners, when studying abroad in the U.S., Germany, France, and Great Britain, or from videos they brought home with them from abroad. Thanh himself initially learned how to break from video tapes. He explains that it took him and his crew quite a while, actually until 2003, to understand what they were doing. Then in 2003, the German b-boy Storm came to Hanoi to perform. Storm was invited by the Goethe Institute. Thanh and his crew asked him to practice together and Storm battled against all the crew members, altogether 15 b-boys at the time. While he was in Hanoi, Storm trained them not only in physical skills, but also shared his knowledge about the moves' names and histories. Thanh remembers how Storm pointed out the importance of understanding each move's history, as well as being able to feel the music. As will become clear later, when looking at dancers of other styles, dancing is definitely about skills and particular techniques, but it is primarily a sensory experience.

Born in 1974, Thanh started breaking in 1991. Thanh travelled and still often travels abroad, participating in battles, teaching, performing, and choreographing dance shows. He taught in Canada and Japan, and has performed numerous times in the U.S., Italy, Germany, Denmark, and Holland. As a choreographer, he was invited to the Metropolitan Theater Tokyo to do a show comprising hip hop, locking, and popping. In 2011, he performed *Nhiều Mặt* (Many faces) with other dancers, including Mai Tinh Vi in both Berlin and Hanoi, which was funded and organized by the Goethe Institute.

Thanh has also organized the dance competition "Floorkillers," which occurred several times in the Savico Mega Call Long Bien. After two or three years, however, he stopped organizing the event, since he lost all his money as it was difficult to find event sponsors. According to Thanh, it would be easier to find sponsors for such an event in Ho Chi Minh City. He is also the co-organizer of "Together Time," an international dance competition held annually in Ho Chi Minh City, in which dancers from all over the world participate.

Thanh is so well-known that he was also part of the national TV program, *Vũ Điệu Xanh*, broadcast on VTV 6, as well as *So you think you can dance?*, which was broadcast on local and regional channels, such as HTV7 (HCMC), H1/H2 (Hanoi), VTV Can Tho 1, DRT (Da Nang), Yan TV (Cable), and VTVcab 1 (Cable). The national TV program, *Vũ Điệu Xanh*, targets both "old and young" people, presenting diverse dance styles, such as breaking, popping, waacking, hip hop, belly dance, and dance sports. *So you think you can dance?*, by contrast, is a global television format that has been adopted in many countries, including

Germany. Thanh served as a judge on both shows, and in one show Mai Tinh Vi tutored participants, as well.

Thanh still dances, but today he focuses mainly on teaching. Together with his wife Trang, he owns the Pro G Academy, a dance academy for young people. His wife is also a professional dancer, specializing in sports dance. The name of his academy is a combination of his wife's former dance club, Pro Club, and his former dancing school for children, Golden Horse. The main studios are located on the 4th and 5th floor of a condominium on Minh Khai Street. The space is 500 square metres in size, and the rent is some $10,000 USD per month. Together with his wife and small daughter, Thanh lives in a flat in the same housing complex. Both husband and wife work every day from 3 pm until 10 pm, and on Sundays they start even earlier. During their busy work schedule, his mother-in-law takes care of their young daughter. Growing up in Hoan Kiem District, Thanh actually prefers to live in Hanoi's Ancient Quarter, but for now it is convenient for him and his family to live close to work. Commuting hours have accelerated in Hanoi in recent years, as I learned when returning to my own family's apartment on Thuy Khue Street on one occasion, which took more than an hour by taxi one Saturday evening.

Thanh training at Pro G Academy

Source: Nils Kurfürst (2018)

Thanh still participates in dance battles. He was a participant in the final battle of the 2 vs. 2 house dance at the Juste Debout in Bangkok 2019, and he is recognized by the younger generation of street dancers as an OG (*Đại*) of the Vietnamese hip hop scene. Thanh is also the leader and co-founder of the Big Toe Crew, Vietnam's infamous breaking crew. Originally, Big Toe was founded in 1992. At that time, the crew's founder invited Thanh to become a member of his crew. Soon thereafter, the crew dissolved and Thanh asked the founder for approval to revive the crew. After its reestablishment, Thanh became leader of the Big Toe Crew. The name "Big Toe," which translates as *ngón chân cái* in Vietnamese, refers to the part of the body that is most important in dancing, as the big toe renders stability. Some people in Vietnam still refer to the crew by the Vietnamese name, but Thanh deliberately chose an English name in order to attend international competitions.

At its height, Big Toe was internationally renowned. The crew won major international competitions, such as the Battle of The Year (BOTY) SOUTH-EAST & SOUTH ASIA in 2010, was champion in China, made top five at BOTY in France, and was awarded third place in the international b-boy R16 tournament, organized in Korea in 2010. At that time, the winning crew was comprised only of b-boys, with no b-girls. The crew was very successful because, as Thanh says, they mixed breaking with a bit of hip hop and popping. Many times during our conversations, Thanh emphasized how important it was to him to combine different dance styles. For him dancing was never about breaking only.

While Big Toe was founded in Hanoi, it soon expanded to Central and Southern Vietnam, with branches in Da Nang and Ho Chi Minh City. In Ho Chi Minh City, the Big South Crew, led by Viet Max, emerged as a major breaking crew. Viet Max was one of Thanh's first students in 1994. Thanh taught him for one year, after which they began performing together and became friends. When Viet Max went to Ho Chi Minh City, he built his own crew there and helped to develop the hip hop scene. Thanh explains that he named Viet Max's crew Big South, as a way of indexing Big Toe in the South. Apart from breaking, the Big Toe Crew integrates dance styles as diverse as popping, waacking, and house.

When I met Thanh for the first time in 2015, he told me that each dance style had its own group within Big Toe. At that time, Big Toe had a group of 10 constant members engaged in breaking, sometimes expanding up to 20 breakers, with only one of them being female. The only b-girl among the breakers was Mai Tinh Vi. Apart from breaking, 20 members were engaged in popping, 15 in waacking, and only five members in house dance. Female dancers could particularly be found in the popping and waacking groups. The Big Toe organization was decentralized, but still hierarchical. All of the sub-groups had their own leader, with Thanh being the overall leader of Big Toe. In a 2015 interview, Thanh described his leadership responsibilities to me as follows: listening to the opinions of group leaders, discussing various issues with them, and mediating among them in cases of conflict. In 2011, one year after the crew's great international success, the crew broke up, at least according to Thanh. As Thanh explained earlier, he felt that as a leader, he needed to focus on more than just winning, as he also hoped to provide livelihoods to his crew members. Thus, while Thanh formally dates the crew's break-up to 2011, the next generation of Hanoi's dancers keeps the crew alive, as they claim to be members of Big Toe. To Thanh, this is not a contradiction, as he understands that dancers long to be part of Big Toe. In other words, the crew is kept alive, yet with new actors. Every year, old members like Thanh, Mai, and many new members celebrate the anniversary of Big Toe, both on the ground and online via social media platforms. On the 25th anniversary in 2017, a celebration took place with Thanh as the MC, introducing all the old members of the crew, among them Viet Max, anh Ha, Phuong Silver Monkey, anh Long, among others. All the old timers reunited on the stage. On the occasion of the crew's 26th anniversary in 2018, Mai Tinh Vi posted on Facebook, "Happy Birthday to all the big brothers of hip hop in Vietnam. BIGTOE CREW. 21/11/1992 - 21/11/2018." The post was followed by the hashtags #Longl iveheking #NgónChânCái #26thAnniversary #BigtoeCrew.

The photo accompanying the post shows Mai in a pose, preparing to strike in a battle with an opponent outside the frame of the picture. In the picture, Mai appears to head the crew, while all male dancers comprising her back-up. In this narration of the crew's birthday, the break-up that occurred in 2011 is not mentioned, whereas the post instead suggests that the crew has been in existence since 1992. In reaction, Thanh responded to Mai's post stating: *Xong đi đâu mất.* (Well... where has it gone?)

In other words, Big Toe has evolved into a hip hop icon in Vietnam, which is revived over and over again, yet by different actors. Already in 1992, in the beginning, Thanh revived the crew, asking permission from its original founder. In the meantime, the name Big Toe was also used to found a new breaking crew in 2014, the bboyz Big Toe, which uses the self-chosen motto "Keep Moving." Virtually, the crew claims a lineage with the 1992 Big Toe Crew, although the mission statement on its Facebook page states that the crew is

Big Toe Anniversary 2018

Source: Facebook Mai Tinh Vi (2018)

independent from Big Toe and has its own studio at De La Thanh nho Street. Among others, the crew is comprised of Bun-X, who used to be a member of the Big Toe Crew, and FuJi Pop, a contemporary of Thanh, who is the owner of ASDJ dance studio, where Nguyet teaches, and Mai Tinh Vi. Consequently, as the first (internationally known) Vietnamese hip hop formation, many performers feel the need to keep the Big Toe Crew alive. More precisely, references that different groups of dancers make to the Big Toe Crew gradually generate a common history and shared sense of belonging. In other words, these references allow for cooperation without consensus in the Vietnamese hip hop community of practice. The name Big Toe thus serves as a signifier for different signifieds, signalled by different group members and leaders at different times. Overall, the crew name Big Toe Crew symbolizes the roots of breaking in Vietnam, and has become a temporal marker for the beginnings of hip hop in Vietnam. Whenever I talked to hip hop dancers, they would often refer to Big Toe Crew as the first dance crew in Vietnam, and remember dancers like LionT or Phuong Silver Monkey as members of the first generation of dancers. All other crews and dancers are measured against the zero point of Big Toe Crew's foundation. One of the interviewed dancers considered Linh3T, the leader of SINE Crew, to belong to the second or third generation of dancers following LionT.

In the meantime, the dance landscape in Hanoi and elsewhere in Vietnam has diversified, with crews mushrooming all over the country. Yet, the affiliation with and linkage to Big Toe appears to render legitimacy to newly found crews. While Big South formed as a section in Southern Vietnam many years ago, Big Toe's latest spin-off, B Nashor, is a Hanoi-based allstyle hip hop crew, comprised of members from Big Toe Crew and Milky Way Crew, and constantly looking for new members. What is striking about B Nashor is that the crew is dominated by female dancers, whose leaders are Mai Tinh Vi and Mia Nashor. Their Facebook account and social media representation introduce the name B Nashor, which is quite new in the Vietnamese hip hop landscape.

Breaking in the periphery

Big Toe is thus not only well-known abroad, but it is thus renowned across Vietnam, as a spatiotemporal reference point for many Vietnamese b-boys and b-girls. Bi Max, a b-boy from Quang Tri Province, is also familiar with the name. Born in 1993, Bi Max started out breaking in Quang Tri Province. Today he lives together with his wife, Nguyet, in Hanoi. Back in Quang Tri Province, Bi Max was a member of the 81 Days Crew. In a conversation with Bi Max, he remarked that they changed the crew name three times before coming up with the current name, which references a historic event that occurred in Max's home province during the Vietnam War – or the American War, as it is referred to in Vietnamese. After the Geneva Conference in 1954, conflicting military parties were ordered to retreat to the Northern and Southern parts of the country. As the Viet Minh retreated to the north under governance of the Democratic Republic of Vietnam, and the French troops in the south under the Republic of Vietnam, a demilitarized area emerged in Central Vietnam. Quang Tri Province, the northernmost province of the Republic of Vietnam, was thus the battle ground for two major confrontations that occurred between the two opposing political regimes: the Tet Offensive of 1968 and the Easter Offensive of 1972. On both occasions, North Vietnam's army struck the Southern Vietnamese and U.S. armies. The crew's name, 81 Days, references the second battle of Quang Tri in 1972, shortly after the Easter Offensive. During the Easter Offensive in 1972, the North Vietnamese People's Army of Vietnam captured Quang Tri Province as well as the northern part of Thua Thien-Hue Province. The second battle of Quang Tri began on 28 June

1972, and lasted 81 days until 16 September 1972. On that day, the Army of the Republic of Vietnam defeated the North Vietnamese People's Army of Vietnam on the battle ground of the ancient citadel of Quang Tri, reconquering most of the province. Accordingly, the crew name quotes this historic event. The choice of the crew name also supports Schwenkel's (2011) argument that contemporary Vietnamese youth, although not having experienced the hardships and turmoil of the war, are well aware of their national, and in this particular case, local history. Accordingly, naming the crew after this historic event can be regarded a performative act of identification with the national community. What is more, the crew name's reference to the second battle of Quang Tri is indexical of breaking. The battle is idiosyncratic to breaking since striking "attacks" toward the opponent, and the overall participation in battles, are crucial to the dance style. Thus, the choice of the crew name reveals members' knowledge of hip hop culture, while integrating the crew into the transnational collective of b-boys and b-girls.

In Quang Tri, Bi Max used to practice with his crew outdoors in a square close to his hometown, where they mainly connected with breaking crews from Central Vietnam. Bi Max was the vice leader of the crew, and he noted that, back then, there were many dancers in Central Vietnam. Bi Max primarily practiced breaking and popping. As each dance style did not have its own crew, each crew integrated these different dance styles. This is similar to the TiTan Crew of Ninh Binh Province in the North, which also integrates different dance styles. However, Bi Max notes that, these days, there are fewer and fewer dancers, since the "young generation" is not interested in hip hop any longer. Instead, they like to go out to watch movies. Bi Max was only able to connect with the Big Toe Crew when he moved to Hanoi to live with Nguyet. In Hanoi, he extended his repertoire to include hip hop dance. Thus, Bi Max has become a member of the New York Style Crew, in which his wife Nguyet is also a member. Bi Max has a lot of popping and b-boy friends, who regularly meet in the same public spaces for training.

Material infrastructures of public space

Already with the rise of breaking in the U.S., dancers gathered in New York's public spaces, on street corners and along sidewalks. Through their bodily contortions on concrete sidewalks, they created make-shift youth centres (Rose 1994: 22). Breaking requires a particular materiality, including a smooth and flat surface, as well as sufficient space to perform in a cypher. When dancers "get down" on the dancefloor, they check that the ground is free from any fissures or splinters. In Hanoi, b-boys and b-girls mingle in the city's central public spaces, like Ly Thai To Garden, Lenin Monument, Thong Nhat Park, and previously around the Soviet Vietnamese Friendship Palace. While the materiality of these spaces offers infrastructure for urbanites to engage in dancing, their daily dancing routines create such communal spaces and times (Hamera 2007). In other words, dance practices interweave disparate places within the urban fabric, connecting dancers from different neighbourhoods, social backgrounds, ages, and genders with one another.

The following vignette describes my observations of Ly Thai To Garden one evening in October 2018.

As I arrive at the square together with my husband and my two sons at 8:20 p.m., eight dancers, one of them female, gathered in front of the statue. Throughout the evening, the girl maintained an observer position, not participating in the dancing. When we arrived, the dancers almost seemed to form a circle, taking turns entering the cypher. However, this formation changed quickly and the spatial practices diversified. Dancers turned to focusing on their individual exercises. Further to the left of the square, dancers started practicing power moves on the ground. Before they began breaking on the ground, they wrapped cloths as protection around their heads, such as scarves, hats, or bandana. As new dancers arrived in the square, they first warmed up and then start grooving before entering the footwork and expanding their moves. Later, their spatial practices began to align with the outline of the square, as the dancers positioned themselves not so much in a circle, as in the cypher, but rather in a rectangular. The dancers formed two parallel lines along the square's North-South-axis, facing each other. As a result, five b-boys were standing with their backs to the king's statue and the other five b-boys with their backs towards the lakefront. A closer look at the layout of the garden might explain the arrangement of these bodies in space. After dark, two large spotlights are directed towards the statue facing the lake, providing light for the dancers, creating an imaginary stage or dance floor. Those dancers facing the statue and with the lights in their back, are even able to see their own shadow on the ground. Behind the statue, there is a spot that remains untouched by the spotlights. This area is used as a dressing room, as b-boys changed their clothes under cover of the night.

Legitimate peripheral participation is once again recognizable in space, as two smaller lines of dancers form along the square' east-west axis. One

Ly Thai To Statue in the evening

Source: Nils Kurfürst (2018)

of the dancers in this circle explains that he was from Blue Garden Crew, and that he comes to practice at Ly Thai To Garden when he does not have to work in the evening. At first, he did not feel comfortable coming to the garden, as there were many advanced dance practitioners, but his teacher encouraged him to join. In this public space, many dancers from different crews practice together. The dancer says: "It is very friendly. Everyone who wants can come here." His quotation reminded me of the b-boys I had met at the same place ten years ago. In 2008, B-boy Born told me: "We got to know each other here. Everyone who likes to dance, comes here. Every day it is getting more crowded." Both b-boys indicate the inclusiveness of their practices and their openness to newcomers.

The young man I talked to is joined by a young b-girl along the periphery of the square. She wears sneakers, sweat pants, and a wide blouse. Before she joins him, she walks along the cypher counter-clockwise, shaking the hands of all the b-boys. She greets them in a very polite manner, holding her right hand with her left, and addressing them as *anh*, using the polite suffix *ạ*. She warms up, and then performs some moves by herself. She starts out with some footwork, before taking to the floor to practice some slow moves on her head. In order to prepare for this floorwork, she wraps a black cloth around her head. After 9 p.m., another b-girl joins the group of dancers. While they are dancing, other spatial practitioners are using the space as well, for skateboarding, inline skating, football, and prayer, as people light incense sticks in front of Ly Thai To. Although other spatial practitioners are allowed entry, the dancers create a well-demarcated space for themselves with their spatial practices and the positioning of everyday objects. They place their bags, backpacks, and water bottles in front of the statue, while those taking breaks sit in front of the statue facing the lake.

One week later after this evening at Ly Thai To Garden, on the evening of October 10th, Hanoi municipality celebrated Liberation Day of Hanoi. On this 64th anniversary of Liberation Day, Ly Thai To Garden is decorated with flags presenting a hammer and sickle, while official celebrations take place in front of the statue. On the platform in front of Ly Thai To, dancers and singers perform in turn. To their left and right, spotlights facing the lake as well as large loudspeakers and music equipment have been erected at the site. A female chorus performs two songs, the women all dressed in long blue dresses. A female host leads the evening's events. A rather large crowd comprised of spectators of all ages gathers in front of the scenery. Since the official festivities occupy their usual breaking spot, the young dancers do not gather at Ly Thai To Garden on this evening. However, the official celebration does not seem to disrupt their daily routines, which take place in the park behind the statue, where various groups who regularly dance there have assembled. Most of the groups consist of women doing aerobics, dance sports, and gymnastics, as well as elderly women practicing movements with their fans.

The following Wednesday is a normal working day, and the b-boys and b-girls reassemble at the same spot as they did two weeks before. Yet, the scene lighting is different, as the spotlights that usually shine on the Ly Thai

To statue are turned off. At 8 p.m., only two b-boys practice in front of the statue without music. Fifteen minutes, however, the scene has changed. Loud U.S. rap plays and the b-boys become a multitude. An hour later, 11 b-boys and one b-girl practice individually or in small groups of two to three people. The girl, wearing a white extra-large t-shirt, baseball cap, white sweat pants, and white sneakers, begins practicing alone and then crosses the square, joining a small group of three b-boys. The oldest of the boys instructs the other two boys and the girl.

This evening, the breakers once again do not form a cypher. Most of the dancers practice facing the statue, while only few of them face the lake, with most of them squatting at rest. Breaking is a very intensive and exhaustive bodily practice compared to the other dance styles discussed in this book. During battles, there is usually no need to keep time for breakers, as the dancers are physically exhausted after roughly one minute. That is why breakers take frequent rests.

On a Monday evening two weeks later, seven b-boys and the b-girl from the week before practice in front of Ly Thai To. Once again, the amplifier, their backpacks, and water bottles are placed in front of the statue, demarcating the dance floor. U.S. rap and breaking music is playing the entire time. The big spot lights are switched off, in favour of a more pleasing orange light, shining on the statue. Once again, most of the dancers face Ly Thai To statue while dancing. With the orange light at their backs, they can see their shadows on the ground. The shadow, in fact, functions as a mirror with which the dancers can assess their movements.

Square infrastructures are thus crucial to creating and maintaining communities of practice. The materiality of Ly Thai To Garden allows for different dance practices. I showed that breakers mainly gather on the smooth surfaces surrounding the statue, making use of the space's lightening, while aligning their bodily practices with the outline of the space itself, thereby creating an iconic index. Instead of convening in a round cypher, they instead form a rectangle with two long lines of dancers facing one another. Apart from the materiality of the space itself, the symbolism of the space, including different degrees of state and municipal control, likewise shapes how dancers gather in particular spots. Ly Thai To Garden, as well as Lenin Monument, are places known to all Hanoians, although their symbolism may diverge or even be contested. To members of the hip hop community of practice, these squares and gardens are symbolic spaces as these are sites where dancers first mingled. Moreover, through their dancing in public, they contest common ideas about

Breakers practicing in front of Ly Thai To Statue

Source: Nils Kurfürst (2018)

proper youth conduct in public spaces. First of all, they introduce a kinesthetic vocabulary into public space that diverges from other uses, such as playing football or badminton. Second, dancing allows for "new" intimacies in public space, transgressing the norms of physical proximity. For instance, a b-girl and a b-boy may stand very close to each other, almost kissing. Such physical affection between lovers can be hardly observed in public space, except under the cover of the darkness, such as on Thanh Nhien Street, which translates into "Youth Street." Located between West Lake and Truc Bach Lake, the street is well-known in Hanoi as "lovers' lane," as young couples sit tightly entwined on their motorbikes along the banks of the lake. On this street, however, they would be alone or at most one couple among many. At Ly Thai To, by contrast, they are the only couple among a group of mostly male dancers, and con-stantly watched by the others. Accordingly, such public displays of affection challenge common ideals of youth's proper conduct, thereby creating "scenes of intimacy" in otherwise public spaces (Berlant and Warner 1998: 554).

B-girls: Mai Tinh Vi

When I conducted field work in Hanoi for my research on public space between 2007 and 2008, I had an opportunity to interview Mai Tinh Vi. At that
time, I could not have known that, some 10 years later, she would become
Vietnam's most famous b-girl.

Born in 1991, Lai Sao Mai, popularly known as Mai Tinh Vi, is Vietnam's
most famous b-girl, hip hop, and house dancer. Starting out as a b-girl, she
has expanded her stylistic repertoire to include waacking, locking, hip hop,
house, and soul dance. Since she likes to combine different dance styles, and
is frequently either a participant or judge in freestyle battles. Her b-girl name,
Mai Tinh Vi, already indicates self-confidence, as it literally translates as "Sophisticated Mai," demonstrating both self-confidence as well as authenticity,
since she has become sophisticated in diverse dance styles. Mai explains that
the phrase *tinh vi* has two meanings, first, "I think I am better than you," and
second, that you are good in every detail. This makes her b-girl name ideal for
participation in battles, as it deploys two incremental forms of street rhetoric,
including the taunt and the boast. The taunt is embodied in insulting gestures
toward the opponent, whereas the boast is incorporated in acrobatic virtuosity (Banes 2004: 14). In breaking, the taunt and the boast are analogous to
the stylistic devices of dissing and bragging in rap. Bragging, brought to an
extreme in braggadocio, is a stylistic device used by the MC to verbally elevate
herself above all others (Banes 2004; Bradley 2009). Consequently, the demon-
stration of physical virtuosity and inventiveness is the braggadocio analogue
of breaking, verbally symbolized in the name Mai Tinh Vi. However, like so
many other dancers I spoke to, Mai did not choose the name herself, but rather
received the name from her cousin. One day, Mai's cousin created a Yahoo
messenger account under that name without Mai's knowledge. Her cousin
seemed to have a liking for Tinh Vi, as he also gave this suffix to another
cousin, which Mai only found out later. The other cousin is also a dancer, but
does not participate in battles. In fact, the act of the name-giving matches the
everyday usage of *tinh vi*, as it is usually employed to characterize someone
else. Mai explained how she eventually came to like the name, and has never
considered changing it since.

Mai started dancing in 2003, at age 12. She first encountered hip hop in
a Korean movie. Her personal summary of the movie boils down to a short-
haired girl who does hip hop dance and has a handsome boyfriend. Watching
the movie, she wanted to become like the movie's protagonist. Both love and

the short hair are two recurring themes in her autobiographic narrative of how she became a hip hop dancer. First of all, Mai has always had short hair, which is a statement in itself, since most Vietnamese women, as in many other places around the world, have long hair. Moreover, a well-known Vietnamese pop song, which she describes as one of her favourite Vietnamese songs to dance to, is called *Tóc nắng*, or "Short hair," by the female singer My Linh. This song is often played at dance battles by Vietnamese DJs. Second, during our interview she reflects on the role different boyfriends played in supporting her, and pushing her to become the skilled and sophisticated dancer she is today. While she performs body movements whose aesthetics are associated with masculinity, she also points out the emotional and sometimes professional support she received from boyfriends who encouraged her to believe in herself, and pushed her to new levels. In fact, she stresses the word "love" when suggesting that it "was the love" that made her stronger. Johnson (2014) rightfully points out that while it may seem trite to integrate love into discussions about women and femininity, she nonetheless claims that b-girling could be linked to a more progressive reading of love as a resource, fundamental to building community, while changing one's community to be more receptive to alternative futures and lifestyles. Love not only implies romantic love, moreover, but also love of the self (Nash 2013). Mai thus employs love as a term to denote a resource and communal bond that provided her with strength and power to become who she is today. Not only does she stand out as an individual in the hip hop community of practice, but she is also active in building and supporting the local hip hop scene and market.

Let me return to how Mai got involved in breaking. After she saw the Korean movie, a neighbour's friend took her to the Soviet Vietnamese Friendship Palace to learn hip hop. At that time, there were only a few well-known places for b-boys in Hanoi, one of them being the *cung xô*. Mai tried to gain access to two crews, regularly practicing there, but none of the crews let her participate. When talking about how she was denied access to practice with them, Mai does not make gender an issue. Rather, she refers to the crew members—whether female or male, she does not say—as simply ignoring her, as they were "so cool." Later in 2004, she went to the Big Toe Crew training site in Giang Vo Street. In contrast with her previous experience at the *cung*, in her narrative she now cites gender as a factor that helped her access the Big Toe Crew. At that time, Thanh was already leader of Big Toe. He was receptive to her as a girl who wanted to learn breaking, and he decided to train her and another girl personally. Mai recalls how they cycled every morning to Thanh's house in Hoan Kiem District during the summer holidays. There, Thanh would teach them different moves, including power moves, from 8:30 to 10:30 a.m. After these exercises, an advanced team from the Big Toe Crew came to Thanh's house for further practice. Mai remembers how she longed to become a member of the crew one day, eventually succeeding, as the Big Toe Crew was explicitly seeking women who could dance. Thanh's attitude, willingness to train her, and finally accepting her into the crew diverges from the approach of his male peers in Hong Kong, Taiwan, and China. Chew and Mo (2019) demonstrate that male instructors frequently refuse to teach difficult moves or combos to b-girls, assuming that it would be enough for women to learn footwork. Thanh, by contrast, was excited to teach women these physically challenging postures.

When I first met Thanh in 2015, he told me that Big Toe's breaking team consisted of 10 core members, sometimes extending to 20, but only one of them was female. He suggested that I get to know the only b-girl in the crew, Mai Tinh Vi. In 2005, Mai founded her own crew, named CunCun, which translates as "cute dog," and initially consisted of three female members. As the crew originally wanted to participate in a showcase, they did not put much thought into the crew name. One day when they were called on stage, and asked their crew name, they simply answered CunCun. From 2005 until 2012, CunCun focused on showcase dance. The founding and training of CunCun reveals parallels with the early involvement of women in breaking in the U.S. As Michael Holman (2004) notes, the early b-girls focused more on synchronized movements of the collective body of their crew. Although within these choreographed routines, each b-girl had a solo part to a particular section of music, the b-girls would refrain from doing the same floor moves that the b-boys did. In 2014, CunCun was champion of the Idance competition in Vietnam. Part of the winning team included Mai as well as two other girls who used to practice with her at Ly Thai To Square in 2008. Today, CunCun Crew has its own studio on Thai Thinh Street, where Mai and others regularly offer dance classes. Moreover, the crew annually commemorates its anniversary, if not in real life celebration, then on social media, such as Facebook.

Together with Big Toe Crew, Mai participated in the Battle of the Year South Asia 2014, which took place in Vietnam. Jointly with other Big Toe Crew members, she was part of the company that performed the break dance theatre performance, "Faces," first in Indonesia in 2009, and then in Germany in 2011. The theatre was a collaborative project between the Goethe Institute

Hanoi and L'Espace in Hanoi. In 2012, Mai was awarded second place in the *Vũ điệu Xanh* dance competition on national television.

Interestingly, Mai does not make gender an issue herself. This is also an observation made by Barley Norton in his research on spirit mediums in Northern Vietnam, and Jane Atkinson's study of Wana shamans in Sulawesi. Norton (2006) shows that although women and men assume different ritual roles in the Mother Goddess religion, most followers did not link this differentiation strictly to gender. In a similar vein, Atkinson (1989) explains that most of the Wana of Sulawesi refuse to regard gender as a prerequisite for becoming a shaman, despite the fact that most shaman were male. This suggests that although to the observer gender appears to be a crucial factor in becoming a b-boy or hip hop dancer, the actors themselves do not necessarily agree. In our conversations, Mai refers to gender two times, first when talking about how she became a member of the Big Toe Crew, and second in her self-perception as a dancer. In a conversation we had in October 2018, she adds that she is so used to working together with men, that she would not know what it feels like to work with women. At the time, she would soon find out, since she was planning to participate in the Juste Debout Battle in Bangkok in January 2019, together with a female hip hop dancer from Hanoi, Hoang Phuong.

Mai explains that she receives respect from her male peers, which she links with her drive toward continuous self-improvement – a crucial element in breaking. Sociolinguistically, these expressions of respect are evident in the forms of second person address that Mai's male peers use to address her (see Chapter 3). The October 2018 Red Bull Battle in Hanoi offers an example for the circumvention of hierarchies through peer address. Mai was not only the organizer of this prestigious event, but she was also the only female of three judges in the freestyle category, as well as the only female dancer in the Hanoi House Dance Crew, which performed that evening for the first time ever in Vietnam. The freestyle battle on the first day was moderated by Trung X, a male popper, who was born in 1990. The judges, apart from Mai Tinh Vi, included Tune Tun of the Last Fire Crew and Phuong of the Milky Way Crew. Before the winners of the preliminaries were called on the stage, the MC asked the judges to come to the stage and to share their experiences with hip hop in Vietnam with the audience. Trung X first welcomed Tune Tun from the Last Fire Crew, and then Phuong from Milky Way Crew. He referred to both men, using the pronoun *anh* (older brother), while explicitly addressing Phuong as *anh* Phuong. Phuong said of himself that he is the oldest on the stage. Mai, apparently the youngest dancer on the stage and the only female, was addressed by the MC as Mai Tinh Vi or Mai, instead of using the proper kinship term of *em* (younger sister). By addressing her first with her dance name, Mai Tinh Vi, and then her given name, Mai, Trung avoids conveying a gendered status difference between himself and Mai, and between Mai and the two male judges. By using her given name, the MC expresses his respect for Mai as a peer, the organizer of the event, and as a renowned female dancer.

Mai Tinh Vi judging the Red Bull freestyle battle

Source: Sandra Kurfürst (2018)

Mai's self-perception reveals continuity in an otherwise binary gender system. In our first interview, Mai self-identified as a "b-boy-girl," describing herself as a bit "boyish." In her social media accounts on Facebook and Instagram, moreover, she regularly posts videos and photos with the subtext "dep zai." *Dep Zai* is a dialect form as well as a creative play on words built from the adjective *đẹp trai*. In Vietnamese, *đẹp* means beautiful, pretty. The masculine form, *đẹp trai*, is used for men, and could be translated as "handsome" in English. Moreover, *đẹp trai* is typically used to refer to other people, and not usually to characterize the self. Posting photos of herself, and commenting on them with *dep zai*, thus diverges from the norm in two ways, first, with respect to the gendered usage of the term, and second, by referring to herself in such terms. The creative connotation of the term is further grounded in her substitution of *trai* for *zai*, as the letter z is not part of the Vietnamese alphabet. In other words, she reflects upon her non-hegemonic femininity by using the term, *dep zai*. Mai explicitly identifies herself as a b-boy-girl, not a b-girl-boy or just b-girl. She characterizes herself through creative word play, thereby transgressing gender boundaries fixed by standard Vietnamese language. Performative gender effects are thus realized both through dancing as well as verbally, in the speech act, as both can serve as mediums for change. Performativity can be both a medium of subjugation, and a subversive resource at the same time (Reuter 2011). Like the embodied practice of dance, word play and other creative uses of language can become subversive resources.

Mai Tinh Vi at Red Bull Battle 2018

Source: Sandra Kurfürst (2018)

Breaking gender

According to Johnson (2014), b-girls help us, first, to think about breaking beyond the male body, and second, to expand our understandings of gender performativity. In consideration of the fact that the aesthetics of breaking are usually associated with fit male bodies, b-girls transgress conventional notions of femininity. While both Bragin (2014) and Johnson (2014) are right to point out that they focus on a Western appraisal of gendered aesthetics, the bodily aesthetics of dances, such as popping and breaking, are assessed against a gendered matrix of corporeal postures, as well. In a 2018 interview with a young male dancer, he explained that since his crew specialized in breaking, there were more male than female members. His explanation referred to breakers as being very strong and requiring a lot of energy. The female members of the crew, by contrast, would engage in free style categories because, according to him, "hip hop dance is more comfortable for them than break dance because break dance is very hard very, very, very hard." Likewise, in another 2018 interview a female popper pointed out that the style "looks quite hard for girls," but cited this as the precise reason why she wanted to learn it. As a consequence, breaking has the potential to counter hegemonic and dominant femininities (Johnson 2014: 16; Bragin 2014). In breaking, dancers are able to perform diverse gender, thereby creating something new that literally "breaks" with established gender norms. In other words, the bodily performance makes room for the fluidity of gender. Through performance such gender fluidity and crossings of gender are enacted in the public sphere (Johnson 2014). While female dancers remain outnumbered by male dancers, they are becoming more and more visible in the public sphere, as they appropriate public spaces and can be increasingly seen performing on national television. As a result, marginalized femininities increasingly move to the centre of public attention, such as in b-girls' and female poppers' performances on television shows like *Vũ Điệu Xanh* and *So you think you can dance?* Their flamboyant performances model and may encourage other individuals to perform non-hegemonic femininities, as well. Rufu, a female popper, and Mai, a b-girl, both participated in the national media programs, and were celebrated for their artistic bodily contortions. Their reworking of normative ideas of femininity involve both their appearance or rather representation in public through visual markers such as clothing, tattoos, as well as their body movement in public space. Their popping or breaking in public space diverges first from other activities commonly practiced in public, such as badminton, aerobics, football, as well as from the movement repertoire expected of young women. Moreover, they contest dominant representations of women on a global scale. If there is such a thing as a global hip hop nation, then female poppers and b-girls challenge representations of women as sexual objects – most dominant in rap videos, where men conspicuously consume women in order to elevate their social status, thereby reinforcing the binary system of heteronormativity. Consequently, Johnson (2014: 17) reminds us that b-girls are located between two competing notions of heterosexual femininity: First, expectations that women undertake polite and ladylike behaviour, and second, the pornofication of women (Johnson 2014: 17). I am aware that the first reading of b-girls is based on a Western, especially American, ideal of a woman's proper behaviour. However, drawing on my own and other scholars' analyses of the representation of women in Vietnamese popular culture, advertisement, and state propaganda, b-girls and female poppers are likely to challenge normative ideas of gender in Vietnam, too. An example for the negotiation of ideal femininity in Vietnamese popular culture is the case of Hoang Thuy Linh, which hit the headlines of national newspapers and online media in 2007. Hoang Thuy Linh was the leading actress in the TV soap opera series, *Van Anh's Diary*, which deals with teenage issues. In the daily episode, Thuy Linh played the school girl Vanh Anh who, in spite of her modern appearance, adhered to traditional Confucianist female virtues of *công*, *dung*, *ngôn*, and *hạnh*, which determine woman's labour, appearance, speech, and behaviour. In real life, however, a private sex video of the actress Thuy Linh and a former boyfriend circulated on the internet, initiating a public outcry. In discussion platforms on the internet and in newspapers, people shared their consternation and disappointment that she did not follow her TV character's moral lifestyle in real life (The Associated Press 24.10.07). What is more, the internet scandal led to public debates about morality and gender, as viewers were mobilized to vote on moral and lifestyle issues by short text messages and e-mails (Thanh Nhien 26.10.07). The evaluation of the actress's morality reveals gender norms underlying such an appraisal. While b-girls and female poppers are far from being publicly condemned for their sexual behaviour, they nonetheless diverge from dominant gender norms through their clothing, embodied practices, and not the least their life style. Participating in crew practices and battles means staying out late at night, frequently travelling alone, and thus detaching themselves from social and gender expectations.

In conclusion, being a b-girl anywhere in the world is ultimately political, not in the least because the "private is political" – a concept rooted in the Global North, particularly the U.S., British, and German feminist movements of the 1970s — but because b-girls constantly have to "deal with the sexual politics of being in an incredible minority," in spaces dominated by men (Johnson 2014: 17).

Popping and Locking

"Originally, 'popping' was a term used to describe a sudden muscle contraction executed with the triceps, forearms, neck, chest, and legs. These contractions accented the dancer's movements, causing a quick, jolting effect. Sam's creation, popping, also became known as the unauthorized umbrella title to various forms within the dance, past and present. Some of these forms include Boogaloo, strut, dime stop, wave, tick, twisto-flex, and slides." (Chang 2006: 23).

The styles of locking and popping are closely related, as both involve bodily techniques in which one body part remains stationary, while another part moves (Banes 2004). Popping originated in California and is contemporaneous with waacking. Mainly danced with funk and hip hop music, popping is a style most often practiced in "hetero-oriented" spaces (Bragin 2014). Funk music is considered the progenitor of hip hop, standing in an uneasy relationship with disco music and its associated dance style, waacking. Consequently, popping and breaking are often found in combination with one another, whereas popping is seldom combined with waacking.

Hanoi Popping

Popping, together with breaking, are the most popular dance styles in Vietnam with the most practitioners. Vietnam has well-known poppers such as CK Animation, TF Star, Sin Boogie, and Kirby, all from Hanoi, and Rufu and MT Pop from Ho Chi Minh City. In Hanoi, there are currently some 200 poppers. One of Hanoi's oldest popping crews is the Milky Way Crew, which was founded by TF Star, whose real name is Vu Tung Phuong. In an interview, TF Star recalls how he came into contact with the style in October 2004. Two months later, he founded a dance group at his school together with friends. This school dance group laid the foundation for the Milky Way Crew. Since its founding, the Milky Way Crew, very much like Big Toe Crew, has developed various subgroups, all focusing on one particular style. One of these groups is the Funkstyle team. In 2009, TF Star and his group joined Big Toe. Since then, they have focused on becoming professional dancers. In Hanoi, the Lenin Monument has evolved as an icon of hip hop in general, and popping in particular, as dancers regularly train together there. On 1st June 2011, the Funkstyle team celebrated its 3rd anniversary at the monument. Hoa Duc Cong, known as CK Animation, was one of the first members of the Milky Way Crew's Funkstyle team. Born in 1991, he was 27 years old when I first met him, about to get married and shortly thereafter to have a baby boy. Cong has been popping half of his life, starting out around the age of 15 or 16. At that time, he explained, popping was hardly known in Vietnam, so he began dancing alone or with others, anywhere he could. Like many others, he often practiced at the Soviet Vietnamese Friendship Palace. In 2008, he joined a group at the palace, and learned a style of popping that was referred to as *Việt Style*. Since then, CK Animation has developed his unique style, becoming one of the most famous poppers in Hanoi. In fact, his alias is indexical of his style, since CK specializes in what is called animation. Animation is a particular style of popping, consisting of jerky movements by rapidly contracting the muscles. According to CK, animation particularly involves moving the torso, and bringing it to an abrupt halt. Animation is frequently compared to robotic movement or figures in stop motion animation.

CK promotes and supports the local popping and hip hop scene. For instance, he normally serves as an MC at the local waacking event, Hallowaack, promotes his fashion label called Chatko, and produces promotional dance videos with Mai Tinh Vi. In November 2019, he was invited by the TiTan crew to serve as a judge in Ninh Binh Province. He also travels widely within Southeast Asia, such as to Malaysia and Singapore, although he has yet to travel to Europe or the U.S.

Together with Hoang Phuong, CK Animation co-founded the Wonder Dance Studio where he teaches popping. Later he founded the Chatko Studio. Apart from co-founding these studios, CK Animation also created the Hanoi-based Wonder Brothers Crew. The crew's name first signifies its relationship with the Wonder Dance Studio, and second its all-male membership. The crew has approximately 10 members and regularly meets three or four times a week, around 8 p.m. at the Lenin Monument. CK Animation carefully differentiates between his students and fellow crew members. In order to become a student, those interested in popping merely need to register at his studio. But in order to become a member of his crew, they need long-term experience, dedicated practice, and they must be able to "play" (*chơi*) or work well with the other crew members.

Minh Anh, aka MA and Dung, aka Andrew, are members of the Wonder Brothers Crew. They explain that they chose to dance for fun (*cho vui*). They like to dance to funk, rap, and Viet Rap. Linh, also known as Linh Ping, is a young woman affiliated with the crew, though not a member. Linh is the only woman who regularly hangs out with male poppers from Hanoi. While Bi Max introduces her as his student, she says that she trains with Wonder Sisters, with Hoang Phuong. Linh wears wide joggings, a wide white t-shirt, and a baseball cap. She sells clothes at a clothing store at Pho Hue Street. She also works as a dance instructor at Chatko Studio, teaching the "hard class." In order to promote her class, she posts videos on YouTube. In 2019, she posted choreography of her class dancing to the latest song by Tien Tien, an upcoming Vietnamese singer and producer from Ho Chi Minh City, who collaborates with Den Vau and Suboi, among others. Linh also taught a "sexy dance" class at Unison studio, and acted as a female dancer on rapper Richchoi and Duy Tuan's music video, *Hư Quá Đi* (What a nasty boy/girl). Richchoi is an upcoming, although controversial rapper from the Northside, making his first underground success with the track "Vinagang," which since its publication in 2018 has reached more than 7 million views on YouTube. The track is a parody of Lil Pump's track "Gucci Gang," published in 2017.

I met Linh Ping, MA, and Andrew for the first time at the Ho Thanh Cong Battle in Hanoi on a sunny Sunday in mid-October 2018.

Ho Thanh Cong

In preparation for my first popping battle ever, I faced the epistemological question raised earlier, of how to write and speak about dance. The question is epistemological insofar as it alerts us to different knowledges and diverse ways of producing knowledge. In particular, the question raises the problem of how to represent somatic and kinesthetic understanding into verbal discourse. Following sensory ethnography, scholars suggest alternative forms and formats to generate and represent knowledge, such as in dance (Foster 1995; Spry 2006). In fact, my participation in the large-scale popping event

Bi Max, MA, Quan Ten, Linh Ping and Andrew

Source: Sandra Kurfürst (2018)

was the result of an attempt to bring together two worlds, perceived as separate, in scholarship and dance. Sharing an interest in youth and public space, my Vietnamese colleague and friend Tuan approached a Hanoian dance crew through a younger relative, and asked them to join a workshop at the Vietnam National University on youth, dance and public space. In response, the dance crew members suggested that they would not know how to present their work to academics. Instead, they asked us to join their dance practice, and talk to them while dancing. That is why I found myself together with Tuan, and his eldest son, on a Sunday in Ho Thanh Cong Park, attending a popping battle. The battle is organized by DOD Crew, which regularly practices in the park, and is scheduled to start at 2:30 p.m. Usually a dance contest in the middle of the day would be unthinkable in Hanoi, but since it is already mid-October – commonly said to be the most beautiful time in Hanoi – the sun is no longer so strong. Ho Thanh Cong, as the name indicates, is a lake surrounded by urban green situated between the large Lang Ha Street and the smaller Thanh Cong and Nguyen Hong Streets in Hanoi's Ba Dinh District. Entering the park from the gate at Lang Ha Street, one hour earlier than the scheduled start, the organizers had already gathered to set up. Opposite the socialist-style yellow entrance gate, a small pond and stones arranged according to feng shui principles welcome the park visitors.

DJ and MCs at Ho Thanh Cong Battle

Source: Sandra Kurfürst (2018)

In front of the stone, a sign indicates the name of the park. The organizers are busy transforming the pond-stone arrangement in a backstage for the popping battle, while they turn the paved space between the entrance gate and pond into the dance floor. As we enter, they are hurriedly running cables and fixing them to the technical equipment. Although the battle will not start for another hour, small groups of dancers, most of them boys aged between 18 to 24, have already gathered. They sit and chat or practice dance moves in the shade of a pergola covered with blossoms. Among the young men are members of the Wonder Brothers Crew. Seven of the ten crew members will join today's battle. They all wear wide trousers, sneakers (Vans, Converse All Star), XXL t-shirts, as well as baseball caps. One of them wears a t-shirt with "WONDERFUNK" printed on the front, advertising the local event. Even Linh, who usually posts images of herself wearing figure-hugging outfits, wears Adidas joggings, an XXL t-shirt, and a baseball cap. As I talk with them, the square gets more and more crowded. In another corner of the park, members of the Funky Style Crew, three boys and two girls, gather and chat. The group is headed by the 22-year-old Nam, known as Popsnap, who wears a red bandana around his head, an XL blue t-shirt, and baggy jeans with sneakers. Nam started out popping with the Wonder Dance Studio, and later joined the Milky Way Studio. As a consequence, he considers CK Animation from Wonder Dance Studio, and TF Star from Milky Way, as his teachers, pointing out that the Milky Way Crew is the first popping crew in Vietnam. Together with his crew member Dung, known as ANG, he studies at the University of Transport and Communication in Hanoi. Dung both studies and works to maintain an income. Manh, known as PAC, is 19 years old and also a member of the crew. Manh studies at the University of Industry in Bac Tu Liem. Phuong, is a female member of the crew, who only recently joined and had been practicing with them for two months by the time I met her. Phuong is an example of how newcomers choose their own crews and teachers, as she asked Nam to become a member of the crew. Phuong has rather short hair, wearing a ribbon around her head. She wears a large blue long sleeve shirt, black joggings, and black Converse All Stars. Over her shoulder, she wears an Adidas supreme bumbag with Bart Simpson print. At 23-years-old, Thuy, known as THIT, has already finished her university studies. She and Phuong are the only female members in a crew of eleven. Nam explains that usually more men practice popping than women. All of them introduce themselves, using their legal name, and only offer their alias when I explicitly ask. The only member without an alias is Phuong, as she only recently joined the crew. Her newcomer status becomes clearer as she does not participate in the battle preliminaries, but has instead come support her fellow crew members. Phuong chose popping because she enjoys it and it helps her relax (*để thoải mái*). Mahn, the youngest crew member, explains that he enjoys popping as it makes him physically stronger. The crew regularly meets three times a week, on Monday, Wednesday, and Friday evening at 7 p.m. in Nghia Do Park west of Hanoi. The last 30 to 45 minutes of practice are carried out in a cypher, marking the ritualized organization of dance practice (Hamera 2007). Mirroring the rhythms of everyday life, the cypher itself is cyclical, heralding the end of the day and marking the time when everyone says farewell and returns home.

As we talk, the crew members get restless before the preliminaries start at 2:30 p.m. Already during our conversation, more and more young people assemble, standing in small groups where they finalize their moves. Although the crowd is mostly young men, more and more young women enter the park, although most will remain spectators. They sit around the dance floor on the ground, or in the small chairs of an ice tea stall. The dance floor distinguishes

Funky Style Crew

Source: Sandra Kurfürst (2018)

itself from the rest of the park's morphology through several, almost intangible markers.

First, the dance floor's demarcation results from the alignment of bodies. Much like the Minang *randai*, the popping battle stage is in a circular configuration. Both performative acts are marked by a centripetal orientation, as the arrangement of human bodies around the dance floor discloses the central stage. In the randai, the *lingkaran* is a ring formed by eight to twelve players, who sit to the side during scenes or perform *galombang* dance sequences during songs. Mahjoeddin (2016: 362) describes the lingkaran as a "liminal membrane" that spatially demarcates the borders of the acting area. In a popping battle, the dance area is likewise marked by a liminal membrane. The composition of this membrane varies, as members of the audience shift from being spectators to dancers as they are called onto the floor. This circle of bodies is interrupted by the stone-pond arrangement noted earlier. Second, the dance floor unfolds from the MCs' and judge's vantage point, from their position in front of the large stone – the "backstage" – that faces the entrance toward Lang Ha Street. Third, the dance floor is made from an acoustic field, which emanates from the physical location of the DJ and his equipment, particularly the two music boxes oriented toward the entrance gate. The DJ literally occupies the back stage, since he positions himself slightly behind the MCs and the judge, using the stone pillar – which indicates the park's name – as the DJ desk, where the Numark mixer and tuner are situated. A black umbrella protects the technical equipment from the sun. There are two large speakers to the DJ's left and right, on the elevated stone in front of the park sign. A cable running across the lawn connects the musical and technical infrastructure to the electricity. Members of the organizing committee must constantly ensure that nobody steps or falls on the cable in order to keep the electricity running. As a result, the dance floor is created in the nexus of a liminal membrane that is constituted *corporeally* by the dancers and spectators, *visually* from the vantage point from the MCs' and judge's position, and *acoustically* through the DJ's laptop, mixer, and speakers.

Dance floor at Ho Thanh Cong

Source: Sandra Kurfürst (2018)

Today's judge is Sin Boogie from EccentricMindz Crew, a renowned popper from Hanoi. Two male MCs – whom I will see again as participants in the Red Bull Battle a week later – are hosting the battle. The dancers participating in the popping battle learned about the event from social media. Potential participants needed to sign up online, via Facebook, and then "check-in" once they have arrived at the park. Upon check-in, each dancer receives a number by which they will be called to the dance floor. Naturally, the dancers do not know whom they will battle in advance. Only if another dancer's number is close to theirs, they might have a chance of battling one another. Prior to the start, the MCs briefly explain the battle rules, with each dancer having 45 seconds to perform. By contrast with breaking, where dancers will probably stop on their own after a minute or so owed to the physically challenging and exhausting movements, other dance styles require a preset time for each dancer. Otherwise, dancers could dance on and on.

The first MCs calls the first round of dancers to the floor, using the alias that the participants registered with. For each round, ten dancers are called onto the dance floor, and the MC instructs them to align in two opposite rows of five, facing each other. On being called, the dancers step forward from the crowd and begin lining up to the judge's left side. When this left row is filled with five people, the remaining five dancers will form a line on the judge's righthand side. In other words, the ten dancers form a second liminal membrane, whose composition alternates with each round. The dancer positioned closest to the judge on his left begins, and is then followed by the dancer standing to their left. For each dancer, the second MC keeps time on his phone, counting down the last five seconds after which the popper has to exit the floor and reintegrate into the second membrane. The first MC will then call out the next dancer who takes the centre, sometimes commenting a particular move with a shout out. The dancers all take turns popping clockwise until all ten involved in the round have finished.

The last round of preliminaries stands out from the previous rounds, since not ten but rather fifteen dancers participate. The first MC instructs them how to line up using the microphone. This time, however, the dancers form a rectangular with three sides, opening toward the judge. During the entire battle, the judge stands or sits with his back leaned against the large stone, eyes directed towards the dance floor, taking handwritten notes for each dancer. Most dancers try to align their movements toward the judging gaze of Sin Boogie, yet not all are able to do so, as having the main audience to their backs can cause confusion. Newcomers to the popping community particularly struggle with the orientation of their performance. On the one hand, they are aware that they need to align to the judge's view since he decides who will dance in subsequent rounds. On the other hand, they orient towards the audience, which consists of friends, crew members, and peers.

While the preliminaries are still running, more and more people that regularly frequent the park for sports and social activities enter the park, as Hanoi's parks in the autumn become crowded around 4 to 5 p.m. An elderly man, dressed in sportswear, was somehow able to traverse the liminal membrane of the spectators, suddenly finding himself in the middle of the dancefloor, heading towards the judge. A member of the organizing committee approaches him, gently escorting him away from the dance floor. A young man stands with his baby next to the DJ and watches the show. An older woman, standing close to me, verbally assesses the performance of one of the female poppers, while cab drivers and female vendors climb up the gate at Lang Ha Street to watch the show. The owner of the local ice tea stall has offered her little stools for the audience to sit on. On one occasion, the battle needs to be interrupted due to technical problems.

The preliminaries end around 4 p.m. Of the roughly 100 participants, only four are female, but they receive as much applause and verbal support from the crowd as their male counterparts. Backstage, next to the DJ, judge, and MCs, I also meet CK Animation, who does not participate in the battle himself, but is here to support his students. While we talk, his students continuously approach him, greeting him with polite handshakes, bowing a little, and addressing him with *anh*. One of the students says that he is very anxious. CK responds in a calm and friendly manner, suggesting that there is no need to worry.

Ho Chi Minh City Popping

Like Hanoi, Ho Chi Minh City also has a vibrant popping scene. The Ho Chi Minh City's X-Clown Crew specializes in four styles, including popping, hip hop, house, and krumping. The X-Clown Crew was founded on 30 April 2009 (YouTube 2014). April 30 is a symbolic date in Vietnam, particularly for Southern Vietnam, since on 30 April 1975, Saigon was seized by Northern Vietnamese troops, ending the Vietnam War and resulting in the country's reunification. The day is a public holiday, immediately followed by Labour Day on May 1st, another symbolic holiday in support of socialism. While April 30th celebrations are staged in public spaces of major cities, urbanites increasingly use these short holidays for leisure activities and travelling (Kurfürst 2012). Accordingly, the young people founding the crew chose April 30th, possibly because of its national symbolism but also because it is a day off from school and work. The crew features renowned dancers, with one of the male dancers having been the 2014 winner of the Vietnamese TV show, *So you think you can dance?* Another dancer is Minh Tuan, known as MT Pop, well known in Vietnam and abroad for his popping style. In January 2019, MT Pop won the Juste Debout popping battle in Bangkok and received a free ticket to participate in the Paris finals in March 2019. Juste Debout is touted as the biggest hip hop dance competition worldwide, featuring categories as diverse as locking, popping, hip hop, and house dance. Qualifying rounds take place all over the world. The winner of a regional qualifying competition is invited to participate in the final battle held annually in Paris, France. MT Pop frequently travels abroad to participate in international popping battles, particularly in Europe and across East Asia, frequently visiting Japan. On the whole, the crew has approximately 10 members, three of them female, but only one of the three women engages in popping. Both in Vietnam and around the world, female poppers are rather rare.

#Femalepopper

Delphine Nguyen from France, also known as Dey Dey, is one of the few internationally renowned female poppers. She is the winner of the UK B-Boy Championship solo popping battle of 2009 and Juste Debout in 2010. What is more, she is the first female World Popping Champion. Dey Dey has a Vietnamese family background, but was born and raised in France. Moreover, she was also born into hip hop, as she explains in an interview with Red Bull. She started hip hop dancing at age eight, as her two big sisters were already dancers and her two big brothers were DJs. Dey Dey specializes in locking and popping, focusing on funk style (Kawalik 2018; Vibe 2017). Asked if she ever felt outnumbered by men, she answers:

> "I never really felt any difference. Is it because I come from a family where there's a lot of men? I grew up with four brothers, so I don't know if it's because of that. Even being in hip hop culture back then when it was mainly men, I never really noticed." (Kawalik 2018)

Her assessment is shared by many female dancers in styles otherwise dominated by men in Vietnam, who agree that the gender imbalance in their dance style was not an issue for them. When Dey Dey was the first woman to ever win the world popping championship, she received great applause as a woman changing the game. However, she also received negative comments from male peers, who downgraded her win by attributing it to her sex, rather than her skills, technique, style, and performance. She recalls how disrespected she felt both as a woman and as an artist in those moments. But rather than giving up, she decided to train even harder, signing up for Juste Debout, the biggest 2 vs. 2 popping battle in the world. Her fortitude paid off, as she won the battle, making everyone acknowledge that she did not win the first or second time because she was a woman, but rather because of the level of her performance (Vibe 2017). Dey Dey is aware that many male competitors are intimidated when facing her in battle. Together with friends, she established an all-female crew called Zamounda Crew. Talking about her crew members, she emphasizes the intimate relationships they have as friends as well as the intersubjective depth, energy, and confidence they experience when dancing together. While highly successful, Dey Dey confirms that there are only a few female poppers around, particularly at the highest levels. She lamented that at the largest popping competitions there would only be one woman at most, and sometimes whole line-ups without a single woman. As she is successful, she has often been invited to top events. For instance, after winning at Juste Debout, Dey Dey served as a judge herself. For her judge demo during the Juste Debout Netherlands Tour in 2016, Dey Dey dressed in black Puma sneakers, black trousers, and a long blouse that very much resembles the Vietnamese *áo dài*. The *áo dài* evolved as a dress for Vietnamese women at the beginning of the 20th century. Beginning as an elegant apparel during the colonial era, its meaning shifted during the subsidy period (*bao cấp*), representing feudalism that needed to be abolished. In the 1980s and 1990s, the *áo dài* developed into a national symbol of the stylized Vietnamese woman. This process was particularly promoted by the Vietnamese diaspora residing in the U.S. From there, the *áo dài* was taken up in Vietnam as well as an index of authenticity (Leshkowich 2003; Lieu 2000). Consequently, for an internationally renowned French-Vietnamese female popper to wear an *áo dài* blouse indexes the transcultural circulation and uptake of objects, in this case fashion items, as pointed out by Larkin (2013).

Dey Dey also travelled to Vietnam to lead popping workshops. A female popper named Vy, known as Rufu, joined one of the workshops in Ho Chi Minh City. Today, Rufu is the only female popper of the famous X-Clown Crew, performing solo and sometimes jointly with MT Pop. Before starting her popping career, Rufu already had an affinity towards physical challenges, as she exercised aerobics for ten years. When she entered high school, she learned about popping from her friends. On her first encounter with popping, she did not like it very much because the style seemed difficult, especially for a girl.

But as she realized that there were no female poppers in Vietnam, she took up the challenge to become a female popper.

Rufu explained that she likes a challenge. If something is particularly hard and difficult, she wants to learn even more, as she explained to me. When she started popping around 2010 and 2011, there were not as many workshops offered by international dancers in Vietnam as there are today. That is why she researched popping on the internet, particularly by watching YouTube videos. After training for six months, she finally joined her first battle, where she was among the top 16 and finally lost to a male popper. However, she won the second event that she participated in. This time, the judge of the battle was an international female popper from France of Vietnamese origin. She explains that many female dancers visited Vietnam, such as Dey Dey and her sister Cathy, as well as Sonya who is also from France and specializes in waacking and popping. Rufu learned more about popping by participating in their workshops. She was also briefly a member in another crew, but stopped practicing to focus on graduating from high school. When she enrolled to attend university, however, she came across the X-Clown Crew. Since the crew had many great dancers among its members, she longed to become a member herself. In 2012, she finally joined the crew, which is led by DoDo. To become a crew member, she did not have to undergo a casting process, but was accepted outright. Rufu started with an EB-style, the signature popping style of the Electric Boogaloos from Fresno, California. In discussing how the style was brought by OGs from the U.S. to East Asia, mostly Japan and Korea, she says that she first practiced the EB-style, but then got interested in others, too.

Apart from Rufu, there are not many female poppers around. She explains that while Hanoi has a few more female dancers than Ho Chi Minh City, they are not full-time dancers. At the time of our conversation, Rufu had just taken on a full-time job working in an office during the day, while teaching classes at night. A significant part of her life, Rufu is eager to keep dancing. Dancing keeps her active, confident, and happy, she explains, "because when I dance, I feel happy." While she has a full-time job, she teaches three evenings a week and on the other three she practices with her crew in the park. Acknowledging that she is tired from work, and that her time for dancing is limited compared to her time at university, she puts all her effort into crew practice. Rufu participates in local dance battles, like the Together Time in Ho Chi Minh City, as well as in international dance competitions like the Juste Debout in Bangkok. At age 17, she has already travelled to Singapore where she stayed with local dancers to participate in a popping event. Like other dancers, Rufu agreed that it is not only difficult to make a living from dance in Vietnam, but it is also difficult to join international dance competitions, as Vietnamese dancers hardly ever received sponsoring.

International competition thus requires long-term planning, as dancers must earn money to cover their travel expenses. Nowadays, Rufu travels abroad about twice a year, and it is important to her that she is able to finance her travel abroad by herself. That is how she maintains financial autonomy from her parent's household, while simultaneously proving to her parents – who were sceptical of her passion for dance – that she can earn money from dancing. During the COVID-19 pandemic, Rufu stayed in Malaysia for several months, participating in the local hip hop scene. Aiming to develop the Vietnamese hip hop dance community and to make it known worldwide, Rufu hopes to invite more international dancers to Vietnam in the future. What is more, Rufu's aim of fostering a multitude of dancers is more specific than the visions of her other contemporaries presented in this book, as she focuses particularly on female dancers. Acknowledging that women tend to engage more often in waacking or hip hop rather than popping, since these dance styles are all related to "girl style," she emphasizes that she wants more women to practice popping. That is why she teaches a popping class that is primarily attended by girls. Yet, she is aware that some girls only join her class for fun. But in order to develop their skills and technique, she requires her students to spend a lot of time dancing, and to finally take popping seriously.

In sum, Rufu is aware of being one of the few females in Vietnam (and basically around the world, as the interview with Dey Dey suggests) practicing in the male-dominated space of popping. She is the only female member of X-Clown Crew who participates in popping. Moreover, she also engages in infrastructuring work, especially by training and teaching popping to girls. Very active on social media, particularly Instagram, Rufu frequently tags her photos and videos with #femalepopper and #rufupopping, with the latter combining her dance name and style. The use of English in her posts and hashtag metadata indicate her goal to reach the international dance community, as her public presence is not limited to the Vietnamese speech community. While social media is often described as a non-place, Rufu's social media presence shows how language-use shifts according to her positionality and audience—all hallmarks of social situation in (virtual) place. During her time in Malaysia, for example, she mostly posted in English, whereas in

Vietnam she uses Vietnamese. The hashtag #femalepopper, however, is never translated and remains in English.

In the Vietnamese English advertisement on Instagram for a September 2020 dance class, Rufu does not differentiate between beginners or advanced dancers because "experience is never enough." In this class, she promises to show students the difference between foundations, style, and technique. She particularly reaches out to the "young generation," and in particular "all female friends," who wish to learn how to pop. Rufu's posts are always liked by renowned male poppers like MT Pop and CK Animation.

Rufu is not alone in her wish to recruit more women into popping. In 2019, she was invited to the Revolution competition in Malaysia to judge popping and all other dance categories. Organized in Kuala Lumpur, the Revolution 2019 competition aims to connect older and younger generations of dancers so that they may share experiences and inspire each other. The guest line up for popping is comprised of two female poppers out of a total of four. Ker Qian from Malaysia and Ari from Vietnam were the two female guests, whereas Boogie Legz from Vietnam and Chong Jun were the two male guests. Moreover, all three judges at the event were female, with Rufu among them. Rachel Ng, one of the organizers, announced on her Facebook site that Rufu would serve as a judge, with the line:

"Do not limit yourself because you are a woman, you are capable in dancing any style!! Girl power"

Dancers in Malaysia also organize an all-female popping battle, Host of the Dames, or H.O.T Dames, in order "to unite and create a platform for the ladies in our dance community" (Facebook 2020). The event took place in February 2020 in Petaling Jaya, a large Malaysian city near Kuala Lumpur in the state of Selangor. Once again, Rufu was invited to judge to the 1 vs. 1 popping battle. In July 2020, during the COVID-19 pandemic, Rufu reminisced about the event, posting a video of her judging a performance at Host of the Dames earlier that year, writing:

"Online battles are great but
I miss jams
I miss battles
I miss classes
Throwback to the last and great event before MCO @hostofthedames2020"

H.O.T Dames was the "last and great event before MCO," or the Movement Control Order implemented by Malaysia's federal government on 18 March

2020. As in many other places around the world, the MCO was a preventive measure to curtail the spread of COVID-19, prohibiting large gatherings of religious, cultural, and sports activities, the closure of all kindergartens and schools, as well as the restriction of all international immigrants and tourists arriving in or visiting Malaysia. When the MCO was implemented, Rufu was still living in Malaysia, posting videos of her training alone at home or outdoors on the sidewalks.

Infrastructuring work

Like the other dancing communities presented in this book, the popping community also seeks to create platforms to recruit newcomers and for fellow dancers to meet. One such event is called Wonder Funk. The boundaries between styles in the hip hop community are blurred, as the annual event features both two vs. two popping and freestyle battles, thus bringing together poppers from Hanoi and elsewhere with dancers of other styles. The event organizer is the Joy Funk Team, a loose affiliation of people dedicated to the popping community. Each year they invite a famous international dancer to the event to lead a workshop. One of the main organizers is Kirby. However, the last event took place in 2018, as Kirby stopped organizing Wonder Funk since opening his own dance studio, the Low Rider Studio. Nonetheless, Kirby's Low Ridaz Crew still invites internationally renowned dancers to Hanoi. In September 2019, for example, Kirby organized a workshop with Jr. Boogaloo, a celebrated old school popper from Oceanside California. Participating in battles, and teaching diverse popping styles like boogaloo, tutting, waving, animation, strutting, and more, Jr. Boogaloo was invited to give a workshop in Vietnam. The workshop venue was in the New Urban Area of Trung Hoa Nhan Chinh, and the early registration fee was 500,000 VND (18 Euro), while the normal fee was 700, 000 VND (26 Euro).

Another important popping event in southern Vietnam is Together Time. According to its mission statement on social media, Together Time aims to develop the popping community in Vietnam. Taking place annually in Ho Chi Minh City, Together Time was first organized by the Ho-Chi-Minh-based BDM Studio in late October 2018. Together Time features both a popping battle and a freestyle battle. Poppers from Hanoi associated with CK Animation, accompanied by Linh Ping, travelled to Ho Chi Minh City to participate in the battle. Mai served as a judge at the event. That year, MT Pop from X-Clown

Crew won the popping battle, and has participated in Together Time since its foundation.

Locking

The locking community is still quite small in Vietnam. Therefore, lockers often connect with dancers from other dance styles, mostly popping, while participating in freestyle categories at dance events. Other crews integrate locking into their dance routines. The Streetdance Crew, founded in 2003, already drew on the diverse expertise of its crew members to integrate different dance styles. While some practiced hip hop and house dance, others specialized in locking. C-Lock is one of the locking old timers in Hanoi, as he has been practicing for more than 10 years. He learned locking from Chunky, founder of the Lion City Lockers in Singapore. Chunky first learned to lock by watching online videos and was later mentored by the famous Taiwanese locker, Aga. In East Asia, Taiwan used to be ahead of Singapore in developing a vibrant locking scene, but more recently Singapore has caught up. Chunky built up the Lion City Lockers Crew, organized local locking events such as the Lockdown, and hosted the international dance event, Lock City (Teo 2015). As of 2018, C-Lock was the only locking teacher in Hanoi, where he regularly taught a beginner class in the dance studio. Later that same year, he was also teaching at CunCun Studio on Thai Thinh Street, the same studio where Mai teaches her beginner and advanced hip hop classes. C-Lock is teacher of Yen Hanh, a female locker from Hanoi.

> "I keep on locking although I can't spend a lot of time on it since I have to work and make my living, but locking is always a part of my life. Yeah, I think it is one of the things that I live for. I live for locking, for dancing, for dancers, for my friends, for everything I have – dancing has given me a lot of things. Dancing made my life more colourful and meaningful." (Yen Hanh, female locker)

Mai introduced me to Yen Hanh, together with Nguyet, as a female dancer representing funk style. Yen Hanh was born in 1994 and has been living in Hanoi for almost six years. She moved from Ha Tinh Province to study tourism and hospitality management. During her studies, she participated in the university's dance club, which offered sexy, urban style, and hip hop dance, although most students practiced choreography. Initially, Yen Hanh had planned on learning popping, having learned about popping both on television as well as from the old timers of the Milky Way Crew, TF Star and CK Animation. A friend who practiced both popping and locking introduced her to C-Lock, who would eventually become her teacher. This was around 2012. When Yen Hanh first encountered locking, she felt that it was really the right dance style for her, as it resonated with her personality: "I really like the vibe of locking, it's very fun and really peaceful. (...) It's like me, because I like something really peaceful and really fun too, like breaking or hip hop. Yeah, so I started locking, and I really feel like I'm following what I love."

Yen Hanh started attending C-Lock's class in the dance studio, and they later moved to the Lenin Monument. In locking, she prefers and specializes in Japan style. C-Lock, together and some of Yen Hanh's popping friends, chose – what they believe – was a Japanese dance name for her. As they were searching for something similar to her Vietnamese name, they suggested Harin, which similarly starts with Ha-.

Coming from the Central Vietnamese Province of Ha Tinh, Yen Hanh participated in her first battle in 2013, in Vinh City. Together with two poppers from Vinh City, she joined the 3 vs. 3 freestyle battle. This first battle was unforgettable to her, as her team came in second place. "I'm so shocked about it because I'm very new. I don't know how to battle, I just dance with all my heart." While she was not the only woman participating in the battle – the other female participants specialized in girl style or popping – she was the only female locker present. Although she faced social pressure from many people telling her that she could not continue to practice locking, she continued nonetheless, and was quite successful. Ignoring social expectations, and eventually becoming economically independent, she travelled to Singapore to join a large locking battle and was ranked in the top eight of 60 lockers. The battle judge was Patrick Pires, known as P-Lock, a renowned locker from France. Reaching the top eight in international competition, Yen Hanh was convinced that she could continue locking successfully. She has participated in multiple battles ever since.

Yen Hanh is the eldest of two sisters, and lives together with her sister in Hanoi. Leaving their parents in Ha Tinh Province to study at the university, they initially rented a room together. Five years younger, her sister is still studying at the university, but they both share a passion for dancing. Her sister practices breaking with the Big Toe b-boy class. When asked if she influenced her younger sister to engage in hip hop dancing, she insisted that it was her sister's choice, and that she admires her for breaking: "I really like breaking, b-boys, and to watch them. I think it is so pretty, you know, so powerful."

Growing up in the 1990s, Yen Hanh used to listen to U.S. and European funk and disco music (James Brown and Bonnie M.), together with her father. Eventually, the music fostered an emotional connection between Yen Hanh and her father. She admired her father's taste in music, and she explains, "Now I can feel him." Although sharing the same taste in music, her father did not approve of his daughter's passion for dance, instead wanting her to settle down. In fact, her parents do no longer need to worry that dancing will keep her from things like having a career, since Yen Hanh strictly balances work with her passion, as she suggests. She works fulltime for an online fashion company. When we meet one Thursday evening for coffee and conversation about locking, I find her busy at work on her Mac Book in a cosy coffee shop on Ba Trieu Street. She affirms that she really likes her marketing job and wants to advance in her position. Before holding a fulltime position, however, she used to practice every evening. As she is now too busy with work, she only practices with others twice a week, on Monday and Tuesday evenings at the Lenin Monument. For the lockers, the Lenin Monument has also evolved as a symbolic site, as it is the place where C-Lock's class used to take place. Due to her job, she also carefully chooses which international events to participate in. When all of her friends were already planning trips to the January 2019 Juste Debout competition in Bangkok, and later to Singapore in March 2019, Yen Hanh was still indecisive. She jokingly explains that she first has to organize her work so that she can dance during her holidays. Perhaps more importantly, like most dancers, she has to finance trips to international dance competitions on her own.

While she does not "officially" belong to a particular crew, she has friends from C-Lock's class with whom she plays together. They call their group Funky District. Much like in the case of the CunCun Crew, introduced earlier, the group's name arose from necessity. As they decided to join an underground battle as a team, they had to register with a team name. C-Lock's Singaporean teacher finally came up with the name Funky District. The name and naming process are once again indexical of the values, as well as the spatiality, of their community of practice. First of all, "funky" refers to the music to which locking is performed, as well as to the style to which it belongs, as locking falls under the umbrella of funk style. Second, "district" is an administrative unit, both within Vietnamese cities and provinces. However, since the Singaporean locker previously chose names related to urban space (Lion City Lockers), and locking generally is associated with the city (e.g., the international event, Lock City), Funky District suggests reference to an imagined urban neighbourhood. What is more, the naming process also reveals institutional requirements for formal participation. What started out as an informal group of friends was formalized by assigning a name to the group in the process of signing up for a collective competition.

Apart from Funky District, Yen Hanh is connected with dancers of other styles, too. For instance, she got to know Mai – whom she refers to as elder sister – in 2015, when they were practicing soul dance with a group of friends at Mai's CunCun studio. She also dances with Nguyet, a close friend with whom she has participated in 2 vs. 2 battles under the team name "Da Twin." They came up with the name since everybody says they look alike, which is not only attributed to their physical appearance but also to their similar movement repertoire, as both are engaged in soul dance and funk style. In 2016, she participated together with Nguyet in the Urban Jam competition's freestyle category. After the battle, one of the judges, an OG from the Hanoi breaking scene, invited her to serve as a judge for a youth dance event. The event was organized by Blue Dragon in Hanoi, a non-profit organization supporting children from poor families.

Apart from participating in local battles, Yen Hanh occasionally travels abroad. As suggested above, Singapore is an important destination for her and other lockers. She has been to Singapore twice. Much like for hip hop dance, Singapore has evolved as a hub for locking. Yen Hanh counts more than 1,800 lockers in Singapore, far more than in Vietnam where she is only aware of approximately ten lockers. She explains that Singapore appeals to famous international dancers, and therefore the Singaporean hip hop community is able to organize many large dance events, which are particularly attractive to dancers from the Southeast Asian countries like Vietnam. Before the COVID-19 crisis hit, several low budget airlines used to run daily connections from Hanoi and Ho Chi Minh City to Singapore.

While locking is commonly danced to funk music, Yen Hanh likes listening and dancing to rap music, as well, including Viet rap. When I asked about her personal connections to rappers, DJs, and graffiti writers, she recalls hip hop's four elements, suggesting that b-boys and b-girls are more likely to be engaged in them. She explains that the culture of funk is different, characterizing it as *hiền*. While *hiền* translates as gentle and virtuous, it is also an adjective commonly associated with femininity. For instance, one of the three Confucian submissions that specify three types of women's obedience to men is referred to as *mẹ hiền*, meaning virtuous mother. Nonetheless, funk, and particularly locking, is a style in which men predominate, at least in Vietnam. Among the few lockers in Vietnam, and Hanoi in particular, Yen Hanh is one of the rare female dancers. One of her friends used to practice locking with her, but she quit dancing in favour of her career. That is why Yen Hanh appreciates her female peers, Mai and Nguyet, who specialize in other dance styles but also practice locking. Yen Hanh hopes to see the locking community grow and flourish, which is why she frequently participates in battles, to make other dancers aware of her style. Although she is often approached by others to teach locking classes, she is unable to teach while working full time. Sometimes she offers informal instruction to friends, beginning with grooving. She explains that many people know about locking because of grooving, since it is foundational to locking. To Yen Hanh, it is important to extensively practice the basics, which is why in the beginning she always focuses on grooving. She notices that after a few sessions repeating the basics, many students lose interest and drop out of class. She explains: "And the younger ones, I can feel that they don't want to spend the time. So, I think that's one of the reasons why people don't continue practicing locking. And it's so sad, because I want more lockers." Generally, Yen Hanh finds the idea of community, and sharing her passion with others, to be an important feature of hip hop, which is why she enjoys sharing her knowledge about locking with others. After acting as a judge for the Blue Dragon kids breaking event, for example, she taught the children about the history of locking, as she enjoys sharing the life she leads with others.

Hip Hop Dance

"Freestyle hip hop dance" evolved in New York City dance clubs in late 1984. According to Elite Force Crew's Buddha Stretch, freestyle hip hop developed following the stricter styles of b-boying and popping (Crew 2020). In the early years as hip hop dance was adopted in Vietnam, dancers used to refer to the style as rap dance (*nhảy rap*), whereas today they use the English term "hip hop" dance (*nhảy hip hop*), dissociating it from the term "freestyle." Freestyle, by contrast, is used to refer to the battle category in which most hip hop dancers participate. Many of the battles and competitions I witnessed in Vietnam focused on breaking, as it is the most popular style in Vietnam. However, breaking was always accompanied by a freestyle battle category in which dancers of all other styles – such as popping, locking, waacking – could participate.

"We didn't know that what we were doing was hip hop"

One of the main hip hop dance crews in Hanoi is New York Style (NYS) Crew, founded by Phuong Silver Monkey in 2010. The crew's name indicates a return to hip hop's New York City roots. One crew member explains that they chose the name to stand out from other dance crews in Hanoi, for whom the LA style was predominant. The crew's founder, Phuong Silver Monkey, is a contemporary with b-boy LionT, and has been involved in hip hop dancing since 1992. In fact, LionT invited him to join the Big Toe Crew. Phuong Silver Monkey decided to join as Big Toe was a large crew, and he wanted to expand his horizons. Training at the Soviet Vietnamese Friendship Palace, he eventually founded his own crew, the Fantastic Crew. Fantastic Crew consisted of six girls with Phuong Silver Monkey as their teacher. In effect, Hanoi's first hip hop crew was an all-female crew with a male leader. Like LionT, he promoted hip hop dance among young women. His students recall how they exercised different dance moves, but at that time neither Silver Monkey nor the girls were aware that they were practicing hip hop dance. That was around 2008. At that time, b-boying, b-girling, and popping were already known in Vietnam, unlike hip hop dance. Silver Monkey researched dance moves on YouTube, and taught them to his female crew. While he was able to "copy" the motions quite precisely, he did not understand English. That is why they ended up renaming the movements on their own, not knowing that English terms already existed for the movement repertoire. A year later, when a new member entered the crew who was fluent in English, they researched the movements again, familiarizing themselves with English terms like smurfing, grooving, bouncing, and so on, which they had been practicing all along. They realized that what they were doing was part of hip hop dance's foundations.

This narrative shows quite well how information and knowledge in the community of practice is not only shared and transferred from old timers to the newcomers, but newcomers can bring in new knowledge and expand the scope of collective knowledge. Recognizing the standardized corporeal vocabulary, they were able to link and scale up to global hip hop discourse. As a result, newcomers not only assume a marginal position in social learning, but they can come to occupy a central role, for example, by contributing skills that others lack, such as knowledge of the English language. Another turning point in their growing awareness of hip hop was when the crew finally joined a competition for teenagers. Through exchange with others, and by making their practices public beyond their own crew, they realized that what they were doing was hip hop. The narrative of how they got to know hip hop illustrates learning processes within the community of practice. Embodied knowledge is distributed throughout the world in online tutorials – even reaching places that appear to be marginal to hip hop – and shared *in situ* through face-to-face interaction, as dancers form groups in particular times and spaces. Although dance instruction is often mediated by a discursive communicative repertoire, verbal language is not the only mode of conveying dance, as beats and rhythms, clapping hands, flicking fingers and tongues are also key kinesthetic modalities of communication. As Liberman (2013) shows, non-verbal forms of communication are crucial to guiding people's actions and creating order where there appears to be disorder.

While participating in Mai's hip hop class, for example, I quickly realized that although I was able to follow most of her verbal instructions in Vietnamese, the key to learning the motions was to carefully watch her, mimic her movements, feel the beats and music, and to let go. Accordingly, it is not even necessary to know the (discursive) language of instruction while learning hip hop dance. Mimesis or the mimicking of bodily practices is sufficient to begin learning. However, in order to participate in global hip hop discourses, both bodily and linguistically, it is necessary to know specific vocabulary, and to use it correctly. The need to master rap and dance vocabulary is ultimately linked to processes of standardization, for instance, the naming of body motions helps to create cooperation among actors from different social worlds (Star and Griesemer 1989). Evidence for such standardization processes is the use of English language crew names, such as Big Toe, New York Style, Wonder Brothers/Sisters, and so forth.

Another form of standardization in hip hop is the battle mode. To Phuong Silver Monkey, the battle is constitutive of hip hop dance. However, he emphasizes that it is not just about fighting each other, but that the most important outcome of the battle is that competitors become friends again. In this view, Silver Monkey shares an intimate understanding of the battle with Alien Ness, member of the New York City Breakers and Rocksteady Crew. Ness considers the battle as elementary to hip hop together with b-boying and b-girling:

> "Through battle, b-boys and b-girls learn to use humble discipline as a foundation for arrogant creativity. They transform precision and finesse into symbols of raw aggression. They attack without mercy yet still see their opponents as distinct and valuable human beings. Ultimately, battling teaches its disciples how to use style to reconcile opposing forces, a skill that may well be at the heart of hip hop itself." (Schloss 2006: 21)

For Silver Monkey, hip hop's imperative is not to triumph over the other, but to be unique and unrivalled. More than that, hip hop is about helping each other and it should be joyous (Hanyi 2014). Consequently, hip hop is not just about mimicking movement, but making progress in developing the self and community.

Finally, Silver Monkey is one of the few hip hop pioneers in Hanoi who still keeps dancing, while mostly making his living from teaching classes. Many dancers of his generation, by contrast, quit dancing altogether or changed their focus. LionT, for instance, opened an academy and focuses on teaching and arranging choreographies, while only occasionally participating in battles. Silver Monkey explains that it was quite normal for older dancers in other countries to keep dancing, while opening studios and participating in workshops to teach the younger generations. He is quite positive that Vietnamese dancers will also embark on this road in the future.

Generally, Silver Monkey believes that hip hop has a bright future in Vietnam. In a 2014 interview with Dep Online, he was asked to assess the development of hip hop in Vietnam over the last 20 years. He recalls how, in the beginning, they tried to "imitate the American dancers, who went outside to dance in the streets." At that time, however, like their American counterparts in the mid-1980s, Vietnamese dancers were expelled from parks by the police for dancing in public. In the U.S., authorities believed that dance circles disturbed the public order and considered them to be gathering sites for criminals (Johnson 2014). Today, Silver Monkey says that it is much more easy-going (*thoải mái*) to gather and dance in public spaces, for example, in the park. Already by 2008, when I interviewed dancers from the MiNi Shock and Fit Crews, they explained that it was no problem to dance with loud music and late into the evening in front of the Ly Thai To statue. Although the site is monitored by guards in charge of maintaining public order, public dancing did not appear to disturb the well-monitored urban order (*trật tự đô thị*). On the contrary, the guards regularly came to watch the young men and women who assembled to dance. Moreover, hip hop dance in public seems to be accepted by society at large, since elderly people also like to participate and many parents send their children to hip hop class. Silver Monkey concludes the interview suggesting: "Society has developed, people's thinking has become much more open-hearted" (Hanyi 2014). Consequently, he is rather optimistic about hip hop's future in Vietnam, stressing that hip hop will no longer be considered "marginal" (*ngoài lề*) but will rather become recognized.

Infrastructuring work: crews and events

In order to create a wider public and larger community for hip hop, infrastructuring work is essential. Infrastructuring can be achieved through establishing crews, organizing dance events, and most importantly by attaining public visibility, for example, by training in public space or representing a crew at dance battles. Fantastic Crew first practiced indoors in a rented room, but only expanded and recruited new members when they moved outdoors to the Lenin Monument, where male dancers also joined in. As the group became larger, Phuong Silver Monkey founded the New York Style Crew in 2010. Consequently, the public visibility and tangibility of dance practice were essential to expanding the community and raising awareness of hip hop among the urban public. While some of the female members of Fantastic Crew continued with New York Style, others quit in order to focus on careers beyond danc-ing. This is why the recruitment of new members is essential for the crew to survive. Originally coming from other hip hop dance styles, Nguyet and her husband Bi Max joined the New York Style Crew more recently. They are aware that to some onlookers, the New York Style Crew appears old, as Phuong Silver Monkey was born in 1981, while some other crew members were born between 1988 and 1990. Currently, the crew has more than ten members, only two of them female. Apart from Nguyet, Thanh Phuong is the other female mem-ber, whom Nguyet refers to as "elder sister." Against this background, they consider themselves the "new generation," with Bi Max acting as the crew's vice leader. Together with Silver Monkey, they put a lot of effort into develop-ing and rejuvenating the crew, including the recruitment of new and younger dancers. Toward this end, Silver Monkey invites kids around ten or eleven years old to practice with the crew. The old timers are in charge of showing the kids how to develop their skills. Rather than an individual mentor-mentee relationship, however, legitimate peripheral participation appears to be a col-lective effort, requiring the involvement of all the crew members. The teacher-student relationship is also marked linguistically, as the children call Nguyet and Bi Max "teacher" (cô, thầy), while they refer to the children as "child" (con).

To recruit new members and raise awareness about the New York Style Crew among hip hop dancers, Nguyet and Bi Max consider it necessary to represent New York style Crew at battles. However, to date, there are not many hip hop battles as suggested in the introduction to this chapter, but rather events that feature a freestyle category in which hip hop dancers can participate. But the difficulty with freestyle battles, Nguyet suggests, is the music that the DJ plays during the battle. Most DJs not only play hip hop mu-sic, but also other genres that are difficult for many younger crew members to dance to. That is the reason why only Nguyet and Bi Max currently participate in freestyle battles, as the husband and wife team came from waacking and breaking styles, and are used to moving to different beats. By participating in freestyle battles, they thus represent New York Style Crew.

Representation is another important value of hip hop worldwide. Indi-vidual dancers, rappers, or graffiti writers represent their crew, which in turn may represent an entire neighbourhood, community, urban quarter, city, or – at international battles – an entire country. While New York Style Crew typi-cally represents Hanoi, it represents Vietnam in international dance compe-titions, such as the Singapore Arena Dance Competition or the Juste Debout preselection in Bangkok, Thailand. The Singapore Arena is part of a series of worldwide events. According to the Arena website: "The mission of Arena is to create a platform that, through the medium of dance, will connect cultures across the world, promote creative expression, and improve the lives of artists." The platform was founded by the The Kinjaz dance crew from Los Angeles together with the dance studio Sinostage from Chendu, China. In 2017, the New York Style Crew, together with Mai Tinh Vi, submitted a video to the Singapore Arena competition, and were invited to represent Vietnam at the international event. For this event, the crew developed its own choreography, demonstrating Vietnamese cultural elements. They danced to Vietnamese music, wearing costumes resembling the dress of Buddhist monks, embodying a poem by Vietnamese writer, Xuan Dieu. Known for his love poems, short stories, and literary criticism, Xuan Dieu is an important representative of modern Vietnamese literature. In 1943, he joined the League for the Independence of Vietnam (Việt Nam Độc Lập Đồng Minh Hội), or the Viet Minh, and promoted resistance against the French colonial regime in his writings. Accordingly, their choice to incorporate Vietnamese literature and music into their dance choreography indicates a politics of belonging and representation on an international stage. Accordingly, for New York Style Crew "to represent" in Singapore not only meant to represent their crew or the city of Hanoi, but to show to the world that hip hop in Vietnam is alive.

At both the local and national levels, another form of infrastructuring work is in the organization of hip hop events in Hanoi, with the aim of increasing public visibility and pulling hip hop out of its marginal position in Vietnam. A major hip hop dance event organized by New York Style Crew in Hanoi is called Nhiệt, which they organized for the first time between 2011 and 2012. As Mbaye (2014) has pointed out with her reference to peer production, hip hop artists engage in vertical integration, for example, by organizing events that serve as local hubs and markets for hip hop. With Nhiệt, the members of New York Style Crew sought to share their passion for hip hop dance with others, to build social relationships, and to expand their social horizons. Nhiệt literally translates as heat, and thereby references one of five elements of fire, earth, air, water, and ether from the I Ching. B-Boy Alien Ness combines b-boy with fire philosophies to reference the dancers' intensity, their heat, and how they come into the dance (Schloss 2006: 22). Put differently, for Ness the dancer's attitude towards their opponent is the key to winning a battle, even more than their actual movements. The attitude of the dancer becomes even more pronounced as Thanh Phuong, one of the main organizers of Nhiệt, explains the meaning of the event's name, translating it as "hit from fire." Ian

New York Style Crew

Source: Facebook Whassup Sisters (2019)

Condry (2001), in his ethnographic account of hip hop in Japan, likewise puts
the flame metaphor to work. He draws on the lyrics of Japanese rapper ECD,
who employs a metaphor of the spark in describing the arrival of hip hop in
Japan. Overall, Condry (2001: 225) suggests that hip hop never travels between
locales, but suggests that "it is the spark and the local fuel together that make
the fire burn with its own particular range of colors." Condry elaborates that
although popular music tends to travel on the winds of global capitalism, the
local fuel will ultimately determine whether it burns or dies out. The Nhiệt

event was in fact an attempt to ignite passion for hip hop among the public in Hanoi, and to create a larger national hip hop community.

The Nhiệt event in Hanoi was organized three years in a row, bringing together hip hop dancers and b-boys and b-girls, as the latter still formed the majority in Vietnam. The event had two battle categories: b-boy 1 vs. 1 and hip hop 1 vs. 1. The first event took place in a park, and the second time the event was held in a mall. On the third occasion, the NYS Crew invited Henry Link, founding member of the internationally known Elite Force Crew from Brooklyn. Henry Link is an old timer of hip hop who got engaged in locking, popping, and breaking soon after the styles appeared in the U.S. He became popular with his dance style in Michael Jackson and Mariah Carey music videos. One reason for inviting Henry Link was that it is hard for Vietnamese dancers to participate in battles abroad, mostly owed to a lack of financial resources but also due to visa restrictions. Accordingly, NYS crew aims to create a larger public and community for hip hop in Vietnam by inviting international icons like Henry Link to Hanoi. In fact, a lot of former dancers, who had already quit dancing altogether, joined the event with Henry Link (Hanyi 2014). However, after Henry Link's appearance in Hanoi, Nhiệt needed to be put on hold due to a lack of organizational capacity. In 2018, when I was visiting Hanoi, Thanh Phuong explained that she was too busy with work to organize the event this year. While her job kept her from organizing the event this time, the skills she acquired from her job helped her organize the initial event.

Apart from organizational skills, financial resources were another issue. The whole event was pulled off by the New York Style Crew alone, and their major aim was to create a dance floor as a commons of sorts, in which anybody could participate independently of financial resources. While it has become rather common in Vietnam, like elsewhere around the world, to seek sponsors for larger sports events, there was little support for a hip hop event. Phuong Silver Monkey reflects that people might be willing to spend millions for a football match, since football is really popular in Vietnam. But what, he asks, do people get out of a football game? Hip Hop culture attracts young people, provides them with inspiration and joy from dancing. "Like rock, people who love hip hop have passion, and they depend on the passion of those who are able to maintain and make every effort of a difficult life" (Hanyi 2014). Another reason they refused to look for financial sponsors, was that sponsored battles were not "real." A real battle, for them, meant concern for the participants, the dance floor, the sound, and lighting. On the contrary, if a brand sponsored a battle, the sponsor would only be concerned about the number of participants and spectators, and how many celebrities participate, in order to advertise their products. Along similar lines, Mai Tinh Vi explains that sometimes there are larger events like the TV show *Vũ Điệu Xanh*, sponsored by businesses and brands. She attended one such event sponsored by an ice cream company, but emphasized that "it didn't feel like [a real battle], you know." When asked why it did not feel right to her, she explains that no one even started to cypher at the event. In the end, a lot of dancers agreed to keep Nhiệt small, rather than organizing a large event supported by commercial industries.

Mai Tinh Vi's and Silver Monkey's rationale indicate an important shared value in the global hip hop community of practice, which is "keeping it real," in other words maintaining authenticity. Rather than having a commercially sponsored event and getting a lot of attention, members of community prefer smaller events so that all those interested can participate in hip hop. Thus, the inclusiveness of Nhiệt was a major priority, while another goal was to promote hip hop culture to society at large. While Silver Monkey is optimistic about the future development of hip hop in Vietnam, he is mostly concerned that hip hop becomes publicly visible and accepted: "Most important is that people see us when we convey our message, and that they accept and understand it." This overarching goal motivates their use of a communicative repertoire that is also legible outside their community of practice. For instance, Phuong Silver Monkey suggests that flash mobs fitting well with Vietnamese culture, and that they make use of language to convey their gentle message, such as in idioms of peace and love (*tình yêu hòa bình*). While peace and love may be reminiscent of a hippie-esque discourse, the metaphor of peace (*hòa bình*) is a central value to the revolution and in Vietnamese nation-building overall. For instance, Hanoi is referred to as the capital of peace (*thủ đô hòa bình*), a term frequently employed on propaganda posters and flags, such as those welcoming visitors from the International Noi Bai Airport, as they cross the bridge over the Red River. This point once again hints at the embodiment of revolutionary values by postwar Vietnamese youth, expressing them in their own ways and in popular culture.

Almost five years after the last Nhiệt event, the crew organized the fourth round of Nhiệt in October 2019. In the meantime, more and more hip hop dance events have emerged in Vietnam's major cities, such as Floorkillers, Hanoi Unity, Together Time in Ho Chi Minh City, and the Hue Streets Festival. Since 2018, the Red Bull Battle has been held in Ho Chi Minh City and Hanoi. Even during the COVID-19 crisis, dancers remain active, seeking to create alternative formats to the conventional face-to-face battle. Under the government-mandated lockdown that began on 1 April 2020 for 15 days, Mai Tinh Vi organized the Monsta Corona Freestyle Online Battle, which references her own label, Monstarock. On April 6, the registration list for the preliminaries was posted on Instagram. Participants were divided into three categories, each comprised of 26 to 27 dancers. Each category was further divided into groups of three, and each group was assigned a different track number. The track numbers were posted beneath the list, including a link to Google Drive where they could access the music.

The procedure for participating is as follows: Each dancer uses the music track assigned to them to record their dance round. The video is then sent to the organization's email by 5 p.m. on Monday, 6 April. The judges watch each video for one minute and then choose the best five dancers from the group to join the top 16. The last slot would be decided jointly by all three judges. Following the prelims, the top 16 dancers is announced by 10 p.m. on 6 April. The prelims are followed by a live stream at 1 p.m. on 7 April. From the top 16 dancers, eight battles are selected randomly. The post uses the hashtags: #monstarock #onlinebattle #monstacorona #freestyle #dance #proGacademy # hiphop #housedance #locking #breaking #popping #benphan #jokerrock #mcbuck #xClown #maitinhvi. The hashtags make several references, including to the COVID-19 crisis, diverse street dance styles, institutions and individuals prominent in the Vietnamese hip hop scene.

The eldest sister – Chi Bao

Thanh Phuong, aka Bao, is a member of New York Style Crew. Born in 1988, Thanh Phuong holds a degree from the University of Law on Nguyen Chi Thanh Street in Hanoi. She emphasizes that she will never be a lawyer, as she has never worked as such despite her educational background. Instead, she currently works for a major Vietnamese real estate company in marketing, where she has recently been promoted and now leads her own team. On the job, she has to travel quite a bit, both within Vietnam and abroad to other Asian countries. That is why I was quite lucky to meet with her during a lunch break. Stepping outside the office building into the newly developed My Dinh quarter, she wears a tight black dress, no tights, Wellington boots made from genuine leather, as well as a black coat. She is single with no children and lives together with her parents in Hanoi. Originally from Ha Long, her parents moved in with her after she got her first job in the capital. Before her parents moved in, she had already lived on her own while studying at the university. She explains that she does not live with her parents because they expect her to do so, but rather because she herself does not like to live alone. Thanh Phuong is actually the only dancer I met with a fulltime job unrelated to dancing, and which requires her physical presence in headquarter building and in meetings with clients all around Vietnam and Asia. She explains: "You see, I am working for a real estate group, kind of a big group and I love my job and I love dancing too. But I have to arrange the time to bring dancing and working together." That is why she only participates in crew practice once a week, while other crew members regularly practice three times a week.

Thanh Phuong started dancing around 2007 or 2008, in her second year of university. Like her younger crew member Nguyet, she started off with waacking but she soon found hip hop more appealing. She began in the all-female Fantastic Crew, participated in Silver Monkey's open class at the Lenin Monument, and subsequently became a member of New York Style Crew. Thanh Phuong is very fond of the Fantastic and NYS Crews, as the first hip hop dance crews in Hanoi. To her, hip hop is about mixing styles and a way of finding herself: "You can make some uprock or downrock from b-boy, or some foil from locking, or some salsa move from house dance, and the music, too. So many elements from the other kind of music together. And that is why I love hip hop. It's like a kind of mixing, you can find some part of yourself in that."

Being 30 years old at the time of the interview, Thanh Phuong is slightly older than the other female dancers I met. Aware of her seniority in the hip hop community, she also takes responsibility for the community. She appreciates and encourages the skills and styles of her younger peers, and has been dancing with Nguyet and Bi Max for two years. Although both of them only recently started in hip hop, she recognizes their quality and quick development. She admires Mai for her personal style and values how she got into hip hop so early, while still in school. She collaborated with Mai Tinh Vi, participating in a 2 vs. 2 hip hop battle, and in New York Style Crew's choreography at the Singapore Arena hip hop event, representing Vietnam.

The younger peers, in turn, refer to Thanh Phuong as eldest sister, *chị cả Bao*. They appreciate her early involvement in hip hop, and her commitment to the hip hop community. During the King of Basic (K.O.B) event organized at Last Fire Studio in summer 2020, the organizers invited Bao to serve as a judge. The New York Style Crew proudly announced her on their Instagram and Facebook pages as: "Our eldest sister, founder of 'Nhiệt', of 'King

Of Basic K.O.B': Although focusing on her work for some time now, Bao never stopped to support and help the young hip hop generation. Thank you for joining K.O.B this year. RESPECT ♥♥" (Facebook King of Basic, 7 July 2020). The hip hop community acknowledges her support, as she uses cultural and social capital she acquired from her job to organize hip hop events in Hanoi, as she explains: "They like what I am doing because everything is just for our community, no advertising or anything like that, we like it smaller". For example, she writes funding proposals, while carefully monitoring the number of sponsors supporting the event. She only looks for sponsors to balance the co-organizers' personal financial resources, and to keep the event affordable to members of the hip hop community. Apart from Nhiệt, she organizes the Hanoi Unity event. Hanoi Unity is one of the first events in Hanoi to bring together all of hip hop's four elements, DJing, MCing, graffiti, and dancing. Unity, then, signifies the idea of unifying otherwise distributed communities of practice in Hanoi under the banner of hip hop culture. Thanh Phuong organized Hanoi Unity in 2015, which took place in a wedding plaza on Lang Ha Street. She engages in infrastructuring work by archiving the events through video recordings, and distributing them via social media platforms, such as Facebook or YouTube. In this way, the events become searchable and visible online. Recently, she has been thinking about creating an online platform to connect Vietnamese dancers with international dancers. In her wording, she differentiates between "us," as the Vietnamese hip hop community, and "the world." She thereby references the divide between centres of hip hop, like the U.S., and peripheries such as Vietnam, recollecting how much money and effort it took them to invite a renowned dancer like Henry Link to Hanoi. To create a platform for dancers from all over the world to connect and share experiences, she is considering developing a phone app. While showing me videos on her phone inside a noisy lunch counter, she says: "That's a beautiful moment. (...) That's the reason why I wanna organize this kind of event, because of that moment." The video artefact triggers her affective relationship with hip hop culture. Accordingly, information artefacts contribute to infrastructuring work, as they archive events, ephemeral practices, and even evoke affective reactions by those who both watch and share such videos, which convey their passion for dance.

Her attempts at infrastructuring work and commitment to the community also have implications for her career. In her future-making, Thanh Phuong is quite practical, aiming to create synergies between her job and her passion for dancing. She is aware that she cannot have both at the same time, holding a leading position in a large company while practicing hip hop several times a week. That is why she hopes to use her skills, knowledge, and social networks to open her own studio. To do so, however, she needs to acquire financial resources. Consequently, she developed a two-step-plan: First, she started saving part of the money, which she earns from her job. Second, she plans on writing a business plan to find investors. However, while talking about the capital she needs to pull this off, she emphasizes that she does this for the community, whereas for her, "money is just a tool."

Ban Rua – Wonder Sisters

Born in 1989, Hoang Phuong started practicing hip hop dance around 2008. That year she participated in her first hip hop class with Phuong Silver Monkey, although she had already gotten in touch with hip hop several years earlier, around 2004 while she was in high school. Growing up in Hanoi's Dong Da District, she went to Tran Phu school in Hoan Kiem District. In high school, each class was required to perform a show. Together with her friend, she chose to cover the Viet rap track, *Kỉ niệm trường xưa*, by the two male rappers, Lil Knight and Young UNO. The original track name is *Ký ức học trò*[14], and is about school and exams –recurrent themes in Asian rap, for instance, in South Korean rap. Since parents invest a lot of financial resources in their children's education, and education is highly valued, children find themselves under strong social pressure to perform well in school. Accordingly, Hoang Phuong and her friend took up this theme in their own context as high school students. Hoang Phuong rapped Lil Knight's part, while her friend performed Young UNO's part. During their performance, other students started to perform moves from popping and breaking. In that moment, their performance to the rap track functioned as a boundary object, connecting students who had not interacted before, recognizing each other via the word play of rap, and the bodily performance of popping and breaking.

In order to prepare for their performance, she practiced the dance routine with her classmate, who at that time frequently danced at the Soviet Vietnamese Friendship Palace. One day she took Hoang Phuong with her, which was where she met Thanh C.O., the leader of C.O. Crew, who became her first teacher. Thanh went to the same school, but she only got to know him

---

14   https://www.youtube.com/watch?v=xly4iqDAUtM

at the palace. C.O. Crew practiced in the house of culture behind the Soviet Vietnamese Friendship Palace. After practice, Hoang Phuong would join the other dancers to hang out in the palace lobby out front. In the lobby, she saw Phuong Silver Monkey dancing alone. In that moment, she knew that he should become her teacher. When recounting that moment, the pitch of her voice rises. Finally, she and her friend asked him to train them. Phuong Silver Monkey started to teach six girls. That was when Thanh Phuong and Hoang Phuong met, as they were among the first members of the Fantastic Crew, which later became the New York Style Crew.

Hoang Phuong started dancing at high school, when she was still living with her parents. Her parents did not completely approve, but they did not address the issue, as they recognized that dancing made her happy. The awareness of and care for their child's happiness, even if hip hop dancing challenges social conventions, was also shared by Thanh Phuong's parents. Hoang Phuong emphasizes how engaging in hip hop as a teenager completely changed her life. She recalls how she used to be shy, but with hip hop in her life, she gained a lot of freedom. Meeting her today, one would hardly guess that she used to be shy, especially considering her entrepreneurial spirit. Having studied banking and finance at Thang Long University, Hoang Phuong found her own way to earn an income while dancing at the same time. At age 29, she has already tried out various jobs, but most of them were "not good" for her. Finally, some years ago, she quit her previous job and started to work as a fitness instructor for an international fitness studio chain in Hanoi's old quarter. Her new job allows her to make "good money," while being able to practice hip hop dance. Last year, she co-founded her own dance studio together with a well-known popping dancer. When asked if her background in finance and banking helped her establish her own studio, she responds that the studio is not for earning money. While she earns her money by teaching classes in different studios, her own studio serves as a creative space for those who share passion for hip hop. Apart from hip hop classes, under which she subsumes the styles of hip hop, popping, and waacking, her studio offers dance classes that also cater to wider audiences, ranging from urban choreography as well as a girl style or "sexy dance" class. She refers to the latter as being "a little sexy and just fun."

Dance classes that target women by advertising a specific body image – namely, that of an attractive, sexually desirable woman – is a phenomenon that can be observed widely throughout Hanoi. Ann Marie Leshkowich (2008) makes similar observations about Ho Chi Minh City's growing fitness culture, arguing that body images become more important in processes of commodification. Fitness culture is particularly embraced by the growing urban middle class, for whom membership in fitness clubs indicates status and a cosmopolitan life style. Moreover, fitness club membership is a particular form of conspicuous consumption, as it signals that women are free from existential responsibilities like labour or house work, and have enough time and money at their disposal to spend time in fitness clubs. According to Leshkowich (2008: 49), this tendency toward bodily self-disciplining through the consumption of fitness goes hand in hand with the state's promotion of ideals about urban-middle class femininity. Whereas in the post-war era, such conspicuous consumption would have been considered decadent and bourgeois, today images of slim and sexually attractive women are circulated through media such as magazines, books, newspapers and the like. With economic liberalization, women's beauty is consistently marketed as being their own responsibility, for which they need to exert effort in shaping their bodies through physical activity or going on diet.

Such popular images of women in late socialist Vietnam can be read in multiple ways. First of all, the circulation of images is amended by beauty manuals, with one of them evoking the Confucian virtue of *dung*, calling on women to maintain an attractive outer appearance, which is considered appropriate to their economic and social status (Leshkowich 2008: 58). Second, such idealized femininity recalls the three-fold obedience of women, namely, in the relationship between husband and wife. In heterosexual relationships, women need to remain sexually attractive to their husbands. For this purpose, magazines purport to draw on scientific knowledge in providing advice for conjugal relations. Third, such imagined femininity is not unique to Vietnam. Suzanne Brenner (1999: 17) describes virtual and verbal images of women circulating through print media under the New Order in Indonesia. These images evoked the many incarnations of modern Indonesian women: "as happy consumer-housewife, devoted follower of Islam, successful career woman, model citizen of the nation-state, and alluring sex symbol." Apart from the specific time and place of New Order Indonesia, or post-reform Vietnam, such images of women circulate widely across the globe. That said, the adherence to such body images could be seen – for better or worse – as connecting with global imagery of female bodies.

Against this background, we can understand why dance studios offer both girl style or "sexy dance" classes as well as "hard" classes that cater to the demand for normalized bodies. This also provides an explanation for Hoang

Phuong's decision to offer a girl's class, as a strategy for balancing smaller revenues from the hip hop class. Hoang Phuong explains that most people in Vietnam are not acquainted with hip hop at all, thinking that hip hop is some kind of modern dance that will help them shape their bodies. But in her studio, they target participants who are really interested in and share a passion for hip hop's dance styles. The studio is called Wonder Dance Studio, and was founded by Hoang Phuong together with the famous popper CK Animation. Accordingly, the co-founders create synergies through their specialization in different styles, and by representing different sexes.

CK Animation leads his own popping crew, the Wonder Brothers. By contrast, Hoang Phuong created her own all-female hip hop crew, the Wonder Sisters. The choice of English crew names once again hints at standardization, and local efforts to connect with the global hip hop scene. In addition, the names signify a kind of corporate identity, as the crew names relate to their mother dance studio, the Wonder Dance Studio. The Wonder Sisters Crew consists of six girls who have been following Hoang Phuong for several years. There used to be seven, but one girl is currently abroad. The crew members were already her students before Hoang Phuong opened her studio. At that time, they were practicing outdoors in the park behind the Ly Thai To statue. In the pavilion, where I had encountered the first b-girls in 2008, Hoang Phuong offered two classes, one on hip hop foundations while the other was an open class. The aim of the open class was to create space for freestyling, as Hoang Phuong helped her students develop their own style. She emphasizes that what holds them together as a group is not only dance, but that they "share many things about life" in common. As a result, they spend a lot of time together, hanging out and practicing every night. Today, she sometimes still takes her team to the Lenin Monument to practice. However, she is very conscious about both the merits and limits of training in public space. Although Hoang Phuong started out dancing in public space, she acknowledges that it is impossible to train in the park forever, particularly if a dancer wants to advance. She cites the number of other park users, suggesting that parks are overcrowded these days and that it is hard to concentrate in public. In contrast to Nguyet, who emphasizes the sensory experience of dancing in public spaces, Hoang Phuong outlines the sensory methods of learning in the studio, saying that she needs to listen to and see her "posture" in the mirror. That is why she mostly exercises with her team in her studio. When practicing in studio, the crew only needs to pay a small amount of money for using the infrastructure, mainly for electricity. The intimate, and rather informal, relationship between her and her students is also signified in their choice of pronouns, since her students address her as "older sister" (*chị*) rather than referring to her as "teacher" (*cô*). Hoang Phuong's offer for free hip hop classes in a public space aligns with the approaches of many other hip hop icons, who would offer free classes outdoors. Consequently, Hoang Phuong, like her teacher Phuong Silver Monkey, or the waackers WHOWL and C2Low whom I introduce in the next chapter, make their dance practices visible in the city and thus accountable to others. In this way, they introduce diverse dance styles into the public sphere, with the aim of recruiting newcomers into their community of practice.

Hoang Phuong is known in the hip hop community as Bạn Rùa. *Bạn* means friend indexing her participation in a community of peers. *Rùa* translates as tortoise. She received her alias from her first dance teacher, Thanh C.O. My first guess was that he gave her the name in reference to the power move called "turtle" from breaking, but she clarifies that he started calling her turtle due to the position of her neck while dancing. In Vietnamese culture, the tortoise is a sacred animal, indicating wisdom and longevity. For example, in Hanoi's Temple of Literature (*Văn Miếu*), the stone pillars, which display names of the men who passed their doctorate in the temple, stand on tortoises made from stone. Bạn Rùa has participated in multiple competitions and dance battles. While studying at university, she participated in her university's dance club, too. The members mainly practiced K-Pop, while Hoang Phuong and one other girl engaged in hip hop dancing. The club participated in the Vietnam University Games (VUG) under Hoang Phuong's leadership. In 2013, they first won the national round in Hanoi, and were invited to Ho Chi Minh City to battle with the winner of the Southern competition. They beat the team in Ho Chi Minh City to win the first Vietnam University Games ever. That the VUG tends toward hip hop is indicated by the fact that the first competition judges were Mai Tinh Vi and Phuong Silver Monkey. Apart from these national youth competitions, Hoang Phuong also participated in the national TV program, *Vũ Điệu Xanh*. She participated with a friend in a 2 vs. 2 battle, but they lost to a dancer from Ho Chi Minh City, the best dancer in Vietnam at that time. Hoang Phuong recalls that the format of the TV show was really tough.

While VUG and TV programs such as *Vũ Điệu Xanh* point to the commercialization and popularization of hip hop in Vietnam, I ask Hoang Phuong what hip hop means to her, recalling her earlier statement that most people in Vietnam do not know what hip hop really is. Explaining that she does her own internet research on the history and origin of hip hop, she says that she is

Hoang Phuong, Wonder Sisters Crew

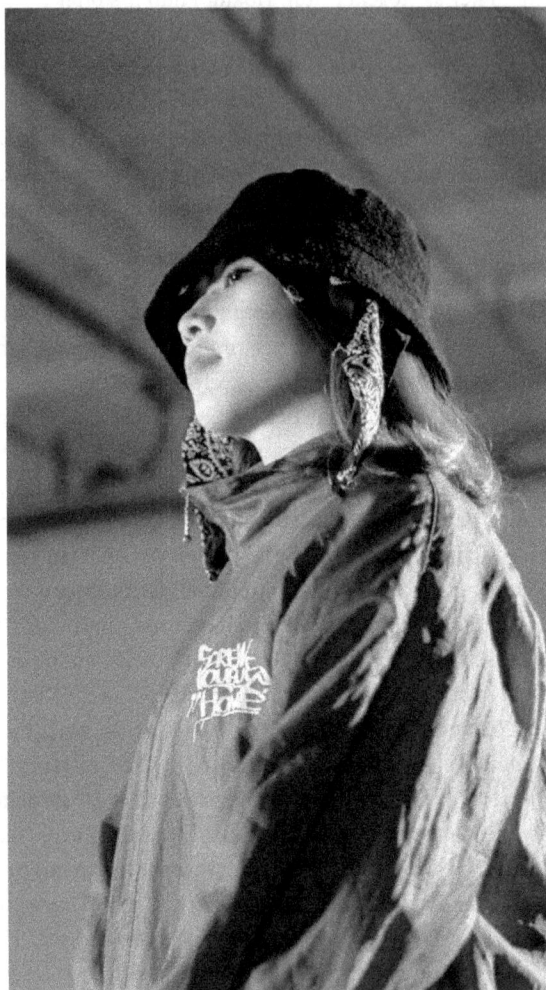

Source: Hoang Phuong (2020)

aware that hip hop is a culture. She explains the origin of the term b-boy, as b-boys used to dance to breakbeat music created by DJs in the 1970s. She recalls how some years ago, she was even able to feel the culture in Hanoi during an event that combined graffiti and rap with dancing. She even started to rap herself, but quickly realized that she was much better at dancing. That was some time ago, however, and both the culture and her feelings have changed. None of that matters to her, she explains, "because I love dance, I love dancing, I love hip hop dance. So, I just practice." That is why she decided to exclusively research hip hop dance. In her research, she found famous videos from the Elite Force Crew. The videos "Old school dictionary," "Middle school dictionary," and "New school dictionary" are retrievable on YouTube. In the videos Buddha Stretch and Henry Link, both members of Elite Force Crew and pioneers of hip hop dance show what they call the "step bible." The videos show the two male protagonists standing in public space, an alley or basketball court, and alternately demonstrating a particular dance move. The only verbal communication in the footage is when Henry Link and Buddha Stretch call out each movement's name. The names are all references to American popular culture, ranging from popular comic figures and actors to sports brands, such as Smurf, Reebok, Fila (old school), Steve Martin, Bart Simpson (middle school), Skeeter, Rabbit, and Harlem Shake (new school).

Hoang Phuong's narrative indicates a combination of different knowledges. On the one hand, she researches hip hop's history on the internet through information artefacts such as video recordings. On the other hand, she "feels" or at least used to feel the presence of hip hop culture in Hanoi. Accordingly, she combines knowledge retrieved through textual and audio-visual sources with her sensory knowledge. This process is also reflected in her assessment of the dance experience. For Hoang Phuong, dance is not only about movement or skills. On the contrary, she states that her dance experience is intimately linked to her life experience, as she draws on, combines, and uses all kinds of inspirations and daily experiences from her job, conversations, and various relationships in dancing. Ultimately, she considers dancing as a tool to express herself: "in a few years, maybe I will try other things to help me to express myself. I don't know. But this time it is only about dance. So, I don't think too much about that." Her sensory approach to dancing also informs her assessment of what it means to be a good dancer. Hoang Phuong often serves as a judge in local and national battles. She identifies two factors that are most important to her as a judge, first, emotions expressed with the body, and second, personal style. First, like so many other dancers I spoke to, she assesses the quality of a dancer not exclusively on their skills, but based on a feeling for the dancer with the music playing, as expressed with their bodies. She explains: "Sometimes I want the music to lift you." Second, dancing is not solely about skill and technique. There may be dancers who have excellent technique, but if they lack their own style, she prefers dancers who may only perform basic moves but with a personal style and feeling.

Hip hop and gender

Thanh Phuong narrates how she longed to be like her teacher the first time she met him at the Soviet Vietnamese Friendship Palace: "I saw him, and I feel like I wanna be him. And I try to do things to make myself look like him. But on the way to being like him, I found so many ways to complete myself (...) I don't want to be him anymore. I want to be myself." Her willingness to imitate a man hints towards gender trouble, the queering of gender in hip hop. Her desire was not about becoming a man, or even behaving like a man. While she started to mimic her teacher, she soon found who she was herself. Thus, gender does not appear as a major factor determining status in the hip hop community of practice, at least when it comes to judging a dancer's quality. Age, for example, is always indicated by an adjective, as when younger dancers refer to their teachers as old, or when they subsume a group of dancers within a particular generation, like first or second generations. Some of the female dancers, like Mai, even seemed surprised about my inquiries into gender. Dancers gain recognition from their peers based on their attitude, style, or technique. Thanh Phuong explains: "It is one reason why they have a different style, because like I'd say dancing is some kind of language and a dancer can prove themselves by that language. And when they present themselves, they show their personality and the style, their activity." Gender, by contrast, is not explicitly discussed. When I asked Mai how she felt surrounded by men, and if she felt respected by them, Mai was astonished, answering that, of course, she received respect from her male peers. In fact, Thanh Phuong was the only dancer who raised the issue of gender herself. One of Thanh Phuong's initial statements when we first met was that female dancers have more power than men, since women have to be responsible for many more things in life than men. Consequently, female dancers are able to practice and blend many different motions and emotions, which, according to Thanh Phuong, is what hip hop is all about. Dancing is also about embodying different emotions, which is something women are better at, as she explains: "a man, he can't feel like a woman, but a woman can feel like a man. They're different. You can see Mai Tinh Vi. She is better than a man."

Although many female dancers did not cite gender as a major issue, gender nonetheless surfaces in a number of other ways. Thanh Phuong's quote shows that she draws on gendered idioms when she evaluates the quality of Mai's performance, raising her above the male dancers she knows. Similarly, gender is used in communicative repertoires on social media. Like Bao, Bạn Rùa was one of the four judges at the King of Basic in 2020. On their Facebook page, the K.O.B. organizers proudly presented her: "Today, we would like to present to you all the first judge of Hip Hop Newbie 1 versus 1, a girl whose name will definitely make male dancer's hearts distressed haha." (Hôm nay, chúng tôi xin được giới thiệu đến các bạn vị Judge đầu tiên của thê loại Hip Hop Newbie 1 vs 1, một cô nàng mà khi nhắc đến cái tên đã làm điêu đứng bao con tim của các chàng trai Dancer haha.)

Linguistically, the author of this post uses a double evocation of gender, by characterizing the female judge as *cô nàng*. Both syllables indicate the female sex, *cô* meaning young woman and *nàng* meaning she, her, or girl. What is more, the author refers to the crowd of dancers, which Rùa obviously stands out from, as *chàng trai Dancer*, denoting the male sex of the majority of dancers.

Waacking

In this chapter, I discuss gender performances within the style of waacking drawing on dance and performative ethnography. In *Between Theatre and Anthropology*, Richard Schechner (2000: 6) alludes to the "liminal qualities of performance," pointing to the transformative aspects of rituals, theatre, and trance dancing. Such performances result in social status changes among performers, and sometimes even among spectators. In the case of initiation rites, permanent transformations can be achieved, whereas in aesthetic theatre and trance dancing, the changes are mostly only temporary in nature – Schechner refers to such temporary changes as transportation. In what follows, I will explore the social changes realized in dance – whether permanently or ephemerally with respect to the performance of gender, as gender bending is central to the style of waacking. As DeFrantz (2016: 69) argues, queer gender articulations, even by non-queer dancers, bring the practices of black social dance to the foreground.

According to Naomi Bragin (2014: 64), "Textual and verbal descriptions of Waacking often obscure its queer[15] (Punk) history, or resort to vague characterizations of the style as 'feminine'." Such characterization of the style as feminine are based on normative gender categories, which inform the bodily practices of waacking, including its perceptions in Vietnam. In her elaboration of gender stereotypes in Vietnam, Nguyen (2019: 57) draws on Herzfeld's (2005) understanding of stereotypes. According to Herzfeld, social groups make use of metaphors to structure their self-representations. Although some individuals may contest stereotypes that inform such representations, they are nonetheless important to social actors' meaning-making,

---

15   In this chapter, queer mainly refers to non-normative genders and sexualities, whereas Johnson (2009) correctly points out that, in academic circles, queer has also come to be deployed in anti-essentialist discussions about non-normative expressions of race and class.

as they employ them consciously to achieve their own goals. Such stereotypes of femininity and masculinity are constantly negotiated in the Vietnamese hip hop dance community. Although this book is focused on hip hop's multipolarity and multi-referentiality (Mbaye 2014), it is particularly relevant to consider waacking's intersections with queer history in the United States.

Initially, waacking or punking evolved in queer Latino and black social spaces, such as gay underground discos in Los Angeles in the 1970s. Waacking draws on freezing and popping gestures, connecting muscular tension in different body parts with brief, transitional flowing movements that might be considered feminine (Bragin 2014; De Frantz 2016).

> "Waacking explores extravagant gestures of punching and hitting, but centers on the preparation for striking rather than striking itself. When waacking, dancers can appear to be executing super-fast warmup exercises for a physical battle. But both forms exalt a decorativeness of gesture, aligning their practice with normative conceptions of femininity as decorative and embellished." (DeFrantz 2016: 68)

Bragin (2014) differentiates between the terms waacking and punking. Waacking refers to rhythmic arm-whipping motions characteristic of the style, whereas punking "indicates a stylized movement behavior that expands beyond set vocabulary, incorporating elements of large locomotion, dramatic gesture and facial expression, and narrative" (Bragin 2014: 63-64; DeFrantz 2016). In fact, the first waacking dancers were inspired by images from early Hollywood movies, mimicking classic Hollywood glamour actresses, such as Greta Garbo, which resulted in a style referred to as "Garbo." The distinction between waacking and punking is thus important with respect to processes of marginalization, since "punk" was originally, in fact, a derogatory term for gay men. Straight dancers would use the term "punking" to parody gay men's movements. By contrast, Tyrone Proctor, one of the pioneers of punking/waacking, used the term "waacking" when teaching outside the gay community. Finally, Jeffrey Daniel, a prominent member of the R&B group, Shalamar, introduced the idiosyncratic orthography to "waacking" with the double "aa" (Bragin 2014: 64, 67). The waacking dance style gained national and international attention through the American TV-show dance, *Soul Train*, which is often referenced by Vietnamese dancers as constituting the roots of hip hop dance.

According to DeFrantz (2016), theatricalized forms of social dance, such as waacking or voguing,[16] emerge in local public spheres where music and dance evolve together, each bringing forward the other. The dance waacking/punking style is closely linked to the disco music soundscape. In contrast to funk, which is considered hip hop's progenitor and the music that accompanies many hip hop dance styles, waacking is performed to disco music. Disco music was embraced by the entertainment industry from 1974 through the end of the 1970s, as it was introduced into the main stream. However, disco quickly came to an end with the so-called "disco sucks campaign," which culminated in 1979 when DJ Steve Dahl, a DJ from Chicago, asked his listeners to bring disco records to a White Sox baseball game at Comiskey Park so that he could blow them up. Disco music was criticized as an artificial, manufactured sound due to the absence of a live band. Moreover, the lyrics of disco music appeared apolitical, particularly compared to the overtly confrontational lyrics of funk music (Bragin 2014; Buckland 2002). As Bragin writes: "Disco lyrics were sparse evocations of a ritualistic dance-floor culture that consumed themes of sex, slavery, and demonic fire, with the sensory affect of heat, fever, and ecstasy" (2014: 69). Accordingly, disco was identified with gay men and gay club culture, and is confronted with anti-queer and racist sentiment to this day (Bragin 2014; Buckland 2002).

While waacking continued to be practiced by queer dancers of colour well into the 21st century, the style was also taken up by white and Asian dancers in international competitions (DeFrantz 2016). Waacking saw a revival in the early 2000s, as street dancers began researching the dance styles of early *Soul Train*. Waacking was made compatible with mass media through the Fox-produced TV dance show, *So You Think You Can Dance*. Bragin (2014: 65) criticizes this mainstreaming of waacking as "an appropriative process by which hegemonic power reconfigures cultural identity, wrapping transgressive relationality and queer practice in hegemonic hetero-normativity." On the one hand, accordingly, the mainstreaming of waacking can be considered an appropriative process, whereby waacking was transformed into a competition style dominated by nonblack cisgender females, meanwhile obscuring its queer history. On the other hand, cisgender female waacking performances may open up possibilities for redefining hegemonic notions of "feminine,"

---

16   Voguing is a dance style that evolved in the 1970s and 1980s in New York City's queer ballroom scene. The dance style consists of a series of stylized poses, imitating the poses of models, thus the name voguing is a reference to the Vogue fashion magazine.

"female," and "woman" (Bragin 2014: 61, 65, 75). As Desmond (2006) reminds us, dance is a performance of cultural and social identity. Furthermore, she suggests to use the concepts of hybridity and syncretism to comprehend interactions between ideology, cultural form, and power differentials, as dance styles move from one social group to another (Desmond 2006: 34). The cultural transmission of dance styles always involves shifts in meaning. Thus, the formerly gay practice of waacking can become a performance of queer femininity. Stereotypes of what is deemed feminine or masculine are thus negotiated in the Vietnamese hip hop community of practice.

Waacking in Vietnam

Waacking was quickly taken up in Vietnam following its revival in the U.S. in the 2000s, as a young Vietnamese dancer named C2Low was among the first to perform waacking in 2011. The year 2010 marked the 40th anniversary of the TV show *Soul Train* in the U.S., and news media about music and street dance culture were quickly spreading to Vietnam, as well. By that time, a large waacking community already existed in East Asia, particularly in Japan, which evolved as a key location for the development of hip hop and street dance early on, especially due to the international travel of early *Soul Train* dancers. Today, Japan has become a major point of reference for Vietnamese popular culture generally, and especially in relation to hip hop.

Whenever I talked with people from Hanoi or Ninh Binh about waacking, they invariably referred to C2Low as the founder of waacking in Vietnam. Born in 1995, C2Low started to practice waacking in 2011, while still in high school. Like Nguyet, he had a longstanding desire to dance and was already practicing hip hop. He stumbled upon waacking via YouTube, and decided to learn this new dance style, too. Given that there were no waacking classes in Hanoi at that time, he studied waacking through YouTube videos. In 2012, he attended a waacking workshop in Singapore. He would not have normally been able to fund such travel, but he had won a dance contest in Vietnam and used the prize money to finance his trip. Upon his return, he started a free waacking class, which took place twice a week in the evenings at the Lenin Monument. Around 2013, C2Low opened his own class at Thai Tinh Street in CunCun Studio, where Mai teaches her hip hop classes. C2Low is not only a renowned waacking teacher, but also the founder and leader of the Soul Waackers Crew, founded in 2012. The crew consists of five women and two

men, including C2Low. Together, they participate in international battles and
regularly practice in the cypher formation. When I met C2Low in 2018, he
taught waacking classes at Wonder Dance Studio and was still the leader of
the Soul Waackers Crew. He frequently travels abroad to participate in international dance battles, particularly in Southeast Asia (Malaysia, Thailand) and
East Asia (Korea, Japan, and China). On his return from the Royal Battle in
Japan, in November 2018, he posted a video on Facebook showing him in a 2
vs. 2 battle with Miyaka. In the text accompanying the video, he writes:

> "Today I would like to share advice with fellow dancers:
> Seven years ago, I was the only one practicing waacking, with all the elder
> hip hop brothers saying 'you dance wrong.' It was hard in the beginning to
> continue in the style that I liked, but I went abroad to battle, learn, and ask.
> After I returned to Vietnam, I finally received recognition.
> The sensation of exerting myself to the utmost, and achieving recognition,
> makes me very happy. Performing dance is freedom. Let's patiently pursue
> the style we like, even if others may be against us.
> Hack the clip, which shows recognition from Uncle Tyrone (OG U.S. waacker)
> after my battle round in Japan."

On the one hand, the post clearly recalls his struggle as the only person (or,
more precisely, the only man) practicing waacking at a time in Vietnam, when
it was little known and hardly appreciated by others. C2Low references other
male hip hop practitioners (*các anh lớn hiphop*), who told him that what he was
doing was "wrong." In the quoted speech, when they said, "you dance wrong,"
they addressed him with the second person singular pronoun *mày*, which is
only used in intimate relationships among friends who have known each other
for a long time, as in *tao* (I) and *mày* (you). However, outside such intimate
relationships, the use of this pronoun is derogatory. Despite such criticisms
from his reference group in hip hop, C2Low continued to follow his aspirations. To develop his technique, it was important to go abroad and learn from
other dancers. Thus, through exerting all of his strength (*nỗ lực*), and developing his style, he finally received recognition from his Vietnamese peers,
as well. Today, he finds freedom in dancing. At the same time, his Facebook
post signals appreciation and recognition from an elder of waacking, the late
Tyrone Proctor, who was a dancer, choreographer, teacher and international
judge in the video shared by C2Low. Tyrone was an official Soul Train Gang
dancer and one of the pioneers of waacking/punking. Together with Jeffrey
Daniels (Shalimar, Soul Train) and Jody Watley, Sharon Hill-Wood, Cleveland

Moses Jr., Tyrone Proctor helped to found The Outrageous Waack Dancers, which toured Canada and Japan (Street Style Lab 2019). Thus, in his post, C2Low refers to Tyrone as a waacking "OG," and was thus honoured to receive his recognition.

Nguyet also mentioned Tyrone when I asked her about the history of waacking. She learned about waacking's origins both from her teacher as well as from international dancers who came to Vietnam to lead workshops. The history of the dance style thus circulates and is exchanged within the community of practice. For Nguyet, the U.S. TV show *Soul Train* was an important reference point that marked the beginning of waacking, and she gives Tyrone credit for developing waacking into street dance.

Waacking Howl

Nguyet was the first waacker I met in Hanoi. Mai introduced me to Nguyet as a female hip hop dancer, representing funk style. We met for the first time in a small coffee shop located in a small alley that meandered along Nui Truc Street. Nui Truc Street had struck me during my first years in Hanoi, in the early 2000s, as a street with some of the few stores that sold street and hip hop apparel. I sat down with Nguyet and she began to recount the story of how she came into contact with both waacking and hip hop, as well as her ongoing participation in multiple crews.

Born in 1993, Nguyet describes herself as a waacker and uses the dance moniker "WHowl," which is short for Waacking Howl. Like most of the dancers I talked to, Nguyet chose her own dance name. As with the locker Harin, described in chapter 5, "POPPING AND LOCKING," her choice of dance name was similarly inspired by Japanese popular culture. She explains that she had come across a Japanese book called *Howl's Flying Castle*. Fascinated by the book's theme, she chose "Howl" as her dance name.[17] To indicate that she is a waacker, she added a "W" to Howl, baptizing herself WHowl. Whenever she is invited as a judge, or participates in a battle, she is referenced by her dance name. On her Facebook profile, WHowl appears beneath her real

---

17   The original title of the book is *Howl's Moving Castle*, written by the English author Diane Wynne Jones. In 2004, the book was adapted as a Japanese Anime film by director Hayao Miyazaki. Both the book and movie narrate the story of a young girl, who is turned into an old woman and later meets a wizard.

name in brackets. Within her community of practice, she is mostly known as WHowl.

Nguyet started waacking in 2013. Before she had already danced K-Pop. In the second year of her undergraduate studies, a friend had taken her to the Lenin Monument one evening to practice with Vietnam's famous waacker, C2Low. But that evening, her bag containing all of her personal belongings, including her motorbike keys, was stolen. She had placed the bag to the side, away from where the group was practicing, where someone must have taken it. She called her father to tell him what had happened, and he reacted by telling her to never return to the class again. Consequently, she stopped attending C2Low's class for a few months. In the meantime, she kept practicing at home by herself, watching YouTube videos, as well as dancing with another group that comprised diverse dance styles. In 2013, she joined her first battle, participating in a 2 vs. 2 battle with her friend. She met C2Low once again, who told her that he was going to teach a class in a dance studio on Thai Tinh Street, which she eventually joined. She has been waacking ever since and recently developed an interest in hip hop dance, as well. She says: "That is why I come to waacking. I think because I like that style, and I want to develop myself in that style. So even if my parents did not allow me to go there, I always want to do it a lot, do it more." Eventually, C2Low invited her to join his crew. She did not have to audition, but he merely appointed her as a member. Nguyet eventually graduated from Vietnam National University in Hanoi, holding a degree in international business studies, and she continues to dance.

Nguyet is married to Bi Max, a b-boy from Hue, whom she met at a battle in Da Nang. After the event, they stayed in contact by texting. In 2017, at the international Dance Asia festival held in Singapore, Bi Max proposed to Nguyet in the cypher. The members of New York Style Crew still recall that moment. Nguyet and Bi Max were married in January 2018. Together, they redefine gendered expectations about a married woman's mobility in Vietnam, where a wife is commonly expected to leave her parents to live with the husband's family. The reason for this is that, both in Vietnam and China, wives are commonly associated with the "outside," and thus integrated "inside" through marriage. By contrast, the husband is considered to be in charge of kin relations on the "inside" (Brandtstädter 2008; Nguyen 2019). This is partly true for Nguyet and Bi Max, since they were married in his home town in Central Vietnam. A photo of their wedding, with the caption "Welcoming the wife home," posted on Facebook shows Nguyet wearing a red *áo dài*, with traditional hair ribbons, and Bi Max wearing a modern blue suit. They are accompanied by two young boys, each carrying a red and yellow canopy above the heads of the bride and groom. The couple is accompanied by two little girls walking in front of them, who hold yellow lanterns. Although the wedding took place in her husband's home province, Nguyet did not move in with her husband. Rather, her husband left Hue and quit his job in the motor industry, and moved to live with his wife and work in Hanoi. Both are members of New York Style Crew and teach dance classes together. For them, working together is joyful. Moreover, Nguyet appreciates having a life partner who shares her lifestyle: "We understand one another, because if we want to travel to a battle or practice late, we understand each other. Because it's not just a hobby, but it's also a job. So yes, we can understand each other."

Living a dancing life often means practicing late into the evening. Most of the crews I met started practice around 8 p.m., and often even later, as most crew members return home from work, eat dinner, and take a rest before they are free for crew practice. Street dancers also frequently travel abroad. Nguyet went to Kuala Lumpur in December 2018, where she participated in a waacking battle. In January 2019, both husband and wife participated in the Juste Debout event in Bangkok. As it is expensive to travel to Japan and Europe, many Vietnamese dancers participate in large battles organized in different parts of Southeast Asia. The winners of the Juste Debout battle were invited to participate in the Paris finals in May 2019 (see chapter 5, "POPPING AND LOCKING"). While Nguyet and Max often travel together, they also make individual trips. As Max embarks on a trip to GS Dance Battle, Nguyet reminds her crew to take good care of her husband during the trip in a Facebook post, as she cannot join them in person.

In dancing, both husband and wife enjoy their own achievements. While Bi Max was the deputy of his b-boying crew back home in Hue, and is now the deputy of New York Style Crew, Nguyet is a successful waacker, having competed in various one-on-one competitions as well as jointly with the Soul Waackers Crew in international freestyle and waacking competitions. Additionally, she is frequently invited to serve as a judge at national and international battles.

Today, together with her teacher C2Low, Nguyet is the only waacking teacher in Hanoi. Overall, she teaches four classes a week, both in waacking and hip hop. These include a kid's class and a preschool class, both at a Japanese dance studio, and a kid's hip hop class that she teaches together with her husband. She also teaches her own waacking class, named WHowl's class, twice a week.

Legitimate peripheral participation in waacking

Once a week, WHowl's class takes place outdoors in the public space surrounding the Lenin Monument, starting at 8 p.m. until "the battery dies," as Bi Max explains. On the other night, the class takes place indoors in the dance studio. For this purpose, Nguyet rented a studio close to Chua Boc Street in Hanoi's Dong Da District. She deliberately chose two locations for her class to convene as she wants her students to practice both in front of a mirror to monitor their movement, as well as to learn how to move in public space. She reveals the sensory dimension to her teaching pedagogy, when she explains that dancing inside or outside feels different. In her explanation, she correlates movement and space, as the differing materiality and spatial arrangement of the studio and public square provide for varied kinesthetic senses. She says: "when you go outside (...) You can feel free to do whatever you want." Her statement recalls Sarah Pink's concept of sensory intersubjectivity, which refers to corporeality occurring in relation to a particular interactional and material environment. To Nguyet, the sensory experience of dancing inside the dance studio, in front of a mirror, differs from dancing outside due to the material infrastructure of public space.

For her outdoor class, she explicitly chose the Lenin Monument as it symbolizes hip hop in Hanoi. Fellow hip hop, popping, locking, and house dancers frequently converge on "Le-nin," as they call it, to practice together. That is why she wants to maintain the monument site as a "traditional space of hip hop," where everyone is welcome to join. By organizing her class in this place, she engages in infrastructuring work, as she continuously recreates a place where newcomers have opportunities to engage in legitimate peripheral participation.

I joined WHowl's class on a rainy evening in October 2018. As I approached the square around 8:30 p.m., coming from Dien Bien Phu Street with my family, I did not immediately see the class. The square in front of the statue was completely empty due to the rain. WHowl's class was instead gathered around the pavilion, southeast of the statue, at the intersection of Dien Bien Phu and Tran Phu Streets. Nguyet and her husband Bi Max welcomed us, and introduced me to four of her students present that evening. The students are

Spatial outline of Lenin Monument

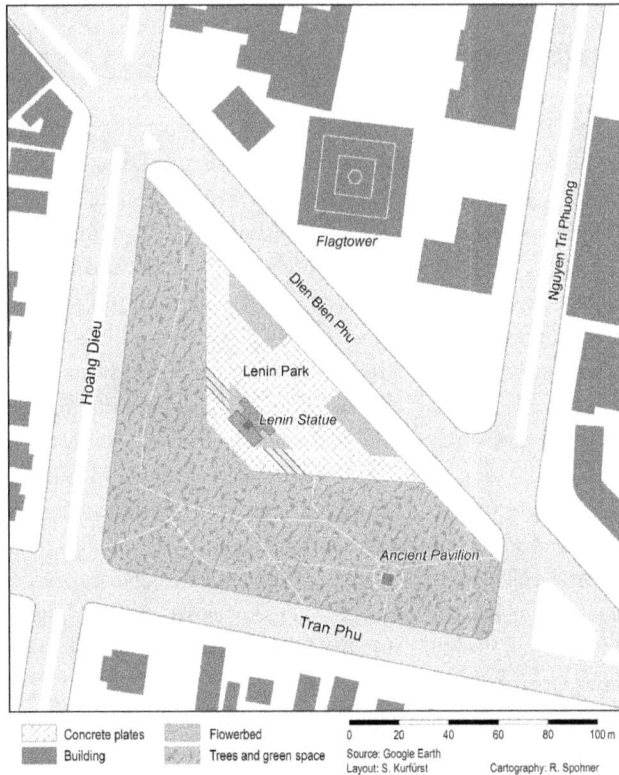

Source: Google Earth, Layout: Sandra Kurfürst, Cartography: Regine Spohner

all female, a little bit younger than Nguyet, in their early twenties. They all wore black joggers, black or white sneakers, as well as hoodies, while one of them wore a crop top. They placed their personal belongings, drinks, and food under the pavilion, within view of the dancers, and protected from the rain. English-language disco music was playing from a mobile phone hooked to an amplifier that Bi Max and Nguyet brought along. After a little conversation, Nguyet called the girls together. The four girls assembled in a line facing the pavilion. Nguyet took her position one-step ahead of them, similarly facing the pavilion. Together, through the individual positioning of their bodies in space, they formed a collective body. As the pavilion became their vanishing point, it seemed like an imagined mirror or at an audience for which they performed. The class began with a warm-up, as Nguyet clapped her hands to either signal a direction change or the beginning of a new movement. After the warm-up, she instructed the girls to practice in pairs of two.

Their spatial configuration again shifted as they collectively entered into a v-shaped formation: two girls standing in the back, two others positioned a step in front of them, aiming toward the apex of the v where Nguyet stood before them in the font. As waacking is primarily about torso movement, Nguyet mostly demonstrates arm and shoulder movements, while moving with her legs up and down, by bending or kneeling on the floor. She enriches her performance with verbal instructions, counting beats, instructing and advising the girls on how and when to move.

The students follow her instructions, while mimicking her bodily movements. As Gershon (2015: 6) notes in her introduction to *A World of Work*: "Many tasks can't be explained with words alone. You learn all sorts of specific ways to hold your body, to sense exactly when to start a motion and when to stop it thanks to touch, smell, hearing, and sight." Nguyet asserts the multisensory experience of learning waacking in declaring to her students that they need to get into the song. She says "I teach my students to get into the song. They need to listen and then do – listen, let [the music] into the body and spread it out."

She identifies listening and kinesthesia as key sensory processes involved in learning waacking, and she describes grooving as an unconscious bodily reaction to the music, explaining "that it is natural" to move to the music because "we feel that. We are happy to do that, not because people say us to do so." In other words, she regards movements of the body as natural responses to music based on feelings of happiness. By referring to the body's reaction as "unconscious," she distinguishes movement based on feelings and emotions from movement based on verbal instructions.

Finally, the girls reassemble in a line. Nguyet alternately moves from the front and through her students' line in order to synchronize their movements. Dance Scholar Judith Hamera (2007) again draws our attention to the importance of technique in dance. She focuses on the lexical function of technique in rendering the body in a shared and legible idiom: "In practical terms, technique provides social bedrock for imagining new ways of being together and being oneself" (Hamera 2007: 13). Thomas Csordas (1999) similarly emphasizes the moment of bodily experience and intersubjective meaning-making.

Dance technique thus evolves as a relational infrastructure, offering templates for sociality in the dance studio and public space. Technique integrates and translates individual bodies into a common communicative repertoire or vernacular among dance class participants (Hamera 2007: 32). Technique opens up conversations about the accurateness of particular moves, their critique, and evaluation. One of the girls repeatedly seeks her teacher's approval, asking if she executes the movements correctly, and how she can improve them. Hamera (2007) also points to the discursive dimension of the voice in dance. The voices of teachers and dance instructors as they count beats, offering praise and distributing advice, and the voices of students asking how to perform particular movements, all constitute the performance space. Accordingly, technique is linked to language in the way that technique as a set of protocols for reading and writing bodies facilitates interpersonal conversations about those bodies (Hamera 2007).

WHowl's class at the Lenin Monument

Source: Nils Kurfürst (2018)

Her students refer to Nguyet as *chị*, elder sister, instead of using *cô*, the honorific address for teacher. The students used to pay to participate in her regular dance class in the studio. The use of first- and second-person pronouns reveals that they have overcome the formal relationship structured of paid instruction. The social structure of the class is marked by more informal relationships, although the hierarchical ordering of master-student relationships still shapes instruction. The students are advanced in the sense that they no longer attend regular dance classes in the studio, but they are not yet members of Soul Waackers, Hanoi's waacking crew. WHowl's class thus constitutes a liminal space structured by formal rules, such as regular practice twice a week, and informal social ties expressed by the fact that they regularly hang out outside of practice. While they are not members of C2Low's crew, they regularly interact with crew members. For instance, on that same October evening, some of the waacking crew members, including C2Low, a 23 year-old woman named Ty Pum, and a young man named Marc, joined them at the pavilion, as well. Yet, instead of joining the class, they practiced waacking on the other side of the pavilion. Situated between the two groups, Bi Max performed footwork on his own.

The distribution of these spatial practices turned legitimate peripheral participation upside down. The novices, the girls in WHowl's class, practice on Tuesday evening at 8 p.m. in front of the Lenin Monument. The most advanced waackers, C2Low, and members of the Soul Waacker's Crew, join the class in this space, but they remain on the periphery, practicing to the music of WHowl's class. They only come together during the small breaks to eat, drink, and chat.

This spatial separation of crew members and non-members is reproduced in the crew's regular cypher practice. C2Low invited me to join one of these cyphers on a Friday evening. Initially, the cypher was to take place at C2Low's dance studio near Ton Duc Thang Street, but as I made my way through rush hour, Nguyet contacted me to redirect me to the Foreign Trade University campus on Chua Lang Street, where the Wonder Dance Studio is located near the students' residential estate. Apart from the Soul Waackers Crew, Bi Max, the four girls from WHowl's class, and a female Malaysian waacker named Bao – whom Nguyet invited for her event Hallowaack – all waited for me outside the dance studio.

As we enter the small studio, a hip hop class was still ongoing. The class is led by Dynamic, a young popper from Hanoi. Dynamic teaches at Wonder Dance Studio and is also a member of CK Animation's Wonder Brothers Crew. Dynamic remains after the hip hop class ends, and all the students leave. Vietnamese music starts playing first, which is then followed by English pop music. The waackers warm up on their own, sometimes helping each other as they stretch. When the music turns to disco music, C2Low claps his hands several times, signalling that the others should convene in the cypher. Bao, the guest from Malaysia, is the first to enter the cypher. She does so without

Soul Waacker's Cypher

Source: Sandra Kurfürst (2018)

any verbal cues. The cypher runs counter clock-wise. Nguyet is next to enter the cypher, followed by C2Low, and then the other crew members. The four students from WHowl's class are the last to enter. Then the cypher restarts. During the first round, the first four dancers waack to Whitney Houston's *So emotional*. Compared to Nguyet and Bao, C2Low makes much more use of the cypher space, as he uses more footwork. He interacts with the cypher participants, pointing to them as Houston sings "Youuuuuuuuuu." The fourth dancer to step into the cypher is a woman, who lies on the floor, curling. While she is in the cypher, the music ends and she laughs but continues to perform, while others encourage her to continue. This fracture in flow demonstrates the necessity of having a DJ who can maintain the sonic flow. That is why, at battle events, such as Hallowaack described below, a DJ is in charge of the music.

Then music kicks in again with Boney M.'s *Sunny*. The fifth dancer replaces her. The sixth is Marc, the only male crew member apart from C2Low, whom I met also during WHowl's class at the Lenin Monument. His facial gestures correspond to his movements. Like C2Low, Marc employs much more space in the cypher than his fellow female dancers, combining wide twists of his arms above his head, alternately with foot work or kneeing down on the floor.

Marc's facial expressions correspond to his body movements, interacting with his mostly female audience. He leaves the cypher and all the others shout. The next dancer is Ty Pum, whom I met three days earlier at Lenin.

As indicated above, the cypher is a socio-spatial formation that indexes the social organization of community and social learning. Overall, the cypher has an integrating effect, as both crew members and non-members are able to join. Nonetheless, the sequencing and ordering of the cypher expresses hierarchies at work in the group. First of all, Bao is allowed to open the cypher. As a crew outsider and international guest, she occupies an exposed position. Bao is followed by her host Nguyet, who is followed by another crew leader, and the other crew members. The last sequences in the cypher are made up by the students of WHowl's class. Dancing in the cypher, they seem to enjoy themselves, showing more self-confidence than during the class held at Lenin. They receive an equal amount of time as the crew members and receive encouraging comments and gestures from other cypher participants. They are not members of the crew, yet they are allowed to join the cypher to practice with the crew. In other words, they are legitimate peripheral participants. Already in the warm-up session, the simultaneous inclusions and exclusions of peripheral participation were at play, as the students of WHowl's class occupied the left side of the studio, remaining spatially separated from the crew members, who practiced to the right close to the technical infrastructure. Consequently, the social hierarchies among veterans and neophytes, crew members and students, express themselves in the spatial positioning of individuals and groups within the collective.

However, such social orders can be negotiated and contested during battles. Battles are generally open to anyone who registers and pays a participation fee. While the reputation of the crew may be at stake, it is the performance of an individual dancer or a group of dancers that is evaluated. Nguyet organized her own event called Hallowaack at the A-Life Angelo Dance School Japan at Sakura Station, where she regularly teaches a children's hip hop and waacking class. Hallowaack featured 2 vs. 2 waacking battles as well as 1 vs.1 non-waacking battles, which were open to dancers of other styles. The event took place on Sunday, October 21, the same weekend as the postponed Red Bull Battle. As the free style Red Bull Battle had taken place the day before on Saturday, many of the Red Bull Battle participants reconvened at WHowl's Sunday waacking event. As I entered the studio, I immediately recognized the Japanese dancer Nemoto, a member of the newly founded Hanoi House Dance Crew, of which Mai is also a member. Hallowaack started at 1 p.m. CK

Animation and Ty Pum acted as MC's. C-Lock served as the DJ while Quan Ten, one of Bi Max's close friends, was in charge of video recording the whole event. Bao, who was invited by Nguyet, was the judge for the 2 vs. 2 waacking battle. C2Low judged the non-waack category, in which dancers from diverse styles, such as popping, hip hop, house, and locking, all participated. Apart from the Vietnamese dancers, a Malaysian team named Queencess, consisting of a young woman and man, also participated in the event. At Hallowaack, WHowl's students split up into different teams of two, battling with members from other crews. Building their own battle teams, the girls performed outside the hierarchical social organization of the waacking crew and class. In the 2 vs. 2 battles, they were able to perform as equal individuals and peers. Two of the students teamed up as Waackerhood, whereas another one cooperated with a renowned female dancer from Milky Way Crew. Nonetheless, they received a special thank you mention from Nguyet in her Facebook caption for the Hallowaack event, thanking her students for their support.

Dancers participating in the non-waack battle needed to form teams and register under a team name. The team names incorporated a multilingual repertoire, including English language terms connoting the dance style like Waackerhood or the Waackers, random English-language names such as Coconut or Jesus, as well as Vietnamese idioms such as "ăn chay," which literally translates as "to eat vegetarian," but also connotes "having sex." According to Nir Avieli (2014), vegetarianism in late socialist Vietnam frequently connotes a moral façade, obscuring something that is not spoken about in public.

Dancers from outside Hanoi were among the waacking battle participants. Tien, a young man from Ninh Binh City, joined Hallowaack, as he was visiting his elder sister in Hanoi and was eager to join the event. He had just started dancing the year before in his high school's dance club. The school team focuses on choreography, performing show cases for school events, such as teacher's day on November 20 or graduation day. He recalls how, after dancing for the first time, he could not stop. Tien first encountered waacking on the TV show, *Vietnam's Got Talent*, and he was fascinated by its beauty. Consequently, he chose to learn waacking for aesthetic reasons. Before Hallowaack, he had just become a student in the TiTan Crew. While there are at least two other hip hop crews in Ninh Binh Province, he chose to train with TiTan as the crew draws on 11 years of experience and meets closer to his home than the other crews. Moreover, TiTan Crew has at least two dancers who specialize in waacking; one of them, a young woman, is now Tien's teacher. In contrast with the high school dance club, the crew practices every day. When dancing, he calls himself CÙ, using the nickname his family gave him. At Hallowaack, he encountered C2Low for the first time, having heard about and watched him a lot before.

Finally, Queencess, from Malaysia, won the waacking battle, whereas Nguyet's fellow Waackerhood crew members won second place. In the 1 vs. 1 non-waack battle, for dancers from other dance styles, mostly poppers participated on this day. CK Animation, who served also as MC during the waacking battle, won in the non-waack category. One thing that is appealing to many people about waacking is that it mingles and combines other dance styles. While there are some exclusively waacking events in Hanoi, such as Hallowaack organized by Nguyet, or the Soul Waackers Crew's anniversary event, Waack your Soul 2020, most waackers are in close and constant exchange with the dancers from other styles in Vietnam, such as popping and hip hop dance. Sometimes they are even members of the same crew. Some dance crews like Big Toe or Milky Way have waackers on their team. Moreover, intimate relationships often evolve from shared passions for dance, as some female waackers develop relationships with male poppers, house dancers, or b-boys. Thus, husbands and boyfriends were also present during the waacking event that day, bringing their peers from their respective dance styles with them. CK Animation, for example, was accompanied by his Wonder Brothers crew members. They participated in the non-waack battle, combining footwork from breaking and popping with the quickly swinging arms characteristic of waacking. Their arm movements did not suggest that they were combining such styles for the first time. As waacking can be readily combined with other styles, they seemed quite comfortable integrating waacking into their dance performance. Indeed, LionT explains that he often combines different dance styles, such as hip hop and house, with waacking.

As one waacker put it: "Waacking is an open style, they have basic moves, but you can combine these with moves from another style. You can do some hip hop moves with your legs and waacking with your hand. And it's okay, you can combine house moves with your legs and combine them with waacking." Waacking is thus recognized by the wider community of practice as part of hip hop culture. While there may be not so many dancers who specialize in waacking, many hip hop dancers integrate waacking motions into their routines.

Queering femininity and masculinity

In Vietnam, waacking is mostly practiced by young cis-gender women, and only a few young men. In dance studios that offer waacking classes, the style falls under the "girl style" category, primarily inviting female students. However, what is particularly striking is growth in the number of children's waacking classes offered at dance studios, which are attended by both male and female children. To be sure, movement vocabulary shifts as middle-class children of diverse genders learn waacking in dance studios (Desmond 2006). While certainly most parents who send their children to such classes know little about waacking's queer history, the old timers in the community of practice do. In the Vietnamese waacking community, queerness is both acknowledged and practiced, as waacking remains a dance style open to practitioners of all gender identities and sexual orientations in Vietnam. Knowledge about the cultural history of waacking is shared and exchanged within the community of practice, largely through transnational networks. C2Low indicates that he learned about waacking while attending a workshop in Singapore. On his return to Vietnam, he shared the knowledge he acquired abroad with his students. Apart from her teacher, a woman dancer claims to have gained knowledge about the history of the dance style and music from international dancers who led workshops in Vietnam. She is aware of waacking's origin in the U.S.-American gay community during the 1970s. Asked about waacking's relation to Vietnam's LGBTIQA community, she says that a lot of different people practice waacking, not just members of the LGBTIQA community. According to her, waacking is easily accessible and everyone is free to join, despite any differences of social status by gender, age, and so on. Nonetheless, she admits that there is a persistent stereotype in Vietnam according to which men who practice waacking are assumed to be gay. Comparing the different perception of boys and girls who practice waacking, she concludes that waacking appears more "normal" for girls in Vietnam. As a consequence, boys who practice waacking are considered queer, while girl waackers appear to conform with heteronormative standards. In his study of the homosexual body in Vietnam's renovation period, Richard Quang-Anh Tran (2014) explains that homosexuality in Vietnam is not so much defined by a person's sexual orientation than by a person's gender. This means that male homosexual practices, desires, and behaviours are considered to belong to a woman, rather than a man. In other words, male homosexuality is assessed against the binary of male and female.

In a similar vein, two young dancers from Ninh Binh – a man and a woman – ascribe waacking to a female gender. While the female dancer associates waacking with femininity (*nữ tính*), the male dancer characterizes waacking's aesthetics as "girly." The idea of waacking being "girly" has been contested by practitioners themselves. In one of his dance classes, Tyrone Proctor dismisses the idea that waacking is simply girly, stating: "This is not an easy dance. Power is most high. If you're gonna just do uh, uh, [waves his arms absentmindedly] and think this is a girly dance? You're in the wrong place. You have to learn how to apply power, attitude, and control. They're everything." (audiotape of dance class 25 March 2012 cited in Bragin 2014: 67). Consequently, Naomi Bragin (2014: 67) distinguishes between "girl-ness as defined by culturally enforced norms of movement that suture (white) femininity and submissiveness and a refigured sense of power that Waacking aesthetics incorporate: radiant energy, vitality, fierceness." Such radiant energy is also what the male waacker refers to when explaining why he enjoys dancing to disco music. By contrast with break beat, which is quite fast and does not affect him very much emotionally, disco music makes him feel like "acting," motivating him to incorporate a bit of drama into his performance.

Referring to all female waackers as his idols, a young Vietnamese male dancer names Lip J from France and the Korean dancer Lia Kim, in particular. He particularly likes how Lip J expresses music with her body – for many dancers, the ability to communicate the feelings of a song through the body was a defining characteristic of a good waacker. To him, Lip J's style is smooth and beautiful. Lia Kim, by contrast, combines waacking with hip hop dance. He explained that her style looks "weird," but still has a lot of beauty in it. By "weird" he refers to the shape of her body during the dance and particularly her poses. In conversation with a fellow female waacker, he refers to C2Low as Vietnam's first waacker. According to the female dancer, C2Low stands out due to his "vanguard" (*tiên phong*) style. Discussing the idiosyncrasies of his style, two waackers from Ninh Binh address the issues of femininity and masculinity. The female dancer admires C2Low exactly for his masculine style (*style Nam*), as it differs from that of female waackers. For her, one indicator that makes him stand out from other, particularly female dancers, is that his style is not sexy, an attribute she ascribes to women. Thus, the waackers' dance styles are assessed based on gendered movement norms and gendered bodily regimes (Elias 1980). In particular, the female body, as well as associated parameters of what is deemed acceptable and proper feminine movement, are highly controlled and defined by specific discourses and ideologies (Desmond 2006; Wolff 2006). In Vietnam, the post-reform discourse stylizes women as providers and family caretakers, institutionalized in the form of "happy mother" and "happy family" campaigns aimed at achieving resilient and happy families. In recent years, dominant modes of representing the female body have focused on the modern middle-class woman as a caring mother and sexually desirable wife (Leshkowich 2008; Nghiem 2004). In her study on fitness culture in Ho Chi Minh City, Ann Marie Leshkowich (2008) shows that middle-class women are required to both master and embody sex. As a consequence, the sexy dress and overtly expressive gestures of waacking challenge persistent body regimes, while also adhering to demands that women – or rather wives –maintain a sexually desirable outer appearance. Naturally, the space of manoeuvre for women to act out their own sexual desires and sexuality is limited and socially sanctioned. Women's bodies remain subject to public scrutiny, as expressed in the scandal around the female model Ngoc Trinh's appearance at the Cannes Film Festival in 2019. On the Film Festival's red carpet, Ngoc Trinh wore a dress made from transparent fabric, with high slits on both sides of the hips. The Vietnamese public considered the dress too sexy. Already in 2012, a far less revealing dress worn by model Hong Que had resulted in public outcry in national and social media (VietnamNetBridge 2012).

While female bodies in the public eye have always been treated as aesthetic objects, and subject to public scrutiny, black queer kinesthetics allow for the negotiation of hegemonic femininity, as women may critically distance their bodies from gendered movement norms (Bragin 2014; Nurka 2013). As Bragin (2014: 73) writes, "Learning to Waack has the potential to redefine the meaning of movement coded 'feminine' within a normative binary gender system." Critical distancing away from movement norms, and thus hegemonic femininity, is something that is constantly practiced by Mai.

Mai, who characterizes herself as a b-boy girl, mostly practices breaking, hip hop, and house dance – all styles dominated by men. However, in her waacking video posted on social media, she wore a neckholder dress that revealed the tattoos on her arms. While dancing is one of the rare occasions that Mai actually wears a dress, as she usually fashions herself in baggy pants, sneakers and XXL t-shirts. Dancing barefoot, she performed a sequence of waacking moves to live punk music. The video posted on Facebook was titled *Bông hoa hồng trên khối bê tông*, "a rose bloom on concrete block." *Hoa hồng* not only means "rose," but is also a popular name for Vietnamese women. With her performance and video title, Mai revokes hegemonic notions of femininity, while simultaneously breaking both gender and waacking conventions. First of all, she dances barefoot, by contrast with most Vietnamese waackers, who wear high heels or sneakers. Second, waacking music is typically disco, Mai chooses to dance to punk music.

According to DeFrantz (2016), normative rhetoric about gender performance operates throughout black social dance practices, whereas the affective force of queer black dance works precisely against such normative categories:

> "A circular recoiling of weight through the hips acted against a dispersed energetic field might constitute a more *feminine* expression of rhythmic bounce than a blockish thrusting of weight sideward and downward, driven by a tensed torso and clenched fists that might be construed as typically *masculine*." (DeFrantz 2016: 66-67)

DeFrantz (2016) concludes that in African American-derived social dances, excellence is achieved through innovative gestures that resists normative gender or sexual identity expectations. Reggie, a US-waacker interviewed by Bragin, explains: "You don't have to take a feminine approach even though that's sometimes something I do... you manipulat[e] people's minds with the ways you danc[e]. I like playing with that kind of gender swap" (Bragin 2014: 70). Particularly within hip hop communities of practice, waacking appears to disrupt gendered (dance) movement norms. In Vietnam, the category of waacking allows for dancers of all gender identities and sexual orientations to creatively engage and play with the normative gender categories. It not only allows for queer creativity, but successful performance explicitly requires the "creative expression of fluid gendered identity" (DeFrantz 2016: 66). Queer gesture is often applied by straight dancers and "others eager to enjoy the social possibilities of queer creativity" (DeFrantz 2016: 66). The fluidity of gender is also required and performed in *lên đồng* rituals in Northern Vietnam. While most spiritual mediums are female, there are also male mediums. Both male and female mediums constantly transgress binary gender categories as they embody both male and female spirits in the ritual. As a result, male mediums may assume both feminine and male postures, whereas female mediums can combine "unfeminine" aspects of their personality with stereotypically feminine aspects, such as a graceful appearance. As a result, mediumship – just like waacking – requires male and female performers to act, move, and ultimately dance outside of prescribed gender conventions (Norton 2006: 68, 75).

The queer movement repertoire is accentuated by the dancers' queer clothing. While b-girls and female poppers often dress in unisex clothing, such as jump suits, XXL t-shirts, baseball caps, and sneakers, both during training and at battles, many waackers in Vietnam wear different outfits when participating in the cypher or in a battle. In the cypher, waackers wore sweat pants, baseball shirts, and sneakers, swapping them for bell-bottoms, skirts, crop tops, bell tops, and leather shoes, high heels, or sneakers at the battle. As a result, the idiosyncrasy of the waacking dance floor lies in the peculiarity of its dress. At 2 vs. 2 battles, the competing pairs often wear glamorous fitted costumes. Dancers identifying as male would wear skirts, crop tops with high heels, as well as make-up and styled hair. As battle apparel in other styles does not substantially differ from practitioners' everyday clothing, there is usually no changing room at battles. At a waacking battle, however, the ladies' room of the dance studio was transformed into a locker room. There, cis-gender female and LGBTIQA dancers mingled, helping each other finalize their hair and make-up, while changing outfits.

The idiosyncrasy of costume change and gender bending in waacking performance deserves further consideration. First of all, the frame of performance offered by the dance floor is key. Erving Goffman's (1986) frame analysis helps us determine "what is going on," and thus what is salient, in any given social interaction. Goffman deploys the frame metaphor to describe how people use frames (structure) to understand their pictures (context). Although often a physical presence, the dance floor is an ephemeral and liminal frame that is demarcated in various ways, perhaps by being slightly elevated, perhaps made of a unique material, or perhaps a different colour. In some cases, however, the dance floor is not materially differentiated from the physical space surrounding it, but it is rather produced socially by the bodies that frame it. In other words, the dance floor is brought into relief by the bodies that surround it, whether in a circle, in rows, and so on. The previously introduced metaphor of the *lingkaran*, the circular formation of players in the Minangkabau *randai*, assists in understanding the situation. According to Mahjoeddin (2016: 362), "the lingkaran is best understood as a liminal membrane that spatially defines the limits of the acting area."

The dance floor is also a space of high exposure, as well. Dancers are under constant evaluation by judges and fellow dancers, who become spectators when they are not dancing. In fact, battle participants constantly oscillate between performer and spectator, as they shift from performing on centre stage, watching or judging other dancers' performances, while continually reproducing the liminal membrane around the dance floor. Theatre director and performance scholar Richard Schechner (2000) has outlined the intimate relationship among performers and spectators, suggesting that no theatre or dance performance can function without an audience. Rather than differentiating between passive and active roles, Schechner suggests a continuum of performative forms that require more or less interactions among performers and spectators. Schechner cites two broad forms of performance: First, where spaces are shared and brought to life through interactions among two or more people, as in the case of the battle dance floor. Second, performances in which spectators may initially appear passive, as in a classical concert, but their sheer presence constitutes a form of interaction, as they long to partake in the performance.

Acting on the dance floor as performers, dancers are evaluated for their technique, physical agility, and the innovative gestures that make their personal style recognizable. They may be evaluated for their gender performance, but this always occurs within the frame of dance performance. The hip hop dance community shares the same value system according to which members evaluate a good dancer. However, as DeFrantz suggested above, waacking not only allows for but even requires gender fluidity in order to achieve innovation. In this sense, the dance floor provides a space for social actions that, outside the frame of the battle, might be non-existent, unauthorized, or socially marginalized. As the dance floor is a socially constructed and thus ephemeral space produced within a performance, the dance floor vanishes as soon as the collective body constituting the liminal membrane dissolves. In terms of theatre, the battle could be compared to a scene, which is similarly liminal as it induces new social roles and conditions (Schechner 2000). Performance and theatre scholar Tracy C. Davis (2009: 3) uses the term theatre as "the institutionalized term for the performance. As a knowledge regime in its own right, theatre 'makes sense' of the reverberation along with the other staged elements in the performance and the 'given circumstances' of the historic artefact on which the event occurred." Similarly, the battle or cypher are institutionalized terms, making sense of the postures and gestures presented to the music. In the battles I attended, all the participants shared common understanding about when the performance began and ended. The rhythm produced as the dancers took turns entering and leaving the dance floor appeared as a ritualized procedure, which was repeated again and again until the winner of the final battle was determined. Organizing the ritual was the MC, who called the dancers to the floor and sometimes counted down to signal the dancer's exit, before finally inviting the judge to declare the outcome. The intimate relationship between theatrical forms and ritual performance has been recognized by sociocultural anthropologists and theatre scholars alike.

The waacking events and practices illustrated above show that waacking fashions a non-normative corporeality (Bragin 2014). While waacking did not develop in any underground gay scene in Vietnam, its uptake by both male and female dancers permitted them to rework hegemonic standards of femininity and masculinity. Although waacking in Vietnam is associated with feminine bodily aesthetics, and although men who practiced waacking are sometimes considered gay, I argue that waacking nonetheless allows for the queering of normative gender categories. Through waacking performances, the boundaries of what is deemed "girly" or feminine and "boyish" and male are constantly blurred. Particularly striking is the performance of LGBTIQA dancers in waacking. Through their membership in hip hop crews and performance in waacking battles, they actively participate in the public sphere. They transform the hyper (in)visibility of being queer by manipulating various social technologies of visibility (Buckland 2002: 26). In the case analysed here, they make themselves visible in the highly exposed space of the dance floor. Further research might consider the intimate relationship between waacking and the LGBTIQA community in Vietnam, as waacking seems to provide a space in which queerness is acknowledged by members of the hip hop community of practice. In a similar vein, Barley Norton (2006: 72) suggests that "awareness of many followers of the Mother Goddess religion that male mediums had homosexual relationships (even if they were married and had children) would seem to suggest that *lên đồng* is one site where, even if not explicitly, a different sexual orientation is acknowledged."

Waacking in Vietnam, as in many other parts of the world, is considered queer, as waacking involves the expression of emotions as well as occasionally sexually coded movements, which deviate from moral codes of public conduct, particularly for young women in Vietnam.

Self-Entrepreneurism and Self-Fashioning

In the *Corrosion of Character*, Richard Sennett (1998) discusses emergent sub-jectivities under regimes of economic flexibility. Sennett explores the effects of post-Fordist capitalism on labour and employment, demonstrating the ne-cessity for workers to quickly and easily reinvent themselves in the work place under new imperatives of flexibility and efficiency. The book was published at a time when Vietnam was undergoing a significant transition, establishing export-oriented industries to attract global capital. In the meantime, Viet-nam has evolved into one of the main global producers and suppliers of tex-tiles, garments, and footwear, and dubbed a middle-income country by the World Bank. Recently, Vietnam has embarked on becoming a major producer of high-tech equipment, as well. Together with the restructuring of the world system, and reconfiguration of the international division of labour, Vietnam's overall transformation from planned to a market economy has had far reach-ing effects at home and in the workplace. Yet, what makes the everyday experi-ences of Vietnamese labourers and consumers differ from the flexible subjec-tivities outlined by Sennett twenty years ago is the marriage of neoliberalism with authoritarianism.

The impacts of so-called "market socialism," "market Leninism," or "late socialism" on living conditions in general, and the labour force in particular, have been of particular concern to scholars working on contemporary Viet-nam (Harms 2016; Nguyen 2015; Nguyen 2019; Schwenkel and Leshkowich 2012). In fact, many of these scholars see many more parallels to develop-ments in China than with (post-)industrialized countries of the West. While the term neoliberalism has been used to describe economic processes of lib-eralization, deregulation, and privatization around the world, Andrew Kipnis (2007) reminds us that the use and analytic value of the term "neoliberalism" needs to be questioned, particularly in the context of socialist histories. What is of particular interest for Vietnam is the continuous conflation of neoliberalist with socialist values. Aihwa Ong (2008) conceptualizes neoliberalism as a travelling logic, which stimulates practices of self-enterprise and self-reflexivity in contexts of market uncertainty. She further argues that neoliberal values promote self-entrepreneurship, self-initiative, and self-investment. Scholars agree that such neoliberal traits merge well with the local culture and post-reform governmentality: in China with the construction of a "harmonious society," and in Vietnam claims for moral personhood (Schwenkel and Leshkowich 2012; Hoffman 2008; Li Zhang 2018). Li Zhang (2012: 661) considers the current political economies of Vietnam and China "a bricolage of practices that best suit the local condition and global order."

As a result of this bricolage of practices and technologies, multiple and oftentimes contradictory logics circulate in contemporary Vietnam, such as the following: discourses about achieving a higher quality of life through market economy and free trade, discourses about optimization achieved through privatization and self-regulation, and finally discourses on the moralization of efficiency, quality, and accountability necessary to produce modern and civilized citizens (Schwenkel and Leshkowich 2012). In such discourses, constant self-assessment, self-optimization and self-advancement under the logic of the free market actually dovetail with ideals propagated by the socialist state, including self-criticism and demands for moral personhood. In her recent monograph *Waste and Wealth*, Minh Nguyen (2019) aptly shows how market socialism poses contradictory demands on individuals, as they must navigate between order and stability on the one hand, and development and prosperity on the other. What she refers to as a moral project pulls together local moral-economic values, neoliberal ideas of self-reliance, and a socialist ethos. The result is a moral subject that is simultaneously enterprising and giving. According to Nguyen, this ethics of striving result in "tireless pursuits of money, wealth, and power," while constantly emphasizing self-responsibility and self-enterprise. In other words, if the modern citizen fails to acquire wealth and power by their means and efforts, it is because they did not enterprise hard enough, they did not dare enough, and they were not responsible enough (Nguyen 2019: 172).

These ethics of striving thus have major implications for the acquisition of skills and the labour market. In her analysis of "patriotic professionalism," Lisa Hoffman (2008) notes that the freedom of job choice in post-Mao China is, indeed, a mechanism of governing and subjectification. Freedom, in this context, does not indicate an absence of power. Rather, following Michel Foucault's analysis of "governmentality," Hoffman considers freedom as a technique of governance that manages and regulates subjects based on the primacy of freedom. Nonetheless, neoliberal governmental forms of China are distinct from those elsewhere in the world, due to the patriotism imbued in the ethos of self-enterprise and freedom of choice. Such patriotism builds on Maoist notions of loyalty and the emphasis for China to be a strong nation on the global stage. Under high socialism, jobs were centrally assigned. This meant that the acquisition of skills served the primary goal of enhancing an organization's performance, which in turn meant pursuing the political objectives of party leaders, rather than personal career aspirations, let alone individual fulfilment. On the contrary, the development of skills to realize personal career goals was deemed politically unacceptable. However, this shifted in the post-Mao area, as the "inefficiencies" of the planned economy came to be described precisely through the disregard of individual skill and the hoarding of labour. Nowadays, graduates in China look for jobs that match the knowledge they acquired at universities, and that offer work environments that advance their individual professional development.

Schwenkel (2011: 133) alludes to a similar development in Vietnam when explaining how contemporary youth in Hanoi make use of global market opportunities to fulfil both their familial and national duties. Schwenkel describes a group of university students from Viet Tri who, when asked about what they desired the most for their future, answered that they wished for the betterment of their families and the nation. They agreed that education was key to achieving such goals. Schwenkel exemplifies this point with the case of Mai, a young Hanoian woman in her mid-twenties who took evening classes in international banking at the university to secure a promotion in her full-time job at a local commercial bank. Mai said: "I'll get promoted through my hard work and education, not from doing favors and socializing with the managers" (Schwenkel 2011: 136). Mai's example demonstrates Hofmann's argument about how jobs are assigned according to skills. In sum, in both China and Vietnam, individuals are considered to be freely choosing subjects, who bear responsibility for their personal wealth and well-being.

Free choice of employment is also embraced by the practitioners of hip hop. In fact, many of the dancers I met in Vietnam held higher education degrees, most of them bachelor's degrees in business or management. However, with the exception of one female practitioner, none of them made their educational background dictate their job choice. Some of the dancers started to work in positions for which their degrees qualified them, but after some time, they chose to quit their jobs in order to make dance their main sources of income. However, they did not completely turn their backs on the formal education they had acquired at university, but rather combined their professional skills with their passion for dance. Many did so, for example, by opening their own dance studios. Such forms of self-entrepreneurism not only require skills, reputation, and social as well as financial capital, but successfully operating a dance studio also requires managerial and financial skills.

Thanh Phuong, whose main source of income comes from her lead position in an internationally operating real estate company, aspires to one day open a dance studio of her own. She plans on making enough money from her current job, so that she will be able to found her own studio, ideally together with her teacher. Similar employment decisions by dancers suggest that a primary motif in their job choices is to pursue something they love and from which they find room for self-development and self-improvement. What dancers in Vietnam thus share with the Chinese workers interviewed by Hoffman is their search for work environments that facilitate self-development and the flourishing of personal abilities. However, while the latter prioritized the search for jobs that matched their university educations, Vietnamese dancers explicitly rejected jobs that might be assigned to them and match their educational background.

This difference in private job choice deserves further attention. In recent years, demand on the Vietnamese labour market has shifted from unskilled to skilled labour. While untrained labour still makes up 83% of the Vietnamese work force, demand for skilled labour is increasing. Professional workers, legislators, senior officials, managers, and technicians require tertiary educational qualifications. While the share of workers with certified training qualifications has not increased since 2007, the number of employees with tertiary education backgrounds has steadily increased (OECD 2014). According to World Bank Education Statistics, gross enrolment in tertiary education in Vietnam increased from 16.2 % in 2005 to 28.5 % in 2016. The gender bias in these enrolment ratios is noteworthy. Gross enrolment for women in tertiary education was 32 % as compared to 26% for men in 2016 (World Bank Education Statistics 2018).[18] Such increase in university enrolment correlates with the cultural value assigned to formal education in Vietnam. In fact, acquiring a tertiary education is highly encouraged by families, including those

---

18   Total female and male enrollment in tertiary education (ISCED 5 to 8), regardless of age, is expressed as a percentage of the total female and male populations for the five-year age group after leaving secondary school.

from rural areas, who spend savings on their children's education. The result is high educational pressure to achieve and keep up with national economic progress, which simultaneously prolongs the period of youth, particularly in urban areas (Hansen 2008). Nguyen (2019: 118) adds to this "classed sense of self that references both the state-sponsored model of personhood centred on modern human capitals and the cultural value placed on formal learning." She presents the example of a married couple of waste traders, who aspire to make enough money to send their children to university. However, as she remarks, the future of their children, even if they are able to get into university, remains uncertain, as the chances of finding an "office job" are decreasing. Accordingly, they have to look for alternative job opportunities, such as opening a streetside restaurant or seeking employment in a factory. Yet, contrary to the example presented by Nguyen, many of the dancers I got to know during my research, had university degrees, and, at least for a time, had held positions that matched their educational background.

For his part, Thanh, aka LionT, holds a bachelor's degree in English Studies from the Foreign Languages University Hanoi, which today is Hanoi National University. Minh Anh, a member of the Wonder Brothers popping crew, graduated from the University of Natural Sciences in Hanoi. Nam and Dung, members of the Funky Style Crew, have degrees from the University of Communications and Transport. Vy, one of the few female poppers from Ho Chi Minh City, studied at Hoa Sen University and works in quality assurance. Tien, a young waacker from Ninh Binh enrolled in an International Business Studies program after graduating from high school. Hoang Phuong graduated from Thang Long University in banking and finance, but then chose to work as a fitness instructor before co-founding the Wonder Dance Studio.

Nguyet studied International Business in Hanoi, combining her online work for a sports company with teaching dance classes. When talking about her university education, she carefully differentiates between what she refers to as "university knowledge," and the process of learning to dance. While she was not fond of her high school and university learning experiences, she stresses how much she enjoys learning to dance as well as foreign languages. She is quite explicit that she merely studied and did not employ her university knowledge for her job. What is more, her parents actually wanted her to become a university teacher, but she decided against their advice. She remarks with irony that she has become a teacher anyway, but a dance instructor rather than a university teacher. In fact, the human capital many of the dancers acquired during their studies of international business or economics assists them in becoming self-entrepreneurs. At the same time, their freedom of choice is partly a function of the kinds of capitals that they control. Accordingly, they act as self-choosing and thence conscious subjects, in an increasingly competitive socialist market economy. Sherry Ortner (2006) considers actors as conscious in the sense that they are partially knowing subjects, as they are self-aware and reflexive. Ortner is particularly interested in understanding subjectivity in its relation to power, particularly those subtle forms of power that pervade our everyday lives. In Ortner's reading, agency is realized in the ways that young people, who have otherwise internalized and reflected the primacy of higher education in Vietnamese society, and are aware of the benefits that could arise from a job that matches their qualifications, nonetheless act against the circumstances and social expectations within which they find themselves, choosing instead to make dance one of their sources of income generation. With such a decision, they counteract social expectations of upward social mobility. Against what Pierre Bourdieu's practice theory might predict, their mobilities take multitudinous pathways from acquiring a university degree to finding a job as they combine and control different kinds of capital, cultural, social, and kinesthetic, to convert it into economic capital. Moreover, they counteract social expectations of moral personhood as enacted in filial piety, as their parents had often envisioned different paths for their children.

Although dance was not the main source of income for all the dancers mentioned above, many of them considered dancing constitutive of their work life, in one way or another. Thanh Phuong, for instance, considers her dance and her work life to have entered a symbiosis. Although expressing a preference for dancing, she nonetheless states that her job helps her maintain a dancing lifestyle, whereas dancing gives her the inspiration and creativity she needs to do her job well. Like Nguyet, she differentiates between "knowledge from school" and the embodied sensory knowledge she gains from dancing and travelling. She explains that "normal" people working in an office would usually apply knowledge that they acquired at school. While she considers such knowledge boring, she says that she puts everything she feels and sees around her into her job. As she works in marketing, she researches what people like and what makes them happy. She says "I can keep my mind vibrant and more creative than normal people because I have dance for balance." She concludes that without hip hop, she would not be able to do her current job: "I love my job and I love dancing together, so I wanna mix them – I can use my knowledge for dancing. So I can help more people." In this way, Thanh Phuong shows her capacity to navigate different knowledges and to capitalize on them across different value regimes.

Ong refers to this art of defining and mixing different kind of knowledges, as well as the capacity to convert information from one sphere into value in another, as self-fashioning: "Self-fashioning thus implies not only fine-tuning oneself but also steering oneself through diverse networks of knowledge and value. Such vigilant self-practices induce an openness to contingency, and possibilities for both strategy and play" (Ong 2008: 187). Thanh Phuong engages in self-fashioning, when she puts money aside from her full-time job, and uses her skills to generate sponsors for the organization of a local hip hop event. For the studio that she hopes to own in the future, she plans to rent a building from the real estate company she works for in order to get a discount.

Dancing labour

Ong applies the term self-fashioning in relation to the growing urban elite of young professionals in China. The application of the term urban elite hints at a more general tendency toward social stratification in late socialist societies. The transformation of non-alienated labour particularly affects the so-called working class, as workers' labour is no longer considered an inalienable part of socially embedded persons, but has rather been turned into a commodity or production input, and thus decoupled from its human subjects (Dunn 2004; Ong and Zhang 2008). However, Ong (2008) qualifies this argument, suggesting that in China's pre-market reform era, workers' bodies were likewise estranged as they were owned by the socialist state. Consequently, labour power and skills were not 'owned' by the individual, but rather considered a national resource and thus as part of the state-owned means of production (Bian 1994; Davis 1990, 2000 in Hoffman 2008). However, the idea of self-ownership – of and being the masters of their own lives and bodies – was a recurrent point made by many interviewees. In other words, dancing appears to maintain its social value, as an expression of non-alienation, as it is intimately linked to the body, emotions, and affect. Of course, such understanding of dance as a form of labour runs the risk of romanticizing dance as a source of income. Dancing is physically challenging, requiring good health and a great deal of self-discipline. As soon as health declines, and as the body begins to age, reliance on dance to make a living becomes a fragile enterprise, indeed. That is why in the long term it is important that dancers own their own studios, as they can provide them with an income after they can no longer dance.

Nonetheless, most dancers were content with their current jobs, and explicitly stressed the value of doing something that they loved. Phuong Silver Monkey recalls how people asked him again and again why he got stuck with dancing, even though it was exhausting, tiring, and didn't provide him with a lot of money. Aware that dancing does not provide him with a stable job or financial rewards, he is nonetheless drawn to dancing. Not able to explain it in words, he compares dancing to love: "Like love, people just do things not knowing why, just because of love" (Hanyi 2014).

Nguyet similarly valued her dancing lifestyle, in marked contrast with her friends who had "normal" day jobs. She further explains: "some of my friends, they are not dancers. They see me now, [and think] dancing is really nice. Because they are just busy at work and then go home. Just no more life. But they cannot experience the feelings of people who join together and dance together." Nguyet's statement touches upon various dimensions, including emotional work and intersubjectivity, as well as self-determination and fulfilment. The point of affection and relationality is also made by Hamera (2007) with regard to Pilates classes, arguing that such classes are not simply physical work, but relational and affective labour, as well. While I will return to the dimensions of emotional work and intersubjectivity later, when discussing conceptions of the self, for now I would like to dwell on the aspect of self-determination or self-ownership.

According to Ong (2008), self-ownership as a neoliberal value transforms and extends the meaning of the private. Drawing on Hegel's (1967) idea of private property as being bound up with power over oneself, Ong (2008: 184) regards privatization as "control over one's property, including one's overall existence as an individual person." In other words, the dancers remain in control of their own bodies, and thus in control of their own lives. Nonetheless, dancers agreed on the difficulty of making a living from just dancing, particularly with respect to the commodification of dance. In her reflection on the status of dancers in Vietnam, Thanh Phuong adopts the metaphor of the alienated worker, recalling the role of workers in the socialist market economy as a production input or commodity:

"... everybody just looks at dancer like a tool, like a worker. They tell me, we can dance one hour (...), I can pay you like this. But they don't know about dancing as an art, too. I need respect from them. That is why I never took any jobs that payed very cheap or do like a worker never."

Thanh Phuong speaks from experience, since she used to earn money from dancing, performing shows with her crew for big brands like Tiger Beer or Heineken. But for Thanh Phuong, it was always important to pitch her own ideas to the companies. Her emphasis on getting respect, on the one hand, indicates the public perception of dance as a commodity. Dancers are considered providers of a particular service in an economic exchange relationship. On the other hand, her demand of respect points to her subjective sense of self-worth as an individual and an artist.

Rufu likewise prefers an office job over making a living from dancing, as this would require her to perform at many weddings, TV shows, or do choreography for pop concerts. She makes it perfectly clear that this was not an option for her, since she wants to decide which events to join on her own, and the countries to which she would like to travel. Like her peer from Hanoi, she is strongly opposed to being told what and how to dance. "Because I know hip hop is worldwide and I want to communicate with [other dancers]. Yeah, I want a dancing life like this – not for performances or to dance for singers. I don't want that." What is more, Rufu's argument points to hip hop's translocal spatiality. As an artform that travels globally, hip hop is a medium that connects practitioners around the world, and Rufu wanted to be a part of it.

Nguyet, by contrast, chose to combine her work as a dance instructor with a stable job, but largely out of economic necessity. While she was still single, income from teaching as a freelancer in multiple dance studios might have been enough, but the income was too little to support a family.

> "(…) not too many dancers can earn money from dancing. So, they have to do other work – and yes, me too. I have a class [that I teach], but since I have family now I think that I have to do more to earn money. So, I work for a fashion company – sport wear – yes, a sport wear company. But it's online, so my time is flexible."

In her job, Nguyet negotiates her passion for dancing with her social responsibility as a married woman who needs to take care of and provide for her family. Yet, as many of the dancers in their twenties were still single, teaching dance classes simply appeared as a viable avenue to earn money. In fact, the mushrooming of dance studios all over Vietnam's larger cities helps many dancers generate income from dancing. One female dancer acknowledges that, although all the studios advertised hip hop classes, they were not "really" hip hop classes to those who were really familiar. Although she could not verify that the classes really taught hip hop dance, she accepted the hip hop label because it would attract more customers, while still providing dancers with an income.

For the most part, dance studios and classes are attended by members of the urban middle-class. The rise of the middle class in Vietnam is testament to the increasing stratification of society under late socialism. Thanh Phuong's comparison of workers to tools, in effect, indicates that a symbolic shift has taken place in relation to the working class. According to Nguyen (2015: 187), the commodification of worker's labour "strips labour of its social values and the workers of their entitlements, thereby depriving the working class of its previous symbolic status and social power." Contemporary propaganda posters include portraits of farmers and industrial workers next to white collar workers and graduate students, propagating imagery of equal citizens, a strong nation, democracy, and civilization. The posters indicate how the formerly contested term "middle class" has become increasingly depoliticized and normalized (Van Nguyen 2012). Previously, the social fact of Vietnam's middle class used to sit uneasily alongside socialist ideology, as political leaders condemned and equated consumption with middle-classness. Consequently, the socialist state has turned to promoting middle-class living as a desired lifestyle. The semantic shift that has occurred with respect to the middle class is further exemplified in the discourse on *dân trí* (intellectual level). The state party aims to develop human resources needed for the country's modernization and industrialization, building on different levels of *dân trí*. Whereas areas inhabited by the educated middle class are considered to have a high level of *dân trí*, remote areas are not. As a result, class distinctions in late socialist Vietnam build on cultural and moral idioms such as *dân trí*, or the urban-rural binary (Nguyen 2019). Elizabeth Vann (2012) points to the ambivalence of modern Vietnamese citizens as economically successful, while simultaneously adhering to official socialist values. The result is a rather ambiguous moral landscape that citizens must navigate, which is coproduced by the state and the market.

In this context, dance instructors in particular evolve as self-determining and entrepreneurial subjects, who help participants in their dance classes maintain healthy and moral lifestyles. When asked about why children's hip hop dance classes have become so popular in urban Vietnam, dance instructors responded that many parents wanted their children to participate in dance in order to keep them from engaging in other leisure activities that are considered morally dubious, such as video gaming. Moreover, they preferred their children to practice in an indoor studio, rather than outdoors in the park where there are many people and distractions. As a result, the provision of dance classes by the private sector offers alternatives to the state-organized youth activities, such as those offered by the Ho Chi Minh Youth Union. One of the primary goals of the youth union is to occupy young people in their spare time, and to keep them away from supposedly dangerous actions and places in the city (Valentin 2008). Social evils, like drug addiction and gambling, are associated with particular social groups, such as adolescent males and particular places in the city (Kurfürst 2012). What is more, social evils are framed as happening during spare time, and thus during leisure time. In contrast to these moral dangers, hip hop dance particularly appeals to young parents, as it involves physical exercise. Physical fitness and bodily health are highly valued in Vietnamese society. Anyone who has visited Hanoi has heard the sound of techno music accompanying vocal instructions during aerobic classes at 6 a.m. and from 5 to 8 p.m., and encountered badminton or football matches on the sidewalks. Dance studio offers such physical exercise in an exclusive, clean, and safe environment. In contrast to public spaces, where youth tend to mingle, and which are often associated with social evils or morally dubious activities (Geertman 2016 et al.; Drummond and Nguyen Thi Hien 2008), the dance studio offers a semi-public space, access to which is granted on the basis of financial transactions. Particularly in the light of increasing child obesity in urban Vietnam, parents express growing demand for exercise programs to slim down children.

Other parents encountered hip hop during their own adolescence and are therefore at ease with hip hop. Some parents who send their children to hip hop class are of my generation. Before they had children, they had practiced dance on their own together with LionT. However, many parents merely consider hip hop as just one among many modern dance styles, and they are not familiar with the hip hop culture, its history, or values. Finally, as politically contested as hip hop may be, dance labour, particularly in the form of teaching dance, has emerged as a service provided to Vietnam's rising urban middle class. The demand is justified precisely by those parents who want their children to develop into cosmopolitan moral subjects. Dance as a form of wage labour is thus a service provided to consumers, which assists others in developing and maintaining moral personhood. Further evidence for the benefits of hip hop dance as physical exercise can be found in its inclusion in curricula at other dance studios and academies, as well as its recognition as an official discipline in the "freestyle" category of the annual Vietnam University Games. As the largest student sporting event nationwide, the 2016 Vietnam University Games were attended by 700,000 students from 68 colleges and universities across Vietnam.

The ethical economy of hip hop

Dance labour is just as much a service provided to customers as it expresses an ethic, thereby simultaneously creating moral and economic opportunities among peers. Arvidsson et al. (2008: 10) consider the hip hop economy an ethical economy in which the entrepreneurial motive extends well beyond monetary incentives of the market economy. The hip hop economy builds on transcultural codes of "proving" oneself and "representing" the community. Describing hip hop communities in Dakar, Senegal, Mbaye (2014: 405) shows that the hip hop economy is organized in a way that allows individual artists to create autonomously within the community, while at the same time becoming aware of themselves as a new generation of entrepreneurs in their city. Mbaye draws on the concepts of "peer production" and communal governance (Bauwens 2009) to emphasize that individual practitioners and the collective hip hop community in Dakar are closely intertwined. The term peer production was coined by Michel Bauwens (2009) who describes a mode of production defined by the following three determinants: 1) 'open and free' availability of raw materials; 2) participatory 'processing'; and 3) commons-oriented output. Following Bauwens, peer production incorporates elements of post-capitalist economies and has the potential to strengthen autonomous production communities. While peer production is reliant on capitalism, it nonetheless bears an emancipatory promise for an alternative logic of life that could replace the current capitalist system. By "peer to peer," Bauwens (2009: 122) refers to "a relational dynamic that emerges through distributed networks." As Mbaye shows, peer production in Dakar's hip hop community helps to sustain as well as to develop the local market. In fact, the rationale expressed by hip hop entrepreneurs in Dakar is to create a market for hip hop in a location of the Global South, which has been largely ignored by global music industry. Aware that their music rarely leaves the country, they therefore try to pave the ground for local music production. Peer production is not based on the dependent relation of wage labour, but rather relies on voluntary self-aggregation. More precisely, peer production builds on self-assigned tasks.

A necessary precondition for such peer production is that the peer producers own or control their productive assets. As a result, the productive assets are managed on the basis of peer governance (Bauwens 2009: 123). Accordingly, hip hop entrepreneurs in Dakar own their instruments and technical infrastructure, such as recording devices, which are necessary for music production. Furthermore, they engage in and have the skills for auto-production. In other words, they own both means of production as well as the skills, techniques, and knowledge necessary to manage the production process.

In Vietnam, for instance, Hoang Phuong founded the Wonder Dance Studio together with CK Animation. On first inspection, this appears to be the next step in her attempt to make money from dance, but she insists that the studio is not to make profit:

> "Because actually, my dance studio now is, how to say, it is not to earn the money from that. (...), because I teach in many, many studio, so there the money comes from. It is not from my studio. It is studio because (...), we educate and we create some people they have the passion on hip hop dance."

In fact, the Wonder Dance Studio offers an excellent example of peer production, as the founders aim to create an environment for dancers to develop skills and their own styles of hip hop and popping. Hoang Phuong recognizes that consumer demand for dance classes like urban choreography or sexy dance is higher than for hip hop classes like waacking, popping, and so on. Therefore, the studio offers the former classes to make money, which balances the lower profits from "real" hip hop classes. Consequently, hip hop dancers engage in what economists call horizontal integration. Moreover, hip hop entrepreneurs also engage in vertical integration, taking advantage of their interconnections with processes of music production. Some dancers, for instance, extend their entrepreneurial activities to festivals, media, audiovisual, and graphic design companies, as well as street wear fashion brands (Mbaye 2014: 405-406). In Vietnam, rappers like Suboi founded their own music labels, and the New York Style Crew builds the festival brand *Nhiệt* to promote hip hop culture in Vietnam. While most hip hop artists have social and business relations abroad, they focus explicitly on developing hip hop in Vietnam. Like the artists in Dakar, dancers and rappers in Hanoi are aware that Vietnam is still located at the periphery of the global music and dance industry. That is why they focus on developing local markets in Vietnam and elsewhere in the Southeast Asian region. The Juste Debout festival in Bangkok, or Whassup Doc in Malaysia, both evidence the development of a regional hip hop scene and market. Moreover, global brands like Red Bull, which also promotes adventure sports apart from producing energy drinks, increasingly recognize Vietnam as an emerging market for investment. Evidence of this global brand's increasing interest in Vietnam is the Red Bull Dance Competition, which was held for the first time in Ho Chi Minh City and Hanoi in 2018, and then again in 2019.

Mbaye (2014: 406) concludes by suggesting that hip hop artists engage with indirect rather than direct reward in the form of monetary compensation. This assumption resonates with earlier the observation that social recognition, such as through "giving back to the community," are characteristic of moral personhood under market socialism generally, and that winning awards and recognition from peers is particularly important to members of the Vietnamese hip hop community of practice. Their efforts to earn respect and recognition from their self-chosen community is aptly captured by the term "reputation economy" (Mbaye 2014: 407). In terms of hip hop music production, such a reputation economy is sometimes rewarded in monetary terms, as when an artist is signed by an international music label or dance company. However, participatory production in the hip hop economy is generally accomplished through intrinsic motivation, and outright passion, rather than extrinsic incentives, whereas the capacity to contribute is measured against demonstrated ability rather than prior formal proof (Bauwens 2009; Mbaye 2014). In other words, knowledge and skill need to be performed and published in some form or the other, such as by performing in public or in videos uploaded on the internet, so that dancers can be recognized by other participants in the hip hop economy.

Finally, the moral project induced by market socialism dovetails with the ethical economy of hip hop, as both build on the accumulation of social recognition and entrepreneurial practices that oscillate between the individual and collective.

Self-fashioning in hip hop

Mbaye (2014: 397) defines hip hop as an "informed product of identity politics and economic deeds." To the dancers with whom I spoke, hip hop is a way of life as they identify themselves with hip hop's sensory codes: visually with hip hop fashion, kinesthetically with breaking, and sonically with hip hop music. Moreover, hip hop has become an entrepreneurial practice for them, as well. They sell and promote hip hop apparel, teach dance classes, and organize events. Since it is difficult to make a living from dance alone, they often combine flexible jobs that match their university degrees with freelancing as dance instructors. For example, Rufu has an office job in which he works in quality assurance during the day, and either practices with her crew in the evening or teaches popping classes. Yen Hanh combines her day job, working online for a fashion company, with her dance practice in the evening. Bi Max, by contrast, felt the need to quit his job as an auto mechanic because this form of employment was not sufficiently flexible to allow him to continue dancing. Other dancers started their own businesses, opening their own dance studios like Hoang Phuong and CK Animation, or a dance academy like Thanh and his wife. However, whether working as freelancers for different studios or as studio owners, the dance instructors take their teaching very seriously. For instance, they would forego participating in a battle if it would interfere with their teaching schedule. Others like Mai Tinh Vi or Mia, who founded their own companies outside the dance field, still related hip hop culture to the fashion industry.

Mai engages in self-entrepreneurism by opening her own fashion label, Monstarock. The label uses the byname *T-Hun Mè Điên Huỷ Diệt* (Mad Cat Destroyer), which she borrowed from her pet. Her fashion label mainly produces t-shirts, baggy pants, and accessories like caps. The name Monstarock already indicates a style that integrates diverse music cultures, like rock and hip hop. The label basically consists of Mai and her boyfriend. The division of labour between the two is as follows: Mai is in charge of the t-shirt print. She learned the printing techniques by herself. Her boyfriend produces the designs for the prints. He works for Boo Shop, one of the first shops to sell hip hop street wear in Hanoi. To build up the fashion label, Mai borrowed money from the bank. When I meet her for coffee for the first time in 2018, she proudly explains that she just paid back the loan last month, saying "I am free." On the one hand, the mere fact that Mai, a young female urbanite, took a loan to build up her own business signals her detachment from the financial resources of her family, as she does not yet have a family of her own. On the other hand, the capital loan indexes the conflation of socialist and neoliberal values, as pointed out by Allison Truitt (2012). In her research on ATM use in Ho Chi Minh City, Truitt poignantly shows how the Vietnamese state initiated the transformation from a dominantly cash-based economy to a transparent and more regulated financial sector. This kind of outcome is usually associated with neoliberalism, as financial regulation and transparency signal that Vietnam is a safe location for foreign direct investments. Since Vietnam's cash-based economy had grown precisely from citizens' mistrust of state banks, the state engineered expansion of ATM networks proceeded by making state salaries only accessible through the local banking system. However, this system was not intended to expand access to financial services, but rather to bolster the local credit system. Despite the popular view of the ATM as a material form of modernity, enabling card-holders as cosmopolitan citizens to transact and interact in the global economy, members of the new middle class found themselves rather disappointed and their individual freedom limited, as they were caught up in the domestic monetary system. The sign "out of money" effectively indexed the local crisis of trust and banking in Vietnam (Truitt 2012). Nonetheless, state engineering allowed ordinary citizens to enrol as banking consumers, and this is how Mai was able to get a loan. Her expression of feeling "free now," having repaid the loan, likewise points toward the ambivalence, on the one hand, of being able to become an entrepreneur based on the possibility of taking out a loan, whereas, on the other hand, personal freedoms are curtailed as debt ties individuals to the anonymous institution of the bank.

Mai advertises her products on social media platforms, including Facebook and Instagram, with the hashtag #Monstarock. She also runs an account named Monstarock on both platforms. For advertisements on social media, she models together with her sister. In addition to the online store, she sells some of her goods through a friend who owns a store in Ho Chi Minh City, as well as via 818 Shop, which is a store located south of Hanoi specializing in street wear.

Mai's self-entrepreneurism is based on self-learning. Other than the dancers presented above, Mai does not have a tertiary education. She recalls how, after graduating from high school, everyone except for her seemed to have a plan about what to do next. This situation really stressed her out. However, although she did not pursue a formal education, this does not mean that she does not enjoy learning. To the contrary, she insists that she can really get into topics she finds interesting. This recalls Nguyet's narrative about not being fond of university learning, but really enjoying to learn dance and foreign languages. In a similar vein, Mai learns in order to develop herself and improve her business. With respect to dance, she continuously develops and extends her dance technique and repertoire. As for her business, she learned t-shirt printing techniques all by herself, and recently began an online marketing class, although she later quit, as the course did not fit with her goal of selling fashion online.

Over the past two years, when she was establishing her own business, Mai mostly stayed in Vietnam, refraining from travelling abroad. What may initially appear as a trade-off between business and dance is not perceived by Mai as such. Although she missed travelling during this time, she suggests that it was actually good for her, as more people in Vietnam got to know her. In fact, she noticed that more and more people enrolled in her dance class. Still she enjoys traveling within Vietnam, such as to Ho Chi Minh City or Da Nang, to either dance in or help to judge competitions.

Mia, a b-girl and co-founder of B Nashor together with Mai, is another self-entrepreneur in the niche sector of hip hop apparel. Mia also runs her own fashion label, called "The MIAT," and sells fashion articles online via Facebook. The Facebook page is comprised of a catalogue that includes images of clothes with their price tags. The clothes can be ordered through the site. According to information available on the site, the store is located in Bac Ninh City, in Bac Ninh Province, some 45 kilometres northeast of Hanoi. In December 2019, the start tab showed a photo of Mia together with a young man, while the info tab included the phrase, "We are not alike" together with a subtext "Street style unisex."

The notion of unisex is important. Nicole R. Fleetwood (2005: 326) considers the "iconic, racialized, adorned male body" at the centre of hip hop's material and visual culture. The masculine construction of hip hop wear is essential to understanding changing gender relations and norms within Vietnam's community of hip hop dancing. Female dancers embody dance aesthetics commonly associated with fit male bodies. Of course, this is a Western reading of aesthetic embodiment (see also Bragin 2014). However, in Vietnamese media reports, hip hop culture generally appears associated with the sphere of masculinity. Hip Hop is described as "rebellious" (*nổi loạn*) and "effervescent" (*sôi động*) (Thu Thuy 2016). According to Helle Rydstrøm (2004), the male character in Vietnamese cosmology is associated with the sphere of *dương*, whereas femininity is ascribed to the sphere of *âm*. *Âm dương*, more commonly known as *yin* and *yang*, constitutes the harmony between the two opposing poles. *Yin* (*âm*) signifies the female, and connotes earth, moon, and shadows, whereas *yang* (*dương*), by contrast, represents the male and connotes heaven, sun, and light (Jochim 1986). Against the background of *âm dương*, characteristics that are "hot," effervescent, and loud are typically assigned to men.

In an interview with Thanh Nhien Online, the interviewer describes female rapper Suboi as "rebellious" (*nổi loạn*) and "mysterious" (*ma mị*). Although these attributes may fit with the rap music genre, the interviewer asks Suboi if she, as a young woman, feels "lost" (*lạc lõng*) in Vietnamese society. Suboi answers confidently: "I have felt lost since I have been going to school." She explains that playing with girls turned out a tragedy, so she instead played with boys, which was a lot more fun. Nonetheless, she remains a woman. She finally concludes that she does not have to be part of a group that assigns her to a particular role in society (Thu Thuy 2016).

As pointed out by the interviewer, Suboi's mysterious and rebellious appearance is further underlined by her clothing choices. In fact, Fleetwood (2005) establishes a mimetic relationship between hip hop fashion and music, and specifically its lyrics. Consequently, Suboi makes use of fashion as a visual identifier of sound. Particularly in her earlier videos and album covers, Suboi mostly dresses in baggy pants, tank tops, baseball shirts, wide t-shirts, and sneakers, sometimes combining these clothes with more feminine fashion items, such as platform sneakers, tights, and earrings. In the YouTube video, *Phục Sinh Cypher* (2015), Suboi is the only female rapper among a group of all-male MCs, wearing an extra-large white t-shirt, a rose coloured baseball shirt, baggy pants, and silver hoop earrings.

Many dancers similarly dress in unisex hip hop apparel, as well. However, clothing styles differ depending on particular dance styles they practice. The chapters on different dance styles indicate that most of participants in the Popping Event at Ho Thanh Cong, and most of the b-boys and b-girls hanging around Ly Thai To, wore baggy pants, jeans, sweatpants, and large t-shirts with appropriate sneakers. As a consequence, the clothing characteristic to popping and breaking appears to either be more male-oriented or unisex. By contrast, participants in waacking events tend to dress in more feminine clothing. Even within a particular style, clothing may vary depending on the setting and occasion. In waacking, for instance, dancers appear to dress according to the occasion. Participating in a crew cypher or class, they dress rather casually in sweatpants, leggings, and t-shirts, whereas they dress up, including hair and make-up, for official events, such as a battle. However, across all the hip hop styles practiced in Vietnam, gender differences are not strongly marked by clothing. In waacking, male and female dancers dress alike. Indeed, an integral part of waacking appears to be gender play, including fashion. On the contrary, male and female practitioners in popping, breaking, and locking wear casual clothing. Mai is a good example, as most of the time she dresses in baggy pants, wide t-shirts, and base cap. The rare times she posts an image or video of herself wearing a dress, she provides the context via the post's metadata, indicating whether she is waacking or freestyling. In one of her posts she addresses her followers using the term *anh em*, omitting *chị*, as the formal version would be *anh chị em*. She asks "Does anyone know of any shop selling old clothes, one with lots of wide trousers to look handsome dancing hip hop?" The last part of the question actually indicates an association of hip hop wear with male bodies, as she uses the adverb *đẹp trai* (handsome), which is indicative of men.

In relation to hip hop wear, the adjective *đẹp trai* is also used by other b-girls on social media. For example, a female dancer from the Milky Way Crew uses the hashtag #Dep_Trai_Thuong_It_Noi when posting fashion photos of the latest hip hop wear on Facebook. *Dep trai thuong it noi* translates as "handsome people usually do not talk too much." The hashtag *đẹp trai* unites both male and female dancers in hip hop wear. The hashtag is followed by the crew names, #Bnahsor #Bigtoe #MKWfamily #Hiphopnevadie #Bboy #Funky. The female dancer who posts the photos and hashtags does not refer to a gendered form of break dancers, but uses b-boy as an inclusive term. The gender-inclusive use of b-boy recalls Asia One's take on b-boying. Asia One is a famous b-girl from the USA. In the video *What is a b-girl?* (2010), Asia One erases the conceptual difference between b-boy and b-girl, as she claims to be a part of hip hop culture, or b-boying. Moreover, she named her crew "No Easy Props," which is a warning against giving easy props (or accolades) to female dancers simply because they are female. Like all others, female dancers are entitled to props if they are good at dancing (Johnson 2014).

In the post presented above, the use of the term b-boy is particularly striking, first of all because the hashtag was employed by a female dancer, and second, because female dancers actually predominate in the photo, which depicts five women and three men. Among the five women are Mai and Mia from B Nashor, both of whom have their own fashion labels. Accordingly, the hashtags #Dep_Trai_Thuong_It_Noi and #dep trai are not only used to refer to the self, but also to promote unisex fashion.

Visual economy and female bodies

Social media facilitates self-entrepreneurism and self-fashioning in the hip hop community of practice. In peer production, social media platforms assist in producing, distributing, and sharing hip hop artists' output. Such output usually consists of images and videos showing portraits, close-ups, or full body pictures of dancers, which are uploaded to individual or collective social media accounts and downloaded, liked, and shared by others. While social media primarily appears to build on visuality, other senses are involved in social media use, as well. Selfies are produced via the haptic experience of clicking on the camera button, while images circulated through social media platforms via the same movement of the fingers. Accordingly, touching and clicking become important haptic devices in order to distribute images of the self. Nina Hien (2012) introduces the term "haptic economy" for such self-representational practices, which builds on Deborah Poole's (1997) term "visual economy." According to Poole, the visual economy involves the production of images, including their exchange as commodities, as well as the cultural and discursive systems against which their meanings, values, and uses are assessed and assigned. In Hien's work on beauty regimes in late socialist Vietnam, haptic denotes the technique of photographic retouching. The process of digital postproduction unites technological progress with the popular belief of *sửa hình, sửa tướng*, which means that by altering an image, one can change the fate of the depicted subject. This belief builds on the art of reading face (*nhân tướng học*), as facial structures are believed to determine one's fate (Hien 2012: 475). Against this background, Hien considers the retouching of photos as a beautification technique that offers both women and men the opportunity to take their lives into their own hands and to transform their personal fates. In other words, digital technologies assist individuals in forming new subject positions through which they can articulate hopes and desires.

The forming of subject positions through social media is an important feature of the hip hop communities of practice in Vietnam. Through the circulation of images, values, and beliefs are created and shared within the community. In social media, however, subject formation is achieved in the combination of (audio-)visual media with hashtag metadata. Hashtags are commonly used in microblogging, taking on a cataloguing function. Hashtags classify and catalogue information as they indicate a post's or tweet's aboutness. Rather than being metadata generated by the microblogging site, hashtags are descriptive annotations produced by users themselves. In posts on Facebook and Instagram, hashtags become part of the linguistic structure of the post. Hashtags build on intertextuality as they link to other texts containing the same hashtags (Zappavigna 2015). The intertextuality of the hashtag is amplified by its intermediality, since hashtags can be used across diverse social networking platforms. Moreover, the use of the hashtag is becoming more and more popular in print media, as well as in graffiti writing on concrete.

From a sociolinguistic stance, hashtags contribute infrastructure for forming communities and publics (Zappavigna 2015). The meanings of hashtags, however, may remain opaque to those outside the community (of practice), as they oftentimes involve abbreviations and concatenation (Posch et al. 2013). Accordingly, the hashtags #Dep_Trai_Thuong_It_Noi or #femalepopper can be easily deciphered by members of the Vietnamese hip hop community of practice or the Global Hip Hop Nation. More importantly, the social metadata of the hashtag assists in retrieving information that the user is interested in:

> "Searchable and aggregatable discourse affords the possibility of new forms of social bonding, such as those seen in mass meme participation, as well as smaller scale performances such as alignment with imagined audiences via hashtagged evaluative metacomment." (Zappavigna 2015: 289)

The adoption of the hashtag #femalepopper indexes information that is targeted toward an audience interested in female popping practitioners or produced by users for whom such content is relevant. The hashtag makes talk about female poppers searchable, while aggregating a field of discourse about the content indexed by the metadata.

The combination of videos and photos uploaded to social media, with hashtags such as #Dep_Trai_Thuong_It_Noi or #femalepopper, signify a gender discourse in hip hop dance, in which female members of the community engage in particular. Fashioning themselves in unisex or male street wear, practicing popping, breaking, locking, or waacking, they re-appropriate their bodily image and inhabit their bodies as their own (Nurka 2013: 486). Consequently, popular culture mediates alternative femininities. The publication and circulation of femininities deviating from the (heteronormative) norm also occurs in rap, particularly in recent rap videos produced by Vietnamese female rapper Suboi. Black feminist approaches to rap have long recognized the contribution of black women to hip hop music. In the early 1980s, all-women crews such as Sequence and the Mercedes Ladies, as well as mixed-gendered crews such as the Funky Four Plus One More (the only woman being the "one more"), were active in the United States. Women were not only active in the rap business as performers, but also as producers. In fact, Silvia Robinson of Sugar Hill Records signed the first widely successful rap crew, the Sugar Hill Gang, producing the 1980 hit, *Rapper's Delight*. Already in the early years of rap's U.S. commercial success, female rappers topped the music charts, such as MC Lyte, Missy Elliott, Salt-n-Pepa, Lauryn Hill. In Germany, likewise, the all-female crew Tic Tac Toe and female rappers Schwester S. and Cora E. were quite successful. However, many of the pioneering female rappers were not as equally recognized by industry managers as were their male counterparts. With rap's increasing homogenization to target a mass audience, women rappers were marginalized and often not offered money-making record deals. As a result, many female rappers had to turn to love and romance rap, which were more in line with disco and R&B at the time, in order to cater to the music industry's demands (Emerson 2002; Forman 1994). This shifted once again in the 2010s, when female rappers such as M.I.A, Cardi B., and Nicky Menage, and Awkwafina in the U.S., or Lady Bitch Ray and Sookee in Germany, as well as queer rappers like Mykki Blanco, reconquered the world stage of hip hop, adding more gender diversity to hip hop music. The year 2019 was particularly successful for German women rappers, such as Ebow, Shirin Davis, SXTN (Juju and Nura), and others. They not only contested the male-dominated linguistic sphere of rap, but also the imagery of women in rap videos. Rap videos have long been known and critiqued for its male gaze and sexist and sexualized stance. Montage shots of single female body parts, in particular, cast women not as individual subjects but as objects of men's conspicuous consumption. Put differently, women in hip hop are often reduced to video dancers embedded with pornographic imagery (Hunter 2011; Johnson 2014). In her essay on consumption and new gender relations in hip hop, Margaret Hunter (2011) alludes to two forms of the representation of women of colour in rap videos, which she refers to as "getting low" and "making it rain." The former position refers to the interchangeable female bodies of colour that bend over (get low), while the latter refers to men throwing money at the women (making it rain) in order for them to shake. Hunter (2011: 18) contends that such displays of women of colour, mainly black women, wearing lingerie and swim suits in rap videos testifies to the "racialized gender politics of mainstream hip hop."

Rana Emerson (2002), in her analysis of U.S. music videos featuring black performers in 1998, similarly shows how stereotypes of black womanhood permeate music videos in the way that such imagery reproduces the institutional contexts of the videos' production. First, the imagery overtly focuses on the women's bodies. Emerson suggests that women's bodies are displayed according to American beauty standards, meaning that most black female performers were rather thin, and mostly under 30 years old. As mentioned earlier, moreover, women's bodies were sometimes rendered into visual pieces, displaying different body parts separately. Second, the videos imply a one-dimensional black womanhood, as female performers are not fashioned as artists in their own right, but rather as objects for the (heterosexual) male gaze. As a consequence, mothers and pregnant women were almost entirely absent from the videos, which is not to mention the nearly complete absence of any sexual diversity in the music videos. Third, the videos deal with the theme of conspicuous consumption outlined above, mostly in the way that women are displayed in the co-presence of men, who act as their sponsors (Emerson 2002: 120, 122-123).

As a result, sexual relations in rap videos are increasingly portrayed as transactional and racialized in nature. The strip club has emerged as a public place in which men can access women's sexual services via financial trans-actions. At the same time, the display of women of colour in these videos reinforces "dominant narratives about African American and Latina women, and the concomitant symbolic protection of white femininity by its absence in these representations." (Hunter 2011: 25). Against this background, the idiom of "getting low" refers to the performance by women (of colour) of a highly sexualized femininity for a male gaze, whereas "making it rain" expresses men's elevated status above women, expressed through their possession of money (in high denomination bills) with which they pay women for sexual services. The result is the reduction of heteronormative sexuality to a trans-actional relationship, while demonstrating power differentials between men and women, both in monetary and sexual terms (Hunter 2011: 25, 29).[19]

The highly sexualized display of femininity for a male gaze has yet to be-come mainstream in Vietnamese rap videos, as most videos are concerned with displaying the rappers' wealth in terms of money, expensive cars, and houses. But one example can be found in the video for the aforementioned track *Hư Quá Đi* by Richchoi, which shows a long sequence of shirtless Viet-namese men fighting each other, followed by a short sequence displaying Viet-namese women in bikini tops. By contrast, the official video of Suboi's track *Công* (2018)[20], produced by Jenni Trang Le and directed by Bao Nguyen, contro-verts the male gaze of mainstream rap videos, thereby undermining the sexu-alized and racialized gender relations described by Hunter. The video follows

---

19   "Making it rain" also has a more explicit and vulgar meaning, as it is also used to denote men's ejaculation on women's bodies – once more a pornographic reference (Hunter 2011; Miller-Young 2008).

20   https://www.youtube.com/watch?v=Z4cQcpOLjxE

the recent trend in displaying female video dancers. However, rather than de-picting women of colour in swim suits and lingerie, the video shows Vietnam's best known b-girls and female hip hop dancers wearing yellow tracksuits. The tracksuits worn in the video are indexical of the industrial setting, as the video was shot in a Toyota assembly plant in Vinh Phuc Province, northeast of Hanoi.

The Japanese brand Toyota is one of the largest supplier of cars and motor-bikes in Vietnam. The female dancers are dressed as workers with the track-suits covering their entire bodies. Beneath their worker uniforms they wear white tank tops and black flat shoes as footwear. The only display of flesh is by the rapper herself. Contrasting with the yellow of the tracksuits, and grey shades of the factory machines, Suboi wears a black bandeau top combined with wide dark-grey, military-like trousers and silver high heel boots. The bandeau top reveals tattoos along the front and back of her upper body. Suboi wears expressive make-up, consisting of dark eye shadow and red lipstick while wearing her long hair open. The female dancers, by contrast, are styled in nude make-up look, with short hair or else long hair pulled back in a pony-tail. Suboi combines her feminine appearance, consisting of stylized make-up and clothing, with hand gestures and an upper body movement repertoire that is well-known in globally circulating rap videos, yet mostly exercised by male rappers. In the track *Công*, rap video and lyrics go hand in hand, yet in-stead of communicating a binary sex-gender ideology (Hunter 2011), the video casts women as active producers of hip hop culture, on the one hand, while lit-erally portraying them as hard-working contributors to Vietnam's economy, on the other. The rap video departs from common pop cultural representa-tions of Vietnamese women, as the female protagonists are "not only hustling hard to make ends meet and take care of the family, but also maintaining their strength, fierceness, swag and vulnerability" (Saigoneer 2018).

The title *Công* refers to work or labour in general, but it also refers to one of the four Confucian virtues that define women's behaviour and conduct. The virtue of *công* stipulates that women must be skilled at cooking and house-keeping, thus assigning them to roles as family caretakers, while delimiting their scope of responsibility to the domestic sphere. However, in the absence of any male protagonists, the video creates a woman's world in which the fe-male protagonists fashion themselves as independent and autonomous sub-jects, whose position in society is not defined in relation to men. According to literary scholar Sabine Sielke (2011), the appropriation of formerly exclusive spaces by women can be achieved through the imitation of – what are con-

All-female crew of Công video with Suboi in the middle

Source: Công Official Music Video, 2018 Suboi Entertainment

sidered to be – "male" attributes, such as clothing or linguistic norms. Both dimensions are apparent in the *Công* video, as Suboi combines her rather feminine outfit with "male" rap gestures and word play. Moreover, through their bodily practices, the female dancers who wear "male" worker outfits appropriate and occupy the space of the factory. In one scene, the collective body of female dancers mimics a robot, aligning their staccato head and leg movements with the industrial-technical setting of the manufacturing plant. This appropriation of male-dominated spaces is, according to Sielke (2011), another dimension of mimicry.

The concept of mimicry has been adopted widely across disciplines. Originating in biology, mimicry signals similarity where there is actually difference. Mimicry thus refers to the superficial resemblance of one organism to another organism, or another natural object among which it lives. Apart from functioning as a mechanism of protection and attraction, African American, postcolonial, performance, and feminist theories consider mimicry as "projecting a space of liminality and liberation that still remains to be mapped" (Sielke 2003: 328). What is important is that the mimicry "echoes and reproduces its pretest with a significant difference" (Sielke 2003: 330). In contrast to cross-dressing and transvestism, which Marjorie Garber (1992) considers as indexical of crisis while simultaneously reaffirming and enhancing the heterosexual norm (Sielke 1998), female hip hop practitioners like Suboi, Mai, and others engage in gender queering, as they transgress binary sex and gender norms, performing multiple identities.

Sociolinguist Ana Deumert's distinction between mimesis and mimicry contributes to a better understanding of what is going on in the hip hop community of practice. Deumert (2018: 10) understands mimesis and mimicry as two processes involved in the production and performance of creativity. Mimesis denotes the creative affirmation of resemblances, whereas mimicry signifies the transgressive creation of dissemblances. The perception of similarity and difference is linked to performance precisely through the ability to imitate, repeat, and mimic. Deumert (2018: 10) understands performance as "the performative, audience-oriented (re-)creation of similarity/difference." In other words, the representation of women in the *Công* video creates semiotic disruption and transgression within the binary gender norm (mimicry), while simultaneously forming an experiential subject through creative forms of re-presentation (mimesis) (Deumert 2018). This combination of mimicry and mimesis works on multiple levels, comprising the following dimensions: (1) gender ideology, (2) lyrics, (3) video montage and aesthetics, and (4) fashion. In what follows, I will present each dimension with respect to the video and gender performance therein:

(1) First of all, gender ideologies inform the various social positions and roles of women, men, among other gendered individuals. The video setting in a manufacturing plant indexes Vietnam's export-oriented industrialization. Since the 1990s, the government has invested in industrial and economic zones with the infrastructure necessary to attract foreign direct investments. Most of these industrial zones are located in the vicinity of Vietnam's largest cities, including Hanoi, Hai Phong, Ho Chi Minh City, and Da Nang. The automotive industry is a fast-growing sector in Vietnam. With increasing levels of income, development, infrastructure upgrading, and rather low market penetration by four-wheeled vehicles, the Vietnam News Agency estimates automobile sales increase of 22 % in the period from 2018 until 2025 (Schmitz-Bauerdick 2019; The Economist 2018). The automotive industry is dominated by male employees. Although women outnumber men in the export-oriented industries of textiles and garments, electronics, and leather and footwear, they still constitute a minority of the workforce in the automobile industry. In general, women workers in labour-intensive export factories are hired as a cheap and flexible labour force. In export-oriented industries, they face worse health and safety conditions than in the Vietnamese formal sector. While the export sector offers employment opportunities to women with low educa-

tional backgrounds, there is little scope for upward mobility due to a lack of skills upgrading or technical training provided by the companies (Kabeer 2011).[21] As Angie Ngoc Tran (2004: 214) shows in her assessment of female garment workers, female criteria on the factory floor include nimble fingers, manual dexterity and docility, whereas male criteria include the strength to handle heavy machinery, self-confidence when cutting fabrics, and responsibility. Resulting from this gendered division of labour is a preference of men over women, especially when it comes to working with specialized machines, such as in the automobile industry. In such contexts, men are consequently more likely to receive on-the-job training, thereby permitting them to improve their skills and receive higher wages.

Thus, the female dancers in the video literally appropriate the male space of the automotive factory, as they manoeuvre heavy equipment and lift large metal hammers. What is more, the video only refers to women's productive rather than reproductive role in society. While socialism has stressed that women make active contributions to economy and society, the appreciation of women's productivity has always been side-lined by their role as family caretakers (Nguyen 2015). This "force of domesticity," as well as the "persistence of the ideology of women's domesticity in the labour market and the family" (Parreñas 2008: 9), is also promoted by women's magazines (Earl 2014; Leshkowich 2008). However, as Nguyen Thu Giang (2019a: 64) reveals, the promotion of good motherhood and women's domesticity is not unique to Vietnamese media or the socialist state, but is rather a dominant trope in lifestyle magazines from the United States, Europe, and other parts of the Global North. Along similar lines, Suzanne Brenner (1999) argues that the state under Indonesia's New Order regime was not the only actor in propagating conservative ideals about women's domestic obligations to the families, but rather that the state set the tone about what could and could not be said in public, thereby stylizing imagery of women.

Thus, the Công music video disrupts stereotypes about gender across cultures, which is, indeed, a major theme in the lyrics.

2) Second, the song lyrics, which alternate between English and Vietnamese, further address common representations of women. The track opens with the English lines:

---

21   For example in 2004 the ratio of female to male workers in textile and garments was 2.85; in electronics 2.30, and 1.80 in leather and footwear (Kabeer 2011).

Imma young Vietnamese lady, who's this?
(Who's this?)
Imma young Vietnamese lady, who's this?
(Ai đó?)
Real Saigonese pop showbiz don't fit
Real Saigonese pop showbiz don't fit
Real Saigonese pop showbiz don't fit
Real Saigonese pop showbiz don't fit

In other words, she opens with awareness of her queer position, as she obviously deviates from the norm. First, she diverges from the "real Saigonese pop showbiz" in which young women are fashioned and fashion themselves according to normative beauty standards, as talented singers who mostly produce love songs, defining themselves in relation to men. Second, she does not fit the Viet rap biz either. Although in the recent years, female Viet rappers like Linh Lam, Kimmese, and Suzie X have taken the stage, male MC's still dominate Viet rap. Although she gets "props" from male MC's for her (international) success, she is simultaneously criticized for her success, as she has gone from "underground" to "overground." Rha Goddess (2005: 342) describes this tendency in the hip hop industry as a crisis of identity, declaring "Artists who move to a place of not struggling or not wanting to struggle face a crisis of identity, or, worse, they get labeled as 'commercial' or a sellout." While many MC's aspire to become well-known rappers who are able to make a living from rap, the 'real' and authentic rappers are considered those who remain underground (Norton 2015).

Suboi lyrically acknowledges her own trespass by comparing herself to Trang Quynh. She raps: *Thông minh hay không đâu cần chứng minh như Trạng Quỳnh* [Clever or (unfounded) not, we need to prove ourselves like Trang Quynh]. Rapping "like" (*như*) Trang Quynh, Suboi deploys the stylistic device of simile. In *Book of Rhymes*, Adam Bradley (2009) differentiates between simile and metaphor in rap. The simile is used to create a direct comparison between two distinct things, establishing the comparison by using 'like' or 'as.' Metaphor, by contrast, is used when one thing is said to be the other (without the use of 'like' or 'as'). Bradley (2009: 94) concludes by suggesting that similes "shine the spotlight on their subject more directly than do metaphors," with the subject usually being the "I" of the MC. Accordingly, Suboi fashions herself as Trang Quynh. Trang Quynh, whose real name was Nguyen Quynh (1677-1748), is a folk satirical character, who criticized the feudal system of the Trinh lords (1545-1787). The Trinh family ruled Northern Vietnam under the late Le Dynasty, while the Nguyen Lords ruled the South. The comparison with Trang Quynh works on at least two levels. First, Suboi compares herself to a folk character, causing dissonance as her sex does not match the folk character's biological sex. Second, the simile is a pop cultural reference. During the lunar new year in 2019, a Vietnamese movie by the same name was released and screened in movie theatres throughout the country. She once again breaks with stereotypes when denying that she is a "cookie cutter bitch." Cookie cutter bitch is an idiom referring to young girls who all look alike, follow the latest trends, and have no individual features or characteristics whatsoever (Urban Dictionary 2014). This is again a pop cultural reference to hip hop, as *Cookie Cutter Bitch* is a rap track by female American rapper, Snow Tha Product. In fact, video and lyrics form a symbiosis, when Suboi drops the line "Stereotype not my social life. In fact, you better say goodbye to this shadow side." The camera shows Suboi gesticulating upside down in the frame. The next shot shows the main female dancer crawling on the floor, and then quickly rising (like phoenix from the ashes), positioning herself in front of a light source.

3) Third, video montage and aesthetics: The interplay of mimicry and mimesis, including mimicry's potential for semiotic disruption and transgression (Deumert 2018), is further substantiated in the close reading of the video against the template of globally circulating rap videos. *Công* references rap video aesthetics, such as close shots of the MC. The artificial lighting emphasizes Suboi's strong make-up and the nude look of the dancers. The video montage includes some counter shots and close-ups. The close-ups are solely focused on the female rapper. Even in the counter shots, when Suboi seems to be in conversation with an interlocutor, it is always her. The first shot is a close-up of the left side of her face, with a focus on her mouth illuminated with red light while rapping, and the counter shot shows the right side of her face in a cold silvery grey light offering a response. The overt focus on the female artist is further highlighted by the all-female cast. Emerson explains that Black female artists are often presented to the public under the guidance of a male sponsor, who is sometimes so dominant that the music video seems to be about the male producer, rather than the female singer or rapper. Emerson writes: "These videos give the impression that women are unable to be successful without the assistance and creative genius of a male impresario" (Emerson 2002: 124).

Suboi's video, by contrast, opens with the logo of her own music label. After signing with and releasing her first studio album *Walk/Bước* in 2010, with the Vietnamese music label Music Faces, she founded her own company in 2012, Suboi Entertainment. While it is common in Viet Rap to have featured artists on one track, and sometimes even several, Suboi raps most of her tracks single-handedly. It is striking that she did some lyrical collaborations in the early stage of her musical career. For instance, she released the track *I Know* featuring Kim, the female hip hop artist also known as Kimmese, in 2011. Additionally, some male artists featured Suboi, such as Anh Khan in *Quê Hương Việt Nam* (2010), American Vietnamese rapper Thai Viet G in *Hold You Down* (2012), or Antoneus Maximus in his track *I Love Viet Nam* (2012), which featured Suboi, Kimmese, Thanh Bui, and others. What is more, in 2015 Suboi released the single *Trò Chơi* featuring Touliver, a major Vietnamese hip hop producer. However, since taking a break from life centre stage, she has mainly focused on rapping and producing her own music, rarely featuring any other singers or rappers. That said, in the *Công* video Suboi features Vietnam's most famous female hip hop dancers. Mai Tinh Vi was responsible for the choreography in the video and she also participated as a dancer herself. Many of the other women dancers are either members of Mai's Cun-Cun or the Big Toe Crew. Other dancers include Nguyet from New York Style Crew and Ho Tung Lam of Milky Way Crew. The lead dancer is actually a young woman from Ho Chi Minh City. While Suboi differs from the dancers in her clothing, make-up, and rapping, she does not overshadow them. One women in particular stands out as she dances solo, combining graceful ballet movements with breaking and popping moves. Yet the other dancers are also shown individually and collectively towards the end of the video, turning into a wild crowd surrounding Suboi. The female dancers express their outrage with quick fighting moves, kicking and jumping around with aggressive faces. In sum, the female rapper shares the spotlight with the main woman dancer, while lead dancer again shares the spotlight with the other female dancers.

4) Fourth, the fashion in the video further indexes the interplay of mimicry and mimesis. In her analysis of black women artists' music videos, Emerson (2002: 129) found that a focus on appearance and physical (sexual) attraction often occurred in combination with themes of independence, strength, agency, toughness, and a streetwise nature. Such combinations are also found in *Công*. While the rapper's make-up and untamed hair particularly suggest a rather sexualized image of the artist, the military-like trousers, together

with her various facial and hand gestures as well as the lyrics, jointly indicate strength, independence, and autonomy. Likewise, the female dancers demonstrate strength when mimicking the hammering of metal in their track suits, which, as shown by Angie Ngoc Tran, is usually a task assigned to men due to their physical strength. In contrast with the often-sexualized representations of female dancers in rap videos, the women dancers wear track suits that cover their whole bodies, not revealing any flesh beyond their hands and faces. In a sense, the track suits are unisex, as they serve as protection in the factory.

Overall, the combination of hip hop wear, the rapper's gestures, an (all) female cast, and the negotiation of gender roles through rap lyrics are recurrent themes in Suboi's oeuvre.

In conclusion, Suboi's self-fashioning as a female rapper must be read against her lyrics, gestures, and performance. Suboi attaches new meanings to global imagery of hip hop, challenging established gender norms, both in Vietnam and in the highly media-saturated world of rap. What is more, Suboi makes use of social media to challenge common ideals of womanhood and female body images. In 2019, Suboi gave birth to her first child. Her post on Instagram the 5th of May that year includes a video with a close-up of her unvarnished face, talking in Vietnamese into the camera. The post beneath in English says:

> "I said: I saw an article included me with a few women in showbiz who got their body back in a short time after birth based on my recent IG post and I want to say it's not true in my case, the last belly post was an old photo. I'm not trying as well as encouraging these type of "incredible" expectation on women on the media. Bearing a child and giving birth is hard work, right after we have to take care of the baby and recover at the same time, not to mention dealing with postpartum depression because the levels of estrogen dramatically decline after pregnancy. Let's just support and give women some love and understand for what they just went through. I want to say to the women who just gave birth that you did something really brave and wonderful by bringing another human being into this world and we are trying our best to raise them to be happy and decent people, that's what matter the most."

Five days later, the post had received 201 comments from both women and men, all giving her credit for telling the truth and for being authentic as a young mother. Four months after she gave birth to her daughter, Suboi reveals the hyperreal, declaring that the photo of her belly was taken before having given birth. Rather than recreating the illusion of a socially valued slender female body (Leshkowich 2012), she uses social media to counter the idea that mothers need to lose weight and quickly return to their prenatal body-shape. Instead, she calls for recognition of women's toughness in giving life and nurturing other human beings. Women should receive credit for this and not for their outer appearance. In this context, Suboi stresses women's role as caretakers of the family. Yet, rather than reducing women to this role or their bodies, she highlights their braveness and courage.

In the neoliberal visual economy, women magazines in Vietnam purport to draw on scientific knowledge when giving advice about how to maintain a decent and sexually attractive body, whether by physical training or diets (Leshkowich 2008). Such discourses about female bodies are side-lined by professionalized obesity discourses, which aim to confront the country's nutrition problems by drawing on medical knowledge in the form of regular health, weight, and body mass index statistics (Ehlert 2019). In her work on obesity, biopower, and the embodiment of caring, sociologist Judith Ehlert shows how the rising problem of child obesity in contemporary Vietnam aligns with dominant discourses about motherhood, holding mothers responsible for their child's eating practices. In dominant discourse, the bodies of both child and mother are closely intertwined, as suggested in expressions such as "fat children and beautiful mothers" (*con béo mẹ xinh*), or "smart children and slim mothers" (*con thông minh mẹ không mập*) (Vietnam's Nutrition Association 2017). Consequently, mothers find themselves caught up with social pressure and expectations about their own as well as their children's bodies, both during and after pregnancy. While mothers are required to quickly return to their prenatal weight, they are also expected to raise healthy children, preventing them from becoming obese. Yet, at the same time, they are constantly confronted with the visual economy of food advertisements that allude to their "maternal affection" and "love" in making their children happy, which often includes pressure to buy products of low quality and unhealthy (Ehlert 2019: 113). As a consequence, mothers are responsible for regulating both their own diets and bodies, as well as their children's food practices and eating behaviours (Ehlert 2019). Suboi addresses this ambiguous state of women's responsibility, shifting the focus from the mother's body to her state of mind. By addressing postpartum depression in her social media post, furthermore, she transgresses the boundaries between what is considered private and public, as she addresses an intimate matter in the public sphere, paving the way for further public discussion.

Class and consumption

Suboi frequently raps about her childhood, adolescence, and the struggles she faced, as she did not follow the "conventional" and valued path for young Vietnamese urban middle-class women. Likewise, judging from their educational backgrounds and consumption patterns, many dancers can be considered as belonging to the middle class. Fashion items in particular have evolved as visual markers, indicating both class status and membership in the community of practice. Baggy pants, XXL-t-shirts, hoodies, baseball caps, and sneakers, all indexical of hip hop culture, are frequently encountered in Hanoi's urban landscape. These markers are not spatially confined to a particular locality, but shared widely around the world. The promotion of consumption and the embrace of capitalism have become crucial features of hip hop culture (Fleetwood 2005; Hunter 2011). In the hip hop studies reader, *That's the Joint!*, Part VII of the book, consisting of eight chapters, is dedicated to the commodification of hip hop. As Hunter writes: "The shift from cultural practice to commodity was solidified with the advent of gangsta rap in the early 1990s" (2011: 16). Especially in rap videos, conspicuous consumption is promoted and enhanced. This "marketing of difference" (Fleetwood 2005: 343) is actually based on an inversion of Thorstein Veblen's concept of conspicuous consumption (Hunter 2011). According to Veblen the so-called leisure class engaged in the consumption of highly prized commodities, yet of little utility, in order to visualize and materialize its distinction from members of the lower class, for whom consumption rested on the need to survive. In rap videos, however, conspicuous consumption is not linked to upper classes, but is in fact linked to the lower class. The videos mostly show male rappers who drive around in expensive cars, wearing designer clothes, and adorning their bodies with jewellery, thus engaging in conspicuous consumption, meanwhile still maintaining a "ghetto" aesthetic that connects their lifestyle and consumption practices to the black and Latino poor (Smith 2003). Appealing to audiences beyond the black community, elites begin to imitate the aesthetics and consumption patterns of the poor. Hunter (2011: 18) is critical of such aesthetic imitation, stating: "White listeners can consume the music and images of a corporate construction of blackness while maintaining a safe distance from black pain and institutional racism." Although the *Công* video mimics the montage and aesthetics of globally circulating rap videos, it also visualizes the complicated relationships of class, consumption, and gender in contemporary Vietnam. The video is set in an automotive factory, alluding to Vietnam's position in the world economy as a production site providing cheap labour. Instead of displaying status markers, the collective body of female dancers is dressed in track suits, leaving no room for individuality. In fact, life on the assembly line, conducting hard labour, is the reality for many Vietnamese men and women. Instead of cruising around in expensive cars, the workers in the video literally build cars that are consumed by the rising middle class. Female rapper Suboi, by contrast, fashions herself in shiny high heel boots and camouflage trousers, showing that her "finger nails are French tips," thus indicating her class position.

According to Fleetwood (2005: 343), the promotion of "cool America" represented by black b-boys, and the global circulation of such imagery, need to be considered in the context of marketing "youthful alterity" as a stylized commodity. Yet, how does consumption in general, and commodities representing cool America in particular, fit the market socialist agenda? In colonial times, consumption practices and patterns used to serve as sensory markers of social distinction, but the perception of consumption changed with the advent of socialism in Vietnam. In her research on food consumption in colonial Vietnam, Erica Peters (2012) explores the social positioning of the Vietnamese élite and middle class through their culinary choices and practices. In the Republic of Vietnam (1955-1975), elite status was expressed through the conspicuous consumption of American goods (Earl 2014). Of course, public perception of consumption has changed with the country's unification and with the overall transformation of socialism. Equating consumption with imperialism, the state aimed to transform Vietnam from a locus of consumption to a site of production. In other words, socialist ideology built on the eradication of consumerism, as it was seen as enabling individuals to acquire markers of social distinction, as well as individual pursuits of false desires. Under market socialism, this official perception of consumption has changed once again. In contemporary Vietnam, conspicuous consumption is acknowledged and even considered moral by the party-state. In other words, consumption has become an index of personal achievement, and the private accumulation of wealth is promoted by the state. Put differently, modern citizens in Vietnam are encouraged to self-fashion, such as through consumption, but only within parameters established by the party-state (Leshkowich 2012; Vann 2012).

Finally, the authors of *Reinvention of Distinction* (2012) describe the delinking of consumption from middle-class lifestyles. As a result, the middle class is considered the normal state of affairs, which, according to Drummond (2012), makes it increasingly difficult to actually see Vietnam's middle class. Consequently, it is also not easy to identify hip hop practitioners as middle class. Conspicuous consumption is part of their lifestyle, however, and particularly includes the consumption of certain branded products and fashion items, such as sneakers and t-shirts, as well as status symbols, such as mobile phones and cameras. Dancers display their latest gifts and purchased commodities in images posted to social media. On the occasion of his birthday, for example, one b-boy posted a photo of all the gifts he had received from his friends, showing two pairs of sneakers, a t-shirt and hoodie, and three different kinds of baseball caps. In short, the photo displayed a showcase of local and global hip hop brands, among them Converse and Reebok, as well as a t-shirt from Monstarock. Another photo showed another branded product that he received as a gift from his wife, the latest Sony camera system, which costs around 800 Euros.

Hip hop fashion, like the music, builds on referentiality and reflexivity. Accordingly, hip hop wear appropriates and references status symbols from the European upper class, as well as European fashion designers such as Gucci, Louis Vuitton, or Givenchy (Fleetwood 2005). In the meantime, hip hop wear has evolved as a profitable business, with American designer companies drafting designs for hip hop artists, rappers, and hip hop moguls starting their own clothing labels (e.g., Wu-Tang Clan, Lil' Kim, Busta Rhymes, Outcast), or cooperating with established sports and fashion labels to promote their own fashion lines. In 2016, the collaboration between the luxury brand Kenzo X and H&M was represented by Chance the Rapper, Somalian model Iman Mohamed Abdulmajid, and female Vietnamese rapper Suboi. The campaign features a video of each celebrity wearing outfits from the fashion line. In one Youtube video from 2016, Suboi comments on the relationship between hip hop wear and her life as a rapper in Vietnam. H&M only recently opened storefronts in Vietnam. On opening day, a large crowd waited in front of the shop in Hanoi, reminding me of lines of people waiting outside Gucci or Louis Vuitton Stores on Hong Kong's Canton Road, and youth gathered in front of the Hollister Shop in Hamburg, as they waited for permission to enter. That H&M is eager to attract more and more Vietnamese customers is evident from its advertisement featuring Suboi. While H&M is typically not a brand consumed by hip hop practitioners, sports brands like Adidas, Vans, Nike, and the like are. Interestingly, many of these sports companies manufacture their goods in Vietnam. Over the last decade, Vietnam has evolved as a major production site for the textile and footwear industry. In 2016, Vietnam was the world's fifth largest exporter of textiles and clothing (Schmitz-Bauerdick 2017). Nike, Adidas, and Timberland are among the companies producing footwear and textiles in Vietnam. While authentic foot wear is still expensive, it is increasingly available in shopping malls, while knockoff products from these brands are all sold along Hang Dau Street in Hanoi's Ancient Quarter. The economy of counterfeit goods in Vietnam is quite large, with markets for counterfeit versions for valued products, ranging from luxury products, such as Gucci bags, to fake waste products that can be traded for money (Nguyen 2019). However, hip hop consumers and practitioners seek out authentic commodities. Vann (2012) shows how Vietnam's recent status as a major production site for global brands complicates Vietnamese consumers' relationship with branded products. She describes how consumers saw themselves as "cut off from the sorts of connections—of information, fashion, ownership, and display—made possible by goods available elsewhere" (Vann 2012: 166), as foreign-branded goods were produced and consumed in Vietnam. In this context, authenticity has evolved as an important value assigned to commodities. For instance, a female hip hop dancer affirmed that she "loved" Adidas, and a few weeks later, she posted a selfie taken at an Adidas Flagship Store opening on social media.

Interlude: Circulation, Standardization, and Technique

Much like the bodily practice of dance, the leading of a dancing life is marked by both mobility and flexibility. The self-entrepreneurism discussed in the previous chapter reveals that dancers must be highly flexibile in their approach to generating income for themselves and their families. On the one hand, the precarity of dancing labour requires them to pool resources and to quickly switch from one occupation to another. On the other hand, they are able to combine different skills and knowledges and make them work to achieve their own aims. What is more, as shown throughout this book, dancers are highly mobile, moving through the city from one public space to another, or to a dance studio, communal house or convention hall, in order to participate in dance practice or dance battles. Overall, the character of a particular place can only be created and understood by linking it with places beyond (Massey 1994). This is how dancers create geographies of dance within the city through their embodied dance practices. Many dancers started out dancing in a particular public place, such as the Soviet Vietnamese Friendship Palace, and from there they moved to Ly Thai To Square or the Lenin Monument, before finally ending up in a private dance studio. Participating in dance battles, they move beyond the confines of their own city, travelling to provincial towns in both northern and southern Vietnam, including the southern hub of Ho Chi Minh City. In the meantime, new dance spaces have evolved in central Vietnam, particularly in the cities of Da Nang and Hue. Hip hop's intimate relationship with place becomes apparent as dancers identify with "their" city.

Hip hop's relationship with the urban has been commented on extensively. In Vietnam, too, there is a bias toward urban areas that seems to persist. Yet, in actual fact, hip hop is practiced anywhere, including in rural and mountainous areas. Whereas Hanoi and Ho Chi Minh City remain the primary sites of hip hop activities, other more localized hot spots have emerged in the country's rural provinces and medium-sized towns, as well. The TiTan Crew in Ninh Binh City, and the 81 Days Crew of Quang Tri Province, are cases in point. In central Vietnam, moreover, Da Nang and Hue have evolved as focal points where the community of hip hop dance assembles. A large crowd of Hanoian dancers travelled to the Hue Street Festival in 2019, where they battled with local hip hop dancers. Social media posts by members of the hip hop dance community also show that battles also take place in the country's peripheral areas, such as in the southern Binh Duong Province. The house of youth in Binh Duong Province was the site of Binh Duong Street Kids Vol. 1 battle, held on December 29, 2019, which offered open-style dance competition for youth from the surrounding area.

Popping has also expanded to the periphery, more precisely, moving to the highlands. In a video on the history of hip hop dance dating from 2014, three Hanoian poppers, TF Star and CK Animation, the MC Trung X from the Red Bull Freestyle Battle, and three other male dancers, all fashioned themselves in the garb of different ethnic groups that traditionally inhabited Vietnam's highlands. Dancing outdoors in front of a mountain range, they combine popping with folklore dance, aiming to make the culture of hip hop more widely known in Vietnam. TF Star says "we want to bring the culture of hip hop closer to everyone, regardless of age, even if people don't like dancing, we'll make them like it" (YouTube 2014). While the community of dance expands geographically across the country, connections with the diverse other communities of practice, including DJing, rap, and graffiti, still remain rare. Where connections do exist, they are mostly with rappers. Although some dancers declare that they like listening to Viet Rap, this is rarely the music to which they dance. Most of the dance styles introduced to Vietnam fit with particular genres of music that have been developed internationally. Locking goes with funk music, waacking with disco music, and popping with electronic music. Hip hop dancers, as well as b-boys and b-girls, will occasionally dance to rap, mostly U.S. rap and sometimes Viet Rap. Nonetheless, they usually do not know rappers personally and rarely meet with them. Moreover, interactions with practitioners of hip hop's other elements of graffiti writing and DJing are rather rare. One exception, however, is the b-boy, Viet Max. Originating from Hanoi, he and his wife moved to Ho Chi Minh City, where he promoted hip hop dance. He connects the different elements of hip hop, as he simultaneously engages in breaking and graffiti writing, having produced the original music video for Northside rapper LK's track, *Thu Dẩm* (2018).

One of the events that created a platform for hip hop culture, integrating these different cultural practices, was the Hanoi Unity event in 2015, organized by Thanh Phuong and her fellow crew members. Hanoi Unity featured all four elements of rap, graffiti writing, DJing, and dancing. A more recent event mentioned by many dancers was the annual Why Not Crew event, *Aixo*, which is an exclamation that translates as, "Oh, my god!" Aixo took place in late September 2018 at the Sidewalk Bar in Hanoi's West Lake District, bringing together rappers, dancers, and live music. The dancers performed to the live rap music. The Why Not Crew is a rather new crew in the Vietnamese hip hop community of practice. A dancer named Hao explains: "The leader of Why Not Crew, he is really cool. He always wants to do really meaningful things for the community." A lot of icons from the Hanoian dance community of practice joined the event. Yen Hanh participated in the freestyle battle together with her "younger brother," a fellow b-boy. Likewise, Mai Tinh Vi as well as Thanh Phuong from New York Style Crew joined the battle. Mai used the video of her performance on her Facebook page for several months. As more and more events emerge in Vietnam, they bring together members of multiple communities of practice, who join forces to promote hip hop culture in the larger cities.

Dancers not only move around the city, and travel within Vietnam, but they also cross national boundaries. However, their travel often remains confined to the Southeast Asia region, due to visa and financial restrictions. Aware of their marginal position in the hip hop cultural industry, they relate to dancers in distant locations through social networking platforms. Moreover, they invite international dancers to Vietnam to give workshops and share their knowledge of hip hop, putting Vietnam on the global map of hip hop. According to sociologist David Farrugia (2018), youth cultures produce fluid topological connections that articulate connections well beyond established territorial boundaries. Through the circulation of information artefacts like mix tapes, music videos, images, and commodities as well as the mobility of people, hip hop has evolved as a transnational practice, creating distributed communities of practice sharing sonic and bodily sensations, aesthetics, language, values, and more. In her research on ballet, Helena Wulff (2015) shows how language facilitates the travelling of ideas and bodily practices. She notes that, despite or perhaps because of its transnational nature, all dancers are aware of nearly 200 ballet steps and their French designations, such that different versions of classical ballet are similar enough to be quickly learned. The use of terminology in a language other than one's own points to the historic-ity of dance, as it shifts in geography and time (Hamera 2007: 69). A similar observation can be made about the different dance styles assembled in this book. Most of the dancers are aware of, and referred to, English movement vocabulary for their particular dance styles. For locking, dancers are aware of the English names of basic moves. Similarly, for hip hop dance, Hoang Phuong quotes the Old/Middle and New School Dictionary, created by members of Elite Force Crew, Henry Link, and Buddha Stretch, as a common point of reference, and thus standardized vocabulary, that she teaches in her hip hop foundations class. Such standardization of linguistic and bodily terms facilitates communication and cooperation between actors from diverse social worlds (Star and Griesemer 1989). At international events like Juste Debout or the Arena Dance Competition, Vietnamese dancers assemble with dancers from Southeast Asia and elsewhere around the world. While they mostly do not share linguistic repertoires beyond English terms for dance moves, they do share a common repertoire of bodily movements. On the basis of such kinesthetic repertoires, they are able to build relationships and friendships across geographies, creating distributed communities of hip hop dance.

Likewise, Hamera (2007: 6, 19) considers dance techniques as codes that govern and standardize dance practice, rendering performing bodies both legible and intelligible, while offering frames for the analysis of those bodies. Dance technique thus evolves as common vocabularies and grammars, assisting in the deciphering dancing bodies and learning to dance. Techniques evolve as a primary language among fellow dancers, translating individual bodies into a common repertoire. In hip hop dance, the common grammar and vocabulary of technique is referred to as basics or foundation. As many dancers put it, the key to success is learning the foundation, on the basis of which it is possible to develop a personal style and thus uniqueness. Yen Hanh put it this way: "All the good dancers, they always say that you need to keep with the basics, you need to have a foundation before you can improve your own style." That is why advanced dancers tell their students to continue exercising the basics, so that they can develop their own style. Once they have incorporated the basics, they are also able to integrate one dance style with another, such as locking with popping or locking with soul dance, thereby generating bodily creativity. Hoang Phuong likewise points to the importance of the foundation, and yet suggested that while some dancers really know these techniques, they still lack their own style. She tends to prefer the dancer who only knows the basics, but has developed her own style and feeling for the music, to a dancer who just masters advanced techniques.

The constant improvement of technique and skill, as well as self-investment, are important to all of the dancers presented in this book. The dance styles presented above are all rather competitive, with their focus being the dance battle. At battles, dancers come together to present themselves to the community, competing with other dancers, while being evaluated by national and international judges. Many of the protagonists in this book, such as Nguyet, Mai, Rufu, C2Low, CK Animation, or Thanh, serve as judges and MCs at the national and international level. So, how do professionals of diverse dance styles assess and evaluate the quality of a dancer's performance? One factor that they all agreed upon was technique and foundation. However, technique was often not the first response they gave. Rather, they referred to somatic qualities that make for a good dancer, while pointing to the intersubjective ties produced through shared sensations, frequently mentioning feelings, emotions, and sounds. Nguyet, for example, quotes the American waacker, Princess Lockeroo, suggesting that waackers are those who guide listeners into the feelings of a song. Consequently, she suggests that the main task of the waacker is to kinesthetically express the feeling of a song:

> "If the song is fun and happy, then we express the same feelings as the song. So for me, when I judge a good waacker, I look to the feelings of the waacker, not just their technique, not just the basics, just some technique or another. The technique is fine, but I want to see the feeling. Because that is the reason why we love waacking."

Similarly, Thanh Phuong emphasizes the relevance of feelings, comparing technique to reading a book. If one repeats the same moves over and over again, she explains, then it is "boring," like reading the same book twice. Consequently, when assessing a good dancer, she explains: "I want to look to their energy, their power, and their feeling (...), I like a dancer with a good feeling more than good technique." Like Thanh Phuong, other dancers agreed that technique is something that anyone can acquire through continuous training and exercise, but that sensations and emotions are important to giving dance a soul. In fact, dance sensations appear to be more highly valued than technique in the evaluation of a dance performance. Likewise, for popping, CK Animation names three capabilities a good dancer needs to have: First, a presentation of one's talent, representing good flow and style; second, good and high-quality technique; and, third, bodily sensation that goes with the music. CK's last point is shared by Hoang Phuong with respect to hip hop dance.

She explains that she needs to see the dancers' "feeling with that music, and with their body." She would like to see that the music really lifts the dancer. Feeling the music, and transmitting the emotion to the audience, was a recurrent theme in conversations that I had with dancers about what makes for a good dancer. Theatre scholar Katharina Rost (2017) discusses this sensory dimension of dance as "body listening" (Körper-Hören), suggesting that dancers' movements on stage are kinesthetic traces of audibly perceived energy currents. Rost's analysis does not rest on the individual body and sensation of the dancer, but expands to the audience's bodies, as they resonate with the dancers' embodiment of what they hear. The dancers are not the only ones to hear the music, as surrounding dancers, judges, and audience members listen as well. Meanwhile, the dancers guide everyone into the song's feelings, as Nguyet puts it.

The locker Yen Hanh linked the capability to feel the music to the performer's confidence, explaining: "When you feel confident, you can follow the music very well." If a dancer is shy, by contrast, it is very difficult for them to follow and feel the music. Overall, Yen Hanh evaluates three factors when watching someone else dance: pace, technique, and "the way they listen to the music." The relevance of listening to learning how to become a good dancer is shared by many dancers. Yen Hanh compares those who do not know how to listen to the music to music without soul. Apart from the value of a performance, others cited listening when it comes to learning dance. In addition to the kinesthetic differences between training indoors with a mirror or outside in public space, Nguyet pinpoints listening as a further dimension of learning: "Now I teach my students, they have to get into the song. Just listen, only listen, and then do, do, do, do, but listen – get into the body and spread it out." Her emphasis on both space and listening recalls Thomas Clifton's (1983: 70) claim that music, very much like space, is experienced "as fields of action for a subject," rather than music being a mere object outside the self.

In his account of the Afro-Brazilian martial art capoeira, ethnomusicologist Greg Downey (2002) emphasizes how the social and individual processes of musical encounter determine the significance of music (Porcello 1998), and outlines an apprenticeship of hearing. According to Downey (2002: 500), the bodily apprenticeship in listening conditions capoeiristas' perception of sound, "leading them to 'discover' the art's kinesthetic, not as an object external to the body, but as a sensitivity immanent in their lived flesh." Consequently, as much as a phenomenological study of music needs to recognize the dimension of corporeality (Downey 2002), a full phenomenological study of body and dance must attend to the dimension of listening. Listening is a social experience as the moving body is informed by mimetic processes of learning from others. As mentioned earlier, all of the dance style practitioners began by training in public space. The bodily knowledge of different dance styles was transmitted through dancing bodies that were visible, audible, and tangible in public space. The early dancers facilitated social learning by making their movements visible and accountable to others, highlighting how learning occurs through bodily interactions with others. The spatial formation in which the attunement of somatic modes of attention occurs is most often the cypher. Consequently, inspired by Downey's (2002: 493) account of the "affective soundscape of the roda [wheel, circle]" in capoeira, I suggest that the cypher formation employed in hip hop battles be understood as an affective, sonic, kinesthetic, and thus a sense-scape.

In conclusion, moving the focus away from technique, as urged by most research participants, opens to the recognition and awareness of the self as constituted through somatic modes of attention. Yen Hanh defines dancing as listening to the music and moving with your body. The energy currents that Rost alludes to are verbally expressed when the dancers refer to "power" or "energy." Stated differently, dance sensations are energetic and intimately linked to emotions. Yet, extending beyond the individual self, dance sensations are also experienced intersubjectively, as Csordas (1999) emphasizes the relationship between the experience of bodily moment and intersubjective meaning-making. In collective practice and performance, dancers realize "strategies of solidarity in difference" (Hamera 2007: 13). Through collective performance in public spaces, they create intimate spaces in which pleasures, mischief, and success are shared.

Cultivating the Hip Hop Self

"Spontaneous movement is the constitutive source of agency, of subject-hood, of selfhood." (Sheets-Johnstone 1999: 138)

The importance of sensation, not only for embodiment but also for conceptions of the self, has been outlined by David Marr in his article, "Concepts of 'Individual' and 'Self' in Twentieth-Century Vietnam." Marr (2000) ascribes an at least 600-year history to conceptions of self in Vietnamese literature. He determines that the use of *thân* and *tâm* derive from the Classical Chinese used in essays and poems. *Thân* can be translated as "body-person," signifying the animate, sensual self, often used in opposition to *thể*, which could be translated as the physical, objective, instrumental body. *Thân* can also be contrasted with *nhân* or *người*, humans in general or other persons. *Thân* retains a bodily connection distinct from the person's spirit or soul. By contrast, *tâm*, translated as "heart-mind," connotes the sentient, perceptive, reflective, and sympathetic dimensions of human nature. *Tâm* is used in poetry to assert the inner self. Body-mind and heart-mind must be considered conjointly, since each holds implications for the other. For instance, diet and physical exercise enhance the mental state, whereas the heart-mind contributes to bodily well-being (Marr 2000: 769-770). The symbiosis of body-mind and heart-mind is apparent in hip hop practitioners' assessments of dance as having an overall positive impact on their lives, as expressed by Yen Hanh: "Dancing gave me a lot of things. Dancing made my life more colourful and meaningful." Here Yen Hanh implies reference to the body-mind. Through dance, the young people introduced in this book are able to realize parts of themselves that cannot be easily expressed in words, let alone be merely achieved through the private accumulation of wealth. They take good care of both their mental and physical health. Aware of the importance of their corporeality, and need for good health, they regularly exercise while taking care of their diet.

Tu thân, or self-cultivation, builds etymologically on the notion of body-person, thus maintaining a connection with corporeality. Self-cultivation comprises a diverse range of techniques in order to achieve personal enlightenment. While the idea and discourse of self-cultivation has a long history in Confucianism, it used to have a clear gender and class bias, as self-cultivation was a "life-long project of elitary men" (Li Zhang 2018: 47). Through literary debates that occurred in the first half of the 20th century, the idea of self-cultivation resurged among writers and literary scholars. However, during the period of collectivization, concern for the self was replaced by concerns for the collective, at least formally. Eventually, the passing of the Doi Moi economic reform program in 1986 can be regarded as the official recognition of practices already occurring on the ground. Benedict Kerkvliet (1995) intriguingly shows how households were much more eager to put their labour power to work in the cultivation of the small lots of land privately allotted to each household, rather than contributing to the cooperative. In post-Mao China, concerns for and with the self particularly re-emerged in the realm of literature and literary criticism, and were further revived in popular psychological education and the revival of Confucianism (Li Zhang 2018). For contemporary Vietnam, Nguyen (2019) outlines the desires produced and shared for collective well-being and social harmony on the one hand, and "fictional expectations" (Beckert 2016) based on consumption and the private accumulation of wealth on the other. For the hip hop self, these desires that at first blush may be considered binary opposites are integrated with one another. Doing what they love most is a main motivation to continue dancing. As I have shown in the chapter "SELF-ENTREPRENEURISM AND SELF-FASHIONING," many are able or at least try to make a living from dancing, while at the same time receiving recognition from their peers. Dance success is also remunerated financially, when dancers win money prizes for coming in first, second, or third place in a battle. The "bringing home of achievements," as Nguyet calls it, referring to the materialisations of success in terms of awards, trophies, and certificates, may also result in the recognition of their aspirations and lifestyles by their parents, who might otherwise prefer that their children were focused on their studies and making money. In fact, their personal and collective success, both as individual dancers or as a collective crew, must be read against the framework of striving in the new economy. According to Nguyen (2019), the dominant ethic of striving encourages and even generates social pressure to continuously pursue and access wealth and power. It means that if an individual fails to accumulate wealth and power, it is because they were not enterprising enough, not daring enough, and not responsible enough. Yet, at the same time, it is important to achieve social recognition, such as by putting such personal profit to work for the poor and marginalized (Nguyen 2019: 152, 172). As Li Zhang (2012: 663) suggests, "while there is a general shift toward a private self and an increased concern with self-care engendered by a new mass consumer culture and an increasingly commodified society, social embeddedness and socialist moralities remain salient in the remaking of the self and living in postreform Vietnam."

Consequently, the hip hop self sits at the intersection of longing for a good and self-determined life, and societal, economic, and state demands on citizens to perform well in the socialist market economy. Youth has to deal with intersecting and sometimes ambivalent demands formulated by market socialism. Consequently, dancing youth navigate the late socialist city by developing mobile, flexible, and precarious lifestyles, having aspirations of their own, while adhering to their social responsibilities.

Meaning of hip hop: self and community

"And when they hear about hip hop, they will think that this kind of dance is not good. Because it's from the street. Some of the dancers is like homeless, don't have any job — like bad people, they always think like that." (popper Rufu)

In the public eye, hip hop dancing is considered "useless," as it does not provide a "good job" or steady income. Rufu recalls how her parents used to tell her that although she was young and fit to dance, they were anxious about her future, asking her what she would do five years in the future. This question became stuck in her mind, as she realized that dancing was not a mere hobby for her. For Rufu hip hop is a lifestyle, which implies making choices about the future. As a result, it has become her aspiration to change people's beliefs about hip hop, transforming the negative image into a positive one. Graduating from university and still dancing, she was able to prove that she remained a "good" person, and was able to earn money from dancing. Rufu's assessment of what it means to be a "good" person expresses her agency. According to Ortner, agency presupposes awareness and self-reflexivity concerning the circumstances in which the subject acts. While Rufu was seeking personal happiness embodied in dancing, she acted within moral constraints imposed by social expectations about her economic success and her moral conduct as a daughter. In fact, she acted against the circumstances she found herself in, as she made enough money from dancing to become financially independent from her family. Like Rufu, many dancers felt the need to somehow "prove" themselves. They aimed to prove that, despite dancing – or perhaps even *because* of dancing – they were able to act as socially responsible citizens, taking on respective roles in family and society.

In my conversations with dancers, both male and female, the good person was a recurrent trope. Good was defined as industrious and money-making, recalling the ethic of striving outlined by Nguyen, and the promotion of moral personhood by the late socialist state. The continuous striving for wealth and power must eventually take place in the moral framework of *thành người* and *làm người*. *Thành người* means becoming a morally and socially responsible person. In order for an individual to become *thành người*, one needs to be cared for, fed, educated, and socialized to assume one's obligations and responsibilities for oneself, for intimate others, and for society at large. The status of *thành người* is achieved when a person is able to reciprocate the care she has received from others. *Làm người*, in turn, refers to the work of leading a moral life. The art of leading a moral life requires "constant work of cultivating moral behaviours, dealing with the moral challenges of life while maintaining a coherent moral orientation as a member of a family, community, and nation, above all, through socially accepted ways of caring" (Nguyen 2019: 106). For instance, Yen Hanh left her home town in Ha Tinh Province, 200 kilometres away from Vinh City, to study in Hanoi. After graduating from university, she continues to live, work, and dance in Hanoi, which she appreciates for its way of life. However, she aspires to return to her home town once she has acquired enough money. With money made in Hanoi, she would like to sponsor the tourism industry in her home province. Her future imagination is intimately linked to skills and knowledge acquired in Hanoi, as she studies tourism and now works in marketing. Acting within the moral framework of *thành/làm người*, she wants to give back to her local community by drawing on the merits she has earned by leaving home and expanding her horizon in Hanoi. Like Yen Hanh, while disagreeing with their parents about the value of dance, many dancers sought to fulfil their responsibilities and obligations as members of a family, community, and the nation.

Consequently, the uptake of hip hop is not only motivated by the desire to develop and explore the self, but is also shaped by the longing for social interaction and communication, resulting in new forms of sociality beyond the family and work place. Sociality denotes the relationship between humans, non-human objects, and the material world, including the meanings that such relations confer (Ortner 2006). Many respondents claimed that, for them, hip hop meant helping each other, talking with one another, being connected, and hanging out with people you like. CK Animation, an icon of the Northern Vietnamese popping scene, says that in order to become a member of his crew, newcomers must practice persistently and be good at training. But equal or more important is that all members must enjoy playing with each other (*chơi với nhau*), which means spending time and having fun together beyond crew practice. As dancers spend a great deal of time together, it is important that they are on good terms with and support each other. In a similar vein, Tien, a young dancer from Ninh Binh, says the following about his high school dance club: "It's very fun, we're very close just like a family, because we have to play and support and practice with each other a lot." Tien's teacher Hien, likewise, considers her fellow dancers family. In the embodied practice of dance, she is able to connect with other dancers, and feels fondness for them. Dey Dey, a female world popping champion, shares Hien's assessment of what it means to dance together, pointing to the energy and confidence her female crew members provided each other when dancing. Nguyet also emphasized moments of intersubjectivity in dancing, explaining that other friends who have normal day jobs, and who are not dancers, "cannot ... experience the feelings of people who join and dance together. " Sensory intersubjectivity refers to the continuous resituating and remaking of oneself in relations to others through face-to-face encounters, and thus through the senses (Pink 2009). Dance techniques render the body legible in a shared idiom, while allowing interpersonal and sometimes intimate conversations about these moving bodies. Additionally, such techniques also offer possibilities for imagining new ways of being oneself, as well as being together (Hamera 2007). As Yen Hanh says, dancers "have beautiful souls. They know how to enjoy life, they know how to follow their passion. (...) I feel that everything in my life is beautiful, everyone and everything, and everyone around me."

Accordingly, dancing becomes a shared experience resulting in the creation of new collectives. The belonging to and identification with a particular crew, team, or club is highly relevant for hip hop practitioners. Success is not only measured in individual performance, but also in terms of giving something back to the community. In fact, the idea of sharing parts of the power and wealth one has achieved as an individual back to the community,

B Nashor/Big Toe Crew

Source: B Nashor (2020)

immanent in the moral framework of becoming a socially responsible person (*thành người*), is also evident in the Vietnamese hip hop community of practice. Thanh Phuong invests her management skills in the organization of dance events, whereas Mai promotes young upcoming dancers at dance battles. However, Phuong Silver Monkey feels a generational rupture between the old timers and the younger generation of dancers with respect to the idea of giving something back to the community:

> "The young generation has great potential and skills, but they have yet to think about contributing to the community. They just want to be champions, and to express themselves. Maybe we need to give them some time to grow up until they think about how they can develop and contribute to the community." (Hanyi 2014)

Rufu, who has seen the Ho Chi Minh City dance community develop, longs to be able to participate in more battles overseas. However, she also wants to invite renowned international dancers to Vietnam to organize workshops and to share their knowledge about their dance styles with Vietnamese dancers. Many younger dancers, in turn, appreciated the support they received from the advanced dancers, and pointed to their social involvement and support for the dancing community. Contributing to the community, among other things, means creating public awareness of hip hop, and raising awareness about the positive impacts of dance for society at large. Particularly for hip hop elders, like Thanh and Phuong Silver Monkey, the coproduction of a positive public image for hip hop is of the utmost importance. Therefore, they promote hip hop as a physical, inclusive, and creative experience. For them, hip hop is neither a youth culture, nor an exclusively urban culture, but it is open to anyone of any age, gender, social background, and place of residence. Recently, a group of young people living in a remote village in the northwestern province of Dien Bien Phu contacted Thanh via social networking, asking him to come to their village to teach them breaking. To Phuong Silver Monkey, hip hop is also about bringing generations together. He once organized a flash mob in Hanoi, for which a number of older people were willing to join, too. That is why they readjusted their practice time to 5 to 6 a.m., when older urbanites usually indulge in their physical exercise in the city's public space. Thanh had similar experiences. Growing up in Hoan Kiem District, he was asked by the elderly women, who routinely conduct their morning exercise on the banks of Hoan Kiem Lake, to teach them some hip hop moves. The next day, he posted photos of himself training with the women by the lake at dawn.

While they are open to newcomers, and seek to create a broader societal basis for hip hop, the elders of hip hop have and still seek to maintain authority over the meaning of hip hop. For instance, they promote drug-free events, and social responsibility among peers. Aware of wider international associations of hip hop with social ills, such as drugs, some dance event organizers have made the renouncement of drugs and cigarettes compulsory to dancers' participation. For instance, the announcement of the Waack your Soul 2020 event on Facebook included a note concerning the prohibition of the use of cigarettes and stimuli (*chất kích thích*) at the dance site. In cases of violation, transgressing participants would have to pay a fine of 1,000,000 VND (36 Euro), equal to the prize money for the freestyle battle winner, and amounting to half the prize money for the waacking battle champion.

The need to assume social responsibility was also emphasized by Thanh, for whom it is important to provide an income to his fellow crew members and students. In his dance academy, he is able to provide some with jobs, allowing them to finish school and dance, while earning money. Similarly, Thanh Phuong seeks to support the hip hop community through her expertise in marketing and finance, allocating financial resources necessary to host events and create platforms for dancers to interact. Fashioning themselves as hard working subjects engaged in life-long learning, they all seek to overcome prevailing images of dancers as "bad" people who hang out late at night while doing useless things. Young people, in particular, struggle with their parents about their decision to lead a dancing life. In late socialist Vietnam, intergenerational struggles are on the rise as the lifestyles and experiences between children and their parents drift apart.

Generations

At the turn of the millennium, Jean and John Comaroff (1999: 284) suggested that, in South Africa, "the dominant line of cleavage here has become generation." By this claim, among other things, the Comaroffs refer to "rapid shifts in experience that create age-conscious cohorts" (Durham 2000: 113). Jennifer Cole (2010: 6) argues that many contemporary, and principally European, analyses of the role of generations in history are characterized by a language of crisis, as indicated by terms such as "post-soviet generation" or "generation X." In Vietnam, my own generation is referred to as 8X, whereas most of the dancers who participated in my research are members of generation 9X. While such generational references were not mentioned by the dancers, I did encounter such self-descriptions – as belonging to generation 8X or 9X – in my earlier research on public space. The generations 8X and 9X refer to those born in the 1980s and the 1990s, respectively. In 2008, the b-boys and b-girls whom I met at Ly Thai To Garden used these time indices as markers of shared experiences, and as terms for belonging. In her research on Madagascar, Cole considers youth modes of agency and activities across multiple temporalities (Cole 2010: 8-9). Here, I consider agency "as the relatively flexible wielding of means toward ends" (Kockelman 2007: 375), or, in Laura Ahearn's terms, "the socioculturally mediated capacity to act" (Ahearn 2001: 112). Youth agency is of particular interest, as it develops under social and cultural constraints, especially during this specific period of the life cycle. According to Sherry Ortner (2006: 127), agency presupposes a complex subjectivity, meaning that subjects partially internalize and partially reflect on in specific circumstances, and thus constraints they find themselves in. Consequently, young people's agency needs to be considered in the larger context of multiple generations. This is particularly the case in Vietnam, where the imperative of filial piety (hiếu) continues to determine intergenerational relationships, and in particular the relationship between parents and children. And, the Vietnam War, as well as the reform process of Doi Moi, created a substantial experiential rift between generations, resulting in (grand) parents' and government officials' belief that young people are no longer acquainted with the hardships of the war and the later famines of the 1980s. As a result, young people are often blamed for engaging in conspicuous consumption and embracing modern urban lifestyles. Such appraisals of youth are not unique to Vietnam, but can be found elsewhere in Southeast Asia and beyond. For instance, sociologist Chua Beng Huat (2002) identifies a conflict between the generation that grew up in Singapore prior to the period of economic growth, and the younger generation from the turn of the millennium, which grew up with relative prosperity and extravagance, marking them off from the thrift of older generations. Schwenkel (2011) suggests that young people engage with values of the revolution, such as development and social betterment, by making use of the tools of capitalism. In fact, recent studies of socioeconomic change, particularly those that undertake gender analysis, show that young people still adhere to familial responsibilities as daughters and sons, while embracing lifestyles that diverge from those of their parents, such as seeking employment in urban areas or even with international corporations abroad. In *Vietnam's New Middle Class: Gender, Career, City*, Catherine Earl (2014) examines the experiences of female family members among the first-generation of Vietnam's middle class. Young women leave their natal homes in the countryside to attend university and pursue professional careers in the city. As a result, the urban lifestyles of well-educated female migrants differ from those of family members who remain in the countryside. Earl identifies consumption patterns, and especially the possession or renovation of houses or motorbikes, as symbols of their newly achieved social status. However, she also remarks that first-generation middle-class women appear to carefully manage their newly won wealth. Most of the women interviewed use their income to provide for their families in rural areas. For instance, some financed the renovation of their parents' house or bought technical equipment to modernise their parents' homes. In a similar vein, yet with a different focus group, Nguyen (2019) identifies the differing spatial orientations of consumption among male and female waste traders. While most waste traders leave their home towns to engage in waste trading in the city, men felt more entitled to engage in ephemeral pleasures of the urban, whereas female waste traders tended to focus on inner-directed consumption patterns, meaning that they abstained from urban consumption in order to focus on the family's needs.

The female dancers presented in this book simultaneously embrace urban consumption, while taking on social responsibilities. Many of the young women had stable employment, while engaging in dancing during leisure time or else making extra income by teaching dance classes. They invested the money they earned to travel abroad, such as to participate in international dance battles, as well as to participate in the conspicuous consumption of branded products, such as iPhones, cameras, and hip hop apparel, including sneakers, hats, hoodies, and so on. They also fulfilled their responsibilities as daughters and wives, by looking after their parents and providing for their families by maintaining stable employment. Thanh Phuong, for instance, invited her parents to leave her home town, Ha Long, to live with her in Hanoi. Nguyet embraces responsibilities as wife and future mother to provide for her family financially, which is why she does online work while teaching dance classes in studios. However, this care-taking and adherence to their social roles does not necessarily imply that their aspirations conform with social expectations, particularly those of their parents. In fact, dance has evolved as a contested field, which is constantly negotiated among children and parents.

Dancers struggling with their parents to continue or even to begin dancing is a recurrent theme in the hip hop community of practice. Several dancers I talked to encountered problems with their parents, who wanted them to focus on their studies and careers rather than on their passion for dance. One young male dancer recalls how his school dance club had difficulties recruiting new members since most parents of his fellow students were afraid that dancing could have a negative impact on their education, ultimately preventing them from thriving in the socialist market economy. Similarly, a female dancer reported that her parents feared that she would not get enough rest for school the next day, as she would go directly from school to dance practice. In Vietnam, it is common for students to pursue extra-curriculum lessons after school. Sometimes the same teachers who taught in the mornings gave private lessons in the afternoons and evenings, for which the parents need to pay extra. This system has become so institutionalized that, without private tutors, many students are reportedly unable to pass their exams. This is why activities such as after school dancing are considered to interfere with academic learning.

Apart from concerns about the potentially negative impact of dance on young people's future, in particular their ability to secure employment, there is also scepticism about dancing in general. Rufu explains that people in Vietnam know little about hip hop, and rather associated it with something bad, such as young people returning home late at night, living on the streets, and being unemployed. Along similar lines, one female dancer in her mid-twenties reported that her father thought dancers are not "good people," and that dancing poses a threat to his daughter's well-being. This belief may be related to a prevalent anxiety that a child might be "broken" (*bị hỏng*) (Nguyen 2019: 19), and could also be informed by representations of youth decadence in the media. Since the early 2000, media reports on youth drug abuse, laziness, lack of financial discipline, and generally their "aimlessness," have mushroomed (Drummond and Nguyen Thi Lien 2008: 179). To this young dancer's father, dancing seems to be an expression of such aimlessness, as an activity that does not pay off, whereas her mother, in contrast, supports her dance activities. Knowing that her father only wants the best for her, she hopes to prove to him that dancing is really important to her and a part of her life. While many dancers reported on the lack of their parental approval, one dancer was physically prevented from dancing. Another female dancer explained that her parents locked her in her room so she would not be able to attend class. On other occasions, they refused to drive her to class and denied her the money needed to participate in a battle.

Apart from general (parental) scepticisms about the dance, young dancers identified further social pressures and gendered expectations as complicating their involvement in dance. C2Low explains that, within a time period of eight years, he is already teaching the second generation of students, since his first-generation students, most of them young women, quickly quit dancing owed to social pressure to marry and start a family. Thuy, a 30-years old female dancer from Hanoi, has yet to marry and still keeps on dancing. She is aware of normative gender ideals when she explains that women her age in Vietnam are usually married, but that she was not. Consequently, Thuy's parents did not initially appreciate her lifestyle. Like many others, her parents did not want her to continue dancing, but rather to get married and have children. Interestingly, they saw a correlation between her dancing life and single status. Thuy recalls how they would yell at her when she returned home from dance practice late at night, dressed in hip hop apparel, telling her to quit dancing and to find a husband. But she kept on dancing without her parent's approval. Then one day, she explains, she invited her parents to go out dancing near their home, where there was a club that offered Latin dance lessons. At first, her parents refused to go, but she insisted on paying for the class. She asked them to give it one try, and if they really did not like it, then she would never ask again. Eventually, they took one lesson and they have been dancing ever since. Sometimes she and her father even go out to dance together in public space. Thuy concludes that she convinced her parents by showing them how dancing makes her, and now them, happy: "Because they understand how happy I am when I am dancing – and how happy they are. And it is super joyful, you know, enjoying music and being yourself."

Thuy's narrative about the resolution of the conflict with her parents hints at a wider change of values within late socialist families, as well. Parents not only long for their children to be successful within the normative framework of striving – which many of the dancers actually are – but parents also cherish their children's pursuit of happiness. Inviting her parents to dance, Thuy showed her parents that they could trust their daughter, and they, in turn, demonstrated the ability to let go of gender stereotypes. Some parents may now even consider dancing as a potential career path. Thanh told me about a 10-years old girl who studies with him, whose mother believes that dance will be a career for her daughter. Having the resources to support her financially, she wants her daughter to participate in international freestyle and waacking competitions, while trusting Thanh to help advance her career in the right direction.

Youth's aspirations

According to Arjun Appadurai (2008: 67), aspirations are never merely individual, but are rather formed in the thick of social life, as he writes: "aspirations form parts of wider ethical and metaphysical ideas which derive from larger cultural norms." The women participating in my research were self-reflective about their positioning as women, both within the community of practice and in society at large. When asked about the four Confucian Virtues, and their relevance for women today, one female hip hop dancer relates the virtues to her personal life, when differentiating between hip hop as an art form and hobby, and job qualities that are measured against the four Confucian Virtues. To her, the four virtues of labour (công), appearance (dung), speech (ngôn), and conduct (hạnh) are ultimately linked to qualities valued in the job market, and do not relate to dancing as an art form or hobby. Therefore, she is able to distance herself from these female ideals, while recognizing that older generations might think that young women have changed a lot. Respecting their point of view, she understands that, to them, the four Confucian virtues may be important, but not in her view in relation to hip hop as an art form. Again, Rufu makes it explicit that dance is more than just a hobby to her, but has become part of her life. That is why she sees herself still dancing in the future. Conscious about her lifestyle, she also seeks to improve and maintain her well-being by developing healthy habits. Particularly with her full-time office job, where she sits for several hours a day, she is eager to work out afterwards while paying attention to her diet.

Overall, many of the dancers I talked with regarded hip hop not just as a hobby, but as a way of life. This way of life requires a particular commitment from dancers. Most of the female dancers who had become icons within their particular style were in the mid- to late-twenties. Except for Nguyet, who had just married the same year I met her, the others had yet to marry and none of them had children. In fact, a large number of them was still single and they did not feel the need to marry or have children, pointing out that they were still young and not in a hurry to start families. Any potential partners had to be open to and supportive of their dancing lives. As shown earlier, leading a dancing life means meeting after work, often late into the evening, hanging out with both female and male peers. Moreover, participation in international dance battles means travelling a lot. Female dancers were looking for equal relationships in which a partner could understand more than their needs, but also their passion, and provide them with emotional and mental support. In contrast to Valentin's (2008) findings on the focus of Vietnamese youth on their responsibilities, such as preparing themselves for professional careers, marriage, or to support their parents financially, the female dancers I spoke to emphasized their freedom and the possibility of making an independent living. Yet, to these women, leading a dancing life does not mean an exclusive focus on dance and generating an income from dancing, but it often entailed aspirations to build a parallel career, while and because of dancing. Thanh Phuong makes it quite clear that, without hip hop dancing, she would not be so successful in her marketing job. Likewise, Yen Hanh says that she wants to focus on her work, but still continues to dance and enjoy the life she leads. What all of the women I talked to shared in common was their financial independence, both from their parent's households and from their boyfriends' or spouses' incomes. They all succeeded in generating income on their own, allowing them also to invest money in dancing, for example, by financing trips to international dance competitions. That said, most of the women were well aware of the social pressure, particularly their parents' expectations, to marry and establish their own household. Nonetheless, they aimed to pursue their vision of the good life, which, to them, meant being independent and continuing to dance.

Overall, the ideas of being oneself in hip hop, gaining self-esteem, and achieving personal completion, were recurrent themes in the conversations that I had with young women. Like Thanh Phuong, Yen Hanh considers dancing as a language that helps her to present who she is. While both dancers participate in different styles, both use language as a metaphor to describe the meanings that dance has for them. To both, dance is a means of representation and communication. Moreover, Hoang Phuong explains that hip hop, to her, is a vehicle for self-expression that works for her today, if not forever: "But I don't know, maybe in a few years, I'll try other things that can help me to express myself. I don't know. I don't think too much about it." While hip hop may be an ephemeral form of representation for Hoang Phuong, she nonetheless has the "capacity to aspire" for self-expression and representation (Appadurai 2008). The intimate relationship mentioned above between body-person and heart-mind is also evident in female dancers' choice of a dance style, as they chose styles based on the fit with their personalities. That is why, for instance, Yen Hanh chose funk, Rufu popping, and Hoang Phuong hip hop dance. Sometimes dancers tried out different styles before finally deciding on the style that was for them. Hien, for example, started out doing cover dance. When she saw breaking for the first time, she was so fascinated that she thought about starting b-girling. However, she soon found that she was not strong enough to practice breaking. Then one day, while at a battle, she saw another dancer doing something that she had not seen before, something that seemed close to sexy dance. She appreciated the beauty of the dance, and later found out the style's name – waacking. As there are only a few waackers in Vietnam, however, and it is hardly featured as a battle category, she chose freestyle. Finally, she found a style that she could really pursue, explaining: "I like to go with freestyle because freestyle – that is really me."

In dance, young people, and particularly young women, are able to realize themselves in ways that both benefit themselves in terms of self-cultivation, as well as benefit society at large. Navigating the ambiguous moral landscape of late socialism, they oscillate between being true to themselves, their aspirations, and desires, and contributing to the community. As Li Zhang (2012: 663) explains, the search for the private self and the good life are deeply intertwined with larger social relationships and moral concerns. Accordingly, female dancers negotiate their roles as aspiring and self-determined subjects, while being socially embedded in hierarchical social relations. However, as many take on responsibilities within their families – as daughters, in-laws, and wives – they simultaneously establish new relationships beyond the home and workplace, departing from both traditional and socialist ideas of community. In other words, the uptake of hip hop is not only motivated by the desire to develop and explore the self, but also by the longing for social interaction and communication. In dance, individuals strive to bring their skills to perfection and to develop a personal style, while simultaneously investing in and building social relations among fellow dancers, both in and outside of Vietnam. At the same time, the bodily practice of dance has a performative function, as it incites action. Dancing in public, performing among mostly male peers, female dancers rework existing notions of femininity, paving the way for gender fluid performances. Through their actions, they rework gendered hierarchies both within the community of practice, and in the Vietnamese (speech) community. In conclusion, hip hop expresses a notion of the good life, which allows female dancers to combine striving for individualized goals and desires, and the reworking of gendered identities, while maintaining the moral personhood necessary to achieve social recognition as well as performance within the socialist market economy.

References

Agarwal, Bina (2003): "Gender and Land Rights Revisited: Exploring New Prospects via the State, Family, and Market", in: Journal of Agrarian Change 3, pp. 184-224.

Ahearn, Laura M. (2001): "Language and Agency", in: Annual Reviews Anthropology 30, pp. 109-137.

Alim, H. Samy (2006): Roc the Mic Right: The Language of Hip Hop Culture, London: Taylor & Francis Ltd.

— (2009): "Straight Outta Compton, Straight aus München: Global Linguistic Flows, Identities, and the Politics of Language in a Global Hip Hop Nation", in: Alim/Ibrahim/Pennycook, Global linguistic flows. Hip hop cultures, youth identities, and the politics of language, pp. 1-24.

Alim, H. Samy/Ibrahim, Awad/Pennycook, Alastair (eds.) (2009): Global linguistic flows. Hip hop cultures, youth identities, and the politics of language, New York, NY: Routledge.

Androutsopoulos, Jannis (2003): HipHop: globale Kultur -lokale Praktiken, Bielefeld: transcript.

Anon (1962): Di tích cách mạng Hà Nội. Hà Nội: Sở Văn Hóa.

Appadurai, Arjun (1996): Modernity At Large: Cultural Dimensions of Globalization, Minneapolis, MN: University of Minnesota Press.

— (2004): "The Capacity to Aspire: Culture and the Terms of Recognition", in: Vijayendra Rao/Michael Walton (eds.), Culture and Public Action, Palo Alto, CA: Stanford University Press, pp. 59-84.

Arvidsson, Adam/Bauwens, Michel/Peitersen, Nicolar (2008): "The crisis of value and the ethical economy", in: Journal of Future Studies 12(4), pp. 9-20.

Atkinson, Jane M. (1989): The Art and Politics of Wana Shamanship, Berkeley, CA: University of California Press.

Attfield, Sarah (2011): "Punk Rock and the Value of Auto-ethnographic Writing about Music", in: PORTAL Journal of Multidisciplinary International Studies 8(1), pp. 1-11.

Avieli, Nir (2014): "Vegetarian Ethics and Politics in Late-Socialist Vietnam", in: Yuson Jung/Jakob Klein/Melissa L. Caldwell (eds.), Ethical eating in the postsocialist and socialist world, Berkeley: University of California Press, pp. 144-166.

Banes, Sally (2004): "Breaking", in: Neal/Forman, That's the joint! The hip hop studies reader, pp. 13–20.

Barbieri, Magali/Bélanger, Danièle (eds.) (2009): Reconfiguring Families in Contemporary Vietnam, Stanford, CA: Stanford University Press.

Bartlett, Andrew (2004): "Airshafts, Loudspeakers, and the Hip Hop Sample: Contexts and African American Musical Aesthetics", in: Neal/Forman, That's the joint! The hip-hop studies reader, pp. 393–406.

Bauwens, Michel (2009): "Class and capital in peer production", in: Capital and Class 33(1), pp. 121-141.

Bayat, Asef (2004): "Globalization and the Politics of the Informals in the Global South", in: Ananya Roy/Nezar AlSayyad, Lanham, MD: Lexington Books, pp. 79-104.

Beckert, Jens (2016): Imagined Futures: Fictional Expectations and Capitalist Dynamics, Cambridge, MA: Harvard University Press.

Bendix, Regina (2006): "Was über das Auge hinausgeht: zur Rolle der Sinne in der ethnographischen Forschung", in: Schweizerisches Archiv für Volkskunde 102(1), pp. 71-84.

Berggren, Kalle (2014): "Hip hop feminism in Sweden: Intersectionality, feminist critique and female masculinity", in: European Journal of Women's Studies 21(3), pp. 233-2.

Berlant, Lauren/Warner, Michael (1998): "Sex in Public", in: Critical Inquiry 24(2), pp. 547-566.

Betz, Elizabeth (2014): "Polynesian youth hip hop: Intersubjectivity and Australia's multicultural audience", in: Ethnomusicology forum 23(2), pp. 247-265.

Bhabha, Homi (1984): "Of Mimicry and Man: The Ambivalence of Colonial Discourse", in: Discipleship: A Special Issue on Psychoanalysis, pp. 125-133.

Bian, Y.J. (1994): "Guanxi and the Allocation of Urban Jobs in China", in: The China Quarterly 140, pp. 971-999.

Blommaert, Jan/Rampton, Ben (2011): "Language and Superdiversity", in: Diversities 13(2), pp. 1-21.

Bourdieu, Pierre (1990): The Logic of Practice, Stanford, CA: Stanford University Press.

Bourrin, Claude (1941): Le vieux Tonkin, Hanoi: Imprimerie d'Extrême-Orient.

Bowker, Geoffrey C. (1994): Science on the run. Information management and industrial geophysics at Schlumberger, 1920-1940, Cambridge, Mass: MIT Press (Inside technology).

Bradley, Adam (2009): Book of rhymes. The poetics of hip hop, New York, NY: Basic Civitas Books.

Bragin, Naomi (2014): "Techniques of black male re/dress. Corporeal drag and kinesthetic politics in the rebirth of Waacking/Punkin", in: Women & Performance: a journal of feminist theory 24, pp. 61-78.

Brandtstädter, Susanne (2008): "The gender of work and the production of kinship value in Taiwan", in: Susanne Brandtstädter/Goncalo D. Santos (eds.), Chinese Kinship, New York, NY: Routledge, pp. 168-192.

Brenner, Suzanne (1999): "On the Public Intimacy of the New Order: Images of Women in the Popular Indonesian Print Media", in: Indonesia 67, pp. 13-37

Brunstad, Endre/Røyneland, Unn/ Opsahl, Toril (2010): "Hip Hop, Ethnicity and Linguistic Practice in Rural and Urban Norway", in: Terkourafi, The languages of global hip hop, pp. 223-255.

Bucholtz, Mary (1999): "'Why Be Normal?': Language and Identity Practices in a Community of Nerd Girls", in: Language in Society 28(2), pp. 203-223.

Buckland, Fiona (2002): Impossible dance. Improvised social dance as queer world-making, Middletown, CT: Wesleyan University Press.

Butler, Judith (1990): Gender Trouble. Feminism and the Subversion of Identity, New York, NY: Routledge.

Casey, Edward (1996): "Embracing Lococentrism: A Response to Thomas Brockelman's Critique", in: Human Studies (19), pp. 459-465.

Chang, Heewon (2016): Autoethnography as method, London: Routledge.

Chang, Jeff (2005): Can't Stop, Won't Stop: A History of the Hip hop Generation, New York, NY: St. Martin's.

— (2006): Total chaos. The art and aesthetics of hip hop, New York, NY: Basic Civitas Books.

Chesneaux, Jean (1955): "Stages in the Development of the Vietnam National Movement 1862-1940", in: Past & Present 7, pp. 63-75.

Chew, Michael Ming-tak /Mo, Sophie Pui Sim (2019): "Towards a Chinese Hip hop Feminism and a Feminist Reassessment of Hip hop with Breakdance:

B-girling in Hong Kong, Taiwan and China", in: Asian Studies Review 43(6), pp. 1-20.

Clarke, John/Hall, Stuart/Jefferson, Tony et al. (1997): "Subcultures, cultures and class", in: Gelder/Thornton (eds.), The Subcultures Reader, pp. 100-111.

Clifton, Thomas (1983): Music as Heard: A Study in Applied Phenomenology, New Haven, CT: Yale University Press.

Cohen, Albert (1955): Delinquent boys; The culture of the gang, New York, NY: Macmillan USA.

— (1997): "A general theory of subcultures", in: Gelder/Thornton (eds.), The Subcultures Reader, pp. 44-54.

Cohen, Phil (1972): "Subcultural Conflict and Working-Class Community", in: Gelder/Thornton (eds.), The Subcultures Reader, 90-99.

Cole, Jennifer (2010): Sex and salvation. Imagining the future in Madagascar, Chicago, IL: University of Chicago Press.

Comaroff, Jean/Comaroff, John L. (1999): "Occult economies and the violence of abstraction: Notes from the South African postcolony", in: American Ethnologist 26(20), pp. 279-303.

— (2012): "Theory from the South: Or, how Euro-America is evolving toward Africa", in: Anthropological Forum 22(2), pp. 113-131.

Condry, Ian (2001): "A History of Japanese Hip hop. Street Dance, Club Scene, Pop Market", in: Tony Mitchell (ed.), Global noise, Middletown, CT: Wesleyan University Press, pp. 222-247.

Connell, Raewyn (2013): "Using southern theory: Decolonizing social thought in theory, research and application", in: Planning Theory 13(2), pp. 210-223.

— (2014a): "The sociology of gender in Southern perspective", in: Current Sociology 62(4), pp. 550-567.

— (2014b): "Rethinking Gender from the South", in: Feminist Studies 40(3), pp. 518-539.

Conquergood, Dwight (1991): "Rethinking ethnography: Towards a critical cultural politics", in: Communication Monographs 58, pp. 179-194.

Coros, Mary (1982): "Sousta", Privately distributed.

Cox, Andrew (2005): "What are communities of practice? A comparative review of four seminal works", in: Journal of Information Science 31(6), pp. 527-540.

Croissant, Aurel (2015): Die politischen Systeme Südostasiens. Eine Einführung, Wiesbaden: Springer VS.

Csordas, Thomas J. (1999): "Embodiment and cultural phenomenology", in: Gail Weiss/Honi Fern Haber (eds.), Perspectives on Embodiment: The Intersections of Nature and Culture, London: Routledge, pp. 143-62.

Cutler, Cecilia (2009): "'You shouldn't be rappin', you should be skateboardin' the X-games': The Coconstruction of Whiteness in an MC Battle", in: Alim/Ibrahim/Pennycook, Global linguistic flows. Hip hop cultures, youth identities, and the politics of language, pp. 79-94.

Dalsgaard, Anne Line/Tranberg Hansen, Karen (eds.) (2008): Youth and the city in the global south, Bloomington, IN: Indiana University Press (Tracking globalization).

Davis, Deborah/Vogel, Ezra (eds.) (1990): Chinese Society on the Eve of Tiananmen: The Impact of Reforms, Cambridge: Harvard University Press.

Davis, Tracy C. (2009): The Cambridge companion to performance studies, Cambridge: Cambridge University Press

De Certeau, Michel (1984): The Practice of Everyday Life, Berkeley, CA: University of California.

DeFrantz, Thomas F. (2004): "The Black Beat Made Visible: Body Power in Hip Hop Dance", in: Andre Lepecki (ed.), Of the Presence of the Body: Essays on Dance and Performance Theory, Middleton, WI: Wesleyan University Press, pp. 64-81.

— (2016): "Bone-Breaking, Black Social Dance, and Queer Corporeal Orature", in: The Black Scholar 46(1), pp. 66-74.

Degen, Monica Montserrat/Rose, Gillian (2012): "The Sensory Experiencing of Urban Design. The Role of Walking and Perceptual Memory", in: Urban Studies 15, pp. 3271-3287.

De Grave, Jean-Marc (2011): "The Training of Perception in Javanese Martial Arts", in: D.-S. Farrer/John Whalen-Bridge (eds.), Martial arts as Embodied Knowledge. Asian Traditions in a Transnational World, Albany, NY: Suny Press, pp. 123-144.

Deleuze, Gilles (2007): Differenz und Wiederholung, München: Fink.

Desmond, Jane (1999): "Engendering Dance: Feminist Inquiry and Dance Research", in: Sondra Horton Fraleigh/Penelope Hanstein (eds.), Researching Dance. Evolving Modes of Inquiry, Pittsburgh, PA: University of Pittsburgh Press, pp. 309-333.

— (2006): Meaning in Motion. New cultural studies of dance, Durham, NC: Duke University Press.

Deumert, Ana (2018): "Mimesis and Mimicry in Language: Creativity and Aesthetics as the Performance of (Dis-)semblances", in: Language Sciences 65, pp. 9-17.

Doanthanhnien (2017): "Tổng Bí thư Nguyễn Phú Trọng: Thanh niên là người chủ tương lai, là giường cột của nước nhà", 11 December 2017, available at: http://tinhdoantuyenquang.vn/DetailView/2143/6/Tong-Bi-thu-Nguyen-Phu-Trong-Thanh-nien-la-nguoi-chu-tuong-lai-la-giuong-cot-cua-nuoc-nha.html (accessed 20 August 2019).

Downey, Greg (2002): "Listening to Capoeira. Phenomenology, Embodiment, and the Materiality of Music", in: Ethnomusicology 46(3), pp. 487-509.

— (2005): Learning Capoeira: Lessons in cunning from an Afro-Brazilian art, Oxford: Oxford University Press.

Drummond, Lisa (2000): "Street Scenes: Practices of Public and Private Space in Urban Vietnam", in: Urban Studies 37(12), pp. 2377-2391.

— (2012): "Middle class landscapes in a transforming city: Hanoi in the 21st century", in: Van Nguyen-Marshall/Lisa Drummond/Danièle Bélanger (eds.), The Reinvention of Distinction, Dordrecht: Springer, pp. 79-93.

Drummond, Lisa/Rydstrøm, Helle (eds.) (2004): Gender practices in contemporary Vietnam, Copenhagen: NIAS.

Drummond, Lisa/Nguyen, Thi Lien (2008): Uses and understandings of public space among young people in Hanoi, Vietnam, London: Routledge.

Duguid, Paul (2008): "Prologue: Community of practice then and now", in: Ash Amin/Joanne Roberts (eds.), Community, economic creativity, and organization, New York, NY: Oxford University Press, pp. 1-10.

Dunn, Elizabeth C. (2004): Privatizing Poland: Baby Food, Big Business, and the Remaking of Labor, Ithaca, NY: Cornell University Press.

Duranti, Alessandro (2001): "Linguistic Anthropology: History, Ideas, and Issues", in: Alessandro Duranti (ed.), Linguistic anthropology. A reader. Hoboken, NJ: Blackwell Publishers 1, pp. 1-38.

Durham, Deborah (2000): "Youth and the Social Imagination in Africa: Introduction", in: Anthropological Quarterly 73(3), pp. 113-20.

— (2004) "Disappearing Youth: Youth as a Social Shifter in Botswana", in: American Ethnologist 31(4), pp. 589-605.

Dutton, George (2012): "Advertising, Modernity and Consumer Culture in Colonial Vietnam", in: Nguyen-Marshall/Drummond/Bélanger, The Reinvention of distinction: modernity and the middle class in urban Vietnam, pp. 21-42.

Earl, Catherine (2014): Vietnam's new middle classes. Gender, career, city, Copenhagen: NIAS.

Eckert, Penelope/McConnell-Ginnet, Sally (1992): "Think practically and look locally: Language and Gender as Community-Based Practice", in: Annual Review of Anthropology 21, pp. 461-490.

— (2003): Language and Gender, Cambridge: Cambridge University Press.

Ehlert, Judith (2019): "Obesity, Biopower, and Embodiment of Caring: Food-work and Maternal Ambivalences in Ho Chi Minh City", in: Judith Ehlert/Nora Katharina Faltmann (eds.), Food Anxiety in Globalising Vietnam, London: Palgrave Macmillan, pp. 105-136.

Elias, Norbert (1980): Über den Prozeß der Zivilisation. Soziogenetische und psychogenetische Untersuchungen. (= Suhrkamp-Taschenbuch Wissenschaft, Wandlungen des Verhaltens in den weltlichen Oberschichten des Abendlandes Band 158), Frankfurt a. M.: Suhrkamp.

Embree, John F. (1950): "Thailand—A Loosely Structured Social System", in: American Anthropologist 52, pp. 181-193.

Emerson, Rana A. (2002): "'WHERE MY GIRLS AT?' Negotiating Black Womanhood in Music Videos", in: Gender & Society 16(1), pp. 115-135.

Endres, Kirsten (2008): "Fate, Memory, and the Postcolonial Construction of the Self: The Life-Narrative of a Vietnamese Spirit Medium", in: Journal of Vietnamese Studies 3(2), pp. 34-65.

Evans, Grant (1985): "Vietnamese Communist Anthropology", in: Canberra Anthropology 3(1,2), pp. 116-147.

Farrugia, David (2018): Spaces of youth. Work, citizenship and culture in a global context, Abingdon, Oxon, New York, NY: Routledge (Youth, young adulthood and society).

Fleetwood, Nicole R. (2005): "Hip hop Fashion, Masculine Anxiety, and the Discourse of Americana", in: Harry J. Elam/Kennell Jackson/Tricia Rose (eds.), Black Cultural Traffic: Crossroads in Global Performance and Popular Culture, Ann Arbor, MI: The University of Michigan Press, pp. 326-45.

Forman, Murray (1994): "Moving Closer to an Independent Funk: Black Feminist Theory, Standpoint and Women in Rap", in: Women's Studies 28, pp. 35-55.

Foster, Susan Leigh (1995) "Choreographing History", in: Susan Leigh Forster (ed.), Choreographing History, Bloomington, IN: Indiana University Press, pp. 3-21.

Fuhrer, Urs (1993) "Behavior setting analysis of situated learning: The case of newcomers", in: Seth Chaiklin/Jean Lave (eds.), Understanding practice.

Perspectives on activity and context, Cambridge: Cambridge University Press, pp. 179-211.

Fuhrmann, Eva (o. J.): Gendered Life Courses: A Review on Gender Research in Vietnam. Unveröffentlicht, Köln.

Gal, Susan/Irvine, Judith T. (1995): "The Boundaries of Languages and Disciplines: How Ideologies Construct Difference", in: Social Research 62(4), pp. 967-1001.

Garfinkel, Harold (1967): Studies in Ethnomethodology, Upper Saddle River, NJ: Prentice-Hall.

Garfinkel, Harold/Rawls, Anne Warfield (2005): Seeing sociologically. The routine grounds of social action, Boulder, CO: Paradigm Publishers.

Gates Jr., Henry Louis (1988): The Signifying Monkey: A Theory of African-American Literary Criticism, Oxford: Oxford University Press.

Geertman, Stephanie/Labbé, Danielle/Boudreau, Julie-Anne et al. (2016): "Youth-Driven Tactics of Public Space Appropriation in Hanoi. The Case of Skateboarding and Parkour", in: Pacific Affairs 89(3), pp. 591-611.

Gelder, Ken/Thornton, Sarah (1997): The Subcultures Reader, London: Routledge.

Gershon, Ilana (2015): A world of work. Imagined manuals for real jobs, Ithaca, NY: ILR Press.

Gillespie, John/Nguyen, Quang Hung (2018): "Between authoritarian governance and urban citizenship: Tree-felling protests in Hanoi", in: Urban Studies 56(5), pp. 977-991.

Goddess, Rha (2005): "Scarcity and Exploitation: The Myth and Reality of the Struggling Hip hop Artist", in: Chang, Total Chaos. The art and aesthetics of hip hop, pp. 340-348.

Goffman, Erving (1986): Frame Analysis, York, PA: Maple Press.

Goheen, Peter G. (1998): "Public space and the geography of the modern city", in: Progress in Human Geography 22(4), pp. 479-496.

Gordon, Milton (1997) [1947]: "The concept of the sub-culture and its application", in: Gelder/Thornton (eds.), The Subcultures Reader, pp. 40-43.

Gupta, Akhil/Ferguson, James (1992): "Beyond 'Culture': Space, Identity, and the Politics of Difference", in: Cultural Anthropology 7(1), pp. 6-23.

Hamera, Judith (2007): Dancing communities. Performance, difference, and connection in the global city, New York: Palgrave Macmillian (Studies in International Performance).

Hansen, Karen Tranberg (2008): "Introduction: Youth and the City", in: Dalsgaard/Hansen, Youth and the city in the global south, pp. 3-23.

Hanyi, Linh (2014): "Phương Silver Monkey, 'Nhiệt' và tình yêu hip hop - Tạp chí Đẹp", in: Dep Online, available at: https://dep.com.vn/phuong-silver-monkey-nhiet-va-tinh-yeu-hiphop/ (accessed 04 June 2021).

Harms, Erik (2011): Saigon's Edge: On the Margins of Ho Chi Minh City. Minneapolis, MN: University of Minneapolis Press.

— (2016): Luxury and Rubble: Civility and Dispossession in the New Saigon, Oakland, CA: University of California Press

Hegel, Georg Wilhelm Friedrich/Knox, Thomas M. (1967): Hegel's Philosophy of right, London: Oxford University Press.

Herzfeld, Michael (2005): Cultural Intimacy: Social Poetics in the Nation State, London & New York: Routledge.

Hien, Nina (2012): "Ho Chi Minh City's Beauty Regime: Haptic Technologies of the Self in the New Millennium", in: Positions: Asia Critique 20(2), pp. 473-493.

Hoffman, Lisa (2008): "Post-Mao professionalism: Self-enterprise and patriotism", in: Zhang Ong (eds.), Privatizing China, Ithaca, NY: Cornell University Press, pp. 168-181.

Holman, Michael (1984): Breaking and the New York City Breakers, New York, NY: Freundlich Books.

— (2004) "Breaking: The History", in: Neal/Forman, That's the joint! The hip hop studies reader, pp. 31-40.

Howes, David/ Classen, Constance (1991): "Sounding sensory profiles", in: David Howes (ed.), The Varieties of Sensory Experience, Toronto: University of Toronto Press.

Hue Tam Ho Tai (ed.) (2001): The Country of Memory: Remaking the Past in Late Socialist Vietnam, Berkeley, CA: University of California Press.

Hunter, Margaret (2011): "Shake it, Baby, shake it: Consumption and The New Gender Relation in Hip hop", in: Sociological Perspectives 54(1), pp. 15-36.

Huu, Ngoc/Borton, Lady (2014): Frequently Asked Questions About Vietnamese Culture: Women's Long Dress, Hanoi: Thế Giới Publishers.

Huynh Boi Tranh (2005): Vietnamese Aesthetics From 1925 Onwards, Sydney: University of Sydney.

Hymes, Dell (1972): "Models of the interaction of language and social life", in: John J. Gumperz/Dell Hymes (eds.), Directions in Sociolinguistics: The Ethnography of Communication. New York, NY: Holt, Rinehart, and Winston, pp. 35-71.

— (1957): "Breakthrough into Performance", in: Dan Ben-Amos/Kenneth Gold-
stein (eds.), Folklore: Performance and communication, The Hague: Mouton, pp. 11–74.

Ingold, Tim (2000): The Perception of the Environment. Essays on Livelihood,
Dwelling and Skill, London: Routledge.

— (2008): "Bindings against Boundaries: Entanglements of Life in an Open
World", in: Environment and Planning A: Economy and Space, 40(8),
pp.1796-1810.

Irigaray, Luce (1979) Das Geschlecht, das nicht eins ist, Berlin: Merve Verlag.

Jacke, Christoph (2009): "John Clarke, Toni Jefferson, Paul Willis und Dick
Hebdige: Subkulturen und Jugendstile", in: Andreas Hepp/Friedrich
Krotz/Tanja Thomas (eds.), Schlüsselwerke der Cultural Studies, Wies-
baden: VS, pp. 138-155.

Jakobson, Roman (1971): "Shifters, verbal categories, and the Russian verb", in:
Selected Writings II, The Hague: Mouton, pp. 130-147.

Jochim, Christian (1986): Chinese Religions - a cultural perspective. New Jersey: Prentice-Hall.

Johnson, Imani Kai (2014): "From blues women to b-girls. Performing badass
femininity", in: Women & Performance: a journal of feminist theory 24,
pp. 15-28.

Johnson, Patrick E. (2009): "Queer Theory", in: Tracy C. Davis (ed.): The Cambridge companion to performance studies, Cambridge: Cambridge University Press (The Cambridge companions to literature and classics), pp.
166-181.

Kabeer, Naila (2011): Vietnam country gender assessment 2011, World Bank.

Kamal, Zahara/Mahjoeddin, Indija (2016): "Dampeang: Social and textual
structure in the performance of Luambek", in: Uwe U. Paetzold/Paul H.
Mason (eds.), The Fighting Art of Pencak Silat and Its Music: From Southeast Asian Village to Global Movement, Leiden: Brill, pp. 265-289.

Kawalik, Tracy (2018): "Get to know French popping champion Dey Dey", in:
Red Bull, 24 April 2018, available at: https://www.redbull.com/int-en/dey
-dey-interview-popping (accessed 2 September 2020).

Kerkvliet, B. J. T. (1995): "Village-state relations in Vietnam: The effect of everyday politics on decollectivization", in: The Journal of Asian Studies 54(2),
396-418.

Keyes, Cheryl L. (2004): "Empowering Self, Making Choices, Creating Spaces.
Black Female Identity via Rap Music Performance", in: Neal/Forman,
That's the joint! The hip hop studies reader, pp. 265-276.

Kim, Annette Miae (2015): Sidewalk city: remapping public space in Ho Chi Minh City, Chicago, IL: University of Chicago Press.

Kockelman, Paul (2007): "Agency. The relation between meaning, power, and knowledge", in: Current Anthropology 48(3), pp. 375-401.

Kurfürst, Sandra (2012): "Redefining Public Space in Hanoi. Places, Practices and Meaning", in: Christoph Antweiler/Claudia Derichs/Rüdiger Korff et al. (eds.), Southeast Asian Modernities 13, Zürich: LIT.

— (2019): "Multiple Publics in the Global South - A Lefebvrian Perspective on the Production of Public Space in Vietnam", in: Geographische Zeitschrift 107(3), pp. 230-250.

Kusenbach, Margarethe (2003): "Street phenomenology. The go-along as ethnographic research tool", in: Ethnography 4(3), pp. 455-485.

Kipnis, Andrew (2007): "Neoliberalism reified: *Suzhi* Discourse and Tropes of Neoliberalism in the People's Republic of China", in: Journal of the Royal Anthropological Institute 13(2), pp. 383-400.

Labbé, Danielle (2011): "Urban destruction and land disputes in periurban Hanoi during the late-socialist period", in: Pacific Affairs 84(3), pp. 435-454.

Langellier, Kristin M. (1989): "Personal narratives: Perspectives on theory and research", in: Text and performance Quarterly 9, pp. 243-276.

Larkin, Brian (2013): "The Politics and Poetics of Infrastructure", in: Annual Review of Anthropology 42, pp. 327-343.

Lave, Jean/Wenger, Etienne (1991): Situated Learning. Legitimate Peripheral Participation, Cambridge: Cambridge University Press.

Lave, Jean (2011): Apprenticeship in critical ethnographic practice, Chicago, IL: University of Chicago Press.

Lefebvre, Henri (1991): The Production of Space, Oxford, England: Blackwell.

Leshkowich, Ann Marie (2003): "The Ao Dai Goes Global: How International Influences and Female Entrepreneurs Have Shaped Vietnam's "National Costume"", in: Sandra Niessen/Ann Marie Leshkowich,/Carla Jones (eds.), Re-Orienting Fashion: The Globalization of Asian Dress, Oxford, New York: Berg Publishers, pp. 79-115.

— (2008): "Working Out Culture: Gender, Body, And Commodification In A Ho Chi Minh City Health Club", in: Urban Anthropology and Studies 37(1), pp. 49-87.

— (2012): "Finances, Family, Fashion, Fitness, and ... Freedom? The Changing Lives of Urban Middle-Class Vietnamese Women", in: Nguyen-

Marshall/Drummond/Bélanger, The Reinvention of distinction: modernity and the middle class in urban Vietnam, pp. 95-114.

Li Zhang (2012): "Afterword: Flexible Postsocialist Assemblages from the Margin", in: Positions: Asia Critique 20(2), pp. 659-667.

— (2018): "Cultivating the Therapeutic Self in China", in: Medical anthropology 37, pp. 45-58.

Liberman, Kenneth (2013): "More Studies in Ethnomethodology", in: Human Studies 37(4), pp. 597-602.

Lieu Nhi T. (2000): "Remembering "The Nation" Through Pageantry: Femininity and the Politics of Vietnamese Womanhood in the "Hoa Hau Ao Dai" Contest", in: Frontiers: A Journal of Women Studies 21(1/2), pp. 127-51.

Lin, Angel (2009): "'Respect for Da Chopstick Hip Hop'. The Politics, Poetics, and Pedagogy of Cantonese Verbal Art in Hong Kong", in: Alim/Ibrahim/Pennycook, Global linguistic flows. Hip hop cultures, youth identities, and the politics of language, pp. 159-177.

Logan, William Stewart (2000): Hanoi: Biography of a City, Seattle, WA: University of Washington Press.

Lugones, Maria (2007): "Heterosexualism and the Colonial. Modern Gender System", in: Hypatia 22(1), pp. 186-209.

Luong Hy Van (1989): "Vietnamese Kinship: Structural Principles and the Socialist Transformation in Northern Vietnam", in: The Journal of Asian Studies 48(4), pp. 741-756.

Madison, D. Soyini (1993): "'That was my occupation': Oral narrative, performance, and Black feminist thought", in: Text and Performance Quarterly 13, pp. 213-232.

Mahjoeddin, Indija (2016): "The Galombang Wave and the Silek Body", in: Uwe Pätzold/Jean-Marc de Grave (eds.), The fighting art of pencak silat and its music. From Southeast Asian village to global movement, Leiden: Brill (Brill's Southeast Asian library), pp. 359-383.

Margara, Andreas/Nguyen, Van (2011): "Zwei Blicke auf HipHop in Vietnam", in: Tanz Connexions, available at: http://www.goethe.de/ins/id/lp/prj/tco/por/hhv/de12792193.htm (accessed: October 25 2019).

— (2011): Urbane Musik in Vietnam: Interview mit DJ Jase aus Saigon, in: regioactive.de, April 5, 2011, available at: http://www.regioactive.de/story/11953/urbanemusikinvietnaminterviewmitdjjaseaussaigon.html (accessed October 24 2019).

Margara, Andreas (2011): "Interview with Saigon based Graffiti artist DAOS 501", in: Blog Part, available at: https://taki183.wordpress.com/201

1/03/31/interview-with-saigon-based-graffiti-artist-daos-501 (accessed 27 August 2015).

— (2014): "B-Boy or die: Hip Hop in Vietnam", in: taz.de January 6, 2014, available at: http://taz.de/Hiphop-in-Vietnam/!130265/ (accessed October 12 2020).

— (2015) "DAOS501, Vietnam and Montana Cans", in: Montana Cans Blog, available at: https://www.montana-cans.blog/daos501-vietnam-montana-cans/ (accessed 16 June 2021).

Marr, David G. (2000): "Concepts of 'Individual' and 'Self' in Twentieth-Century Vietnam", in: Modern Asian Studies 34(4), pp. 769-796.

Massey, Doreen (1994): Space, Place, and Gender, Minneapolis, MN: University of Minnesota Press.

— (2005): For Space, Thousand Oaks, CA: SAGE.

Mauss, Marcel (1973): "Techniques of the body", in: Economy and Society 2(1), pp. 70-88.

Mbaye, Jenny (2014): "Hip Hop Politics. Recognizing Southern complexity", in: Oldfield/Parnell, The Routledge Handbook on Cities of the Global South, p. 398.

McRobbie, Angela (1998): Feminism and youth culture. From "Jackie" to "Just Seventeen", Basingstoke: Macmillan Press.

Mead, Margaret (1928): Coming of age in Samoa; a psychological study of primitive youth for western civilisation, New York, NY: W. Morrow & Company.

Miller-Young, Mireille (2008): "Hip hop Honeys and Da Hustlaz: Black Sexualities in the New Hip hop Pornography", in: Meridians Feminism Race Transnationalism 8(1), pp. 261-292.

Mitchell, J. Clyde (1956): The Kalela dance: Aspects of social relationships among urban Africans in Northern Rhodesia, Manchester: Manchester University Press.

Mitchell, Tony (2007): "The DIY Habitus of Australian Hip Hop", in: Media International Australia, Incorporating Culture and Policy (123), pp. 109-22.

Mohanty, Chandra Talpade (1991): "Under Western Eyes: Feminist Scholarship and Colonial Discourses", in: Chandra Talpade Mohanty/Ann Russo/Lourdes Torres (eds.), Third World Women and the Politics of Feminism, Bloomington, IN: Indiana University Press, pp. 51-80.

Mollenkopf, John H./Castells, Manuel (1991): Dual City: Restructuring New York, New York, NY: Russel Sage Foundation.

Murray, Pearse/Szelenyi, Ivan (1984): "The city in the transition to socialism", in: International Journal of Urban and Regional Research 8(1), pp. 90-107.

Nash, Jennifer C. (2013) "Practicing Love: Black Feminism, Love-Politics, and Post-Intersectionality", in: Meridians 11(2), pp. 1-24.

Neal, Mark Anthony/Forman, Murray (eds.) (2004): That's the joint! The hip hop studies reader. New York, NY: Routledge.

Ness, Sally Ann (1992): Body, Movement, and Culture: Kinesthetic and Visual Symbolism in a Philippine Community, Philadelphia, PA: University of Pennsylvania Press.

Nghiem Lien Huong (2004): "Female Garment Workers: The New Young Volunteers in Vietnam's Modernization", in: Philip Taylor (ed.), Social Inequality in Vietnam and the Challenges to Reform, Singapore: Institute of Southeast Asian Studies, pp. 297-324.

Ngo Thi Nhan Binh (2004): "The Confucian Four Feminine Virtues", in: Rydstrøm/ Drummond, Gender practices in contemporary Vietnam, pp. 47-73.

Nguyen Minh T. N. (2015): Vietnam's socialist servants. Domesticity, class, gender, and identity, Abingdon, Oxon, New York, NY: Routledge (Asia's transformations, 44).

— (2019): Waste and wealth. An ethnography of labor, value, and morality in a Vietnamese recycling economy, New York, NY, Oxford: Oxford University Press (Issues of globalization: case studies in contemporary anthropology).

Nguyen Thu Giang (2019a): Television in post-reform Vietnam. Nation, media, market, Abingdon, Oxon, New York, NY: Routledge (Media, culture and social change in Asia, 19).

— (2019b): "Aspiring for a better life in pre-Reform Vietnam: Forgetting the equality, remembering the misery", Paper presented at the Conference "The Good Life in Late Socialist Asia: Aspirations, Politics and Possibilities", September 16-18, 2019, University of Bielefeld.

Nguyen-Vo, Thu-Huong (2004): "The Class Sense of Bodies: Women Garment Workers Consume Body Products in and around Ho Chi Minh City", in: Rydstrøm/ Drummond, Gender practices in contemporary Vietnam, pp. 179-209.

Norton, Barley (2006): "'Hot-Tempered' Women and 'Effeminate' Men: The Performance of Music and Gender in Vietnamese Mediumship", in: Karen Fjelstad/Thị Hiền Nguyễn (eds.), Possessed by the Spirits. Mediumship in contemporary Vietnamese communities, Ithaca, NY: Southeast Asia Program Publications Southeast Asia Program Cornell University (Southeast Asia Program series, no. 23), pp. 55-75.

— (2015): "Music and Censorship in Vietnam since 1954", in: Patricia Hall (ed.), The Oxford Handbook of Music Censorship, Oxford, New York, NY: Oxford University Press.

Novack, Cynthia (1990): Sharing the Dance: Contact Improvisation and American Culture, Madison, WI: The University of Wisconsin Press

Nurka, Camille (2013): "Public Bodies", in: Feminist Media Studies 14(3), pp. 485-499.

OECD (2014): "Economic Outlook for Southeast Asia, China and India. Beyond the Middle-Income Trap, Structural Policy Country Notes Vietnam", available at: https://www.oecd.org/site/seao/Viet%20Nam.pdf (accessed January 13, 2020).

Oldfield, Sophie/Parnell, Susan (2014): The Routledge Handbook on Cities of the Global South, New York, NY: Routledge.

Ong, Aihwa/Zhang, Li (2008): Privatizing China: Socialism from Afar, Ithaca, NY: Cornell University Press.

Ong, Aihwa (2008): "Self-fashioning Shanghainese. Dancing across Spheres of Value", in: Aihwa/Zhang, Privatizing China: Socialism from Afar, pp. 182-196.

Ortner, Sherry B. (2006): Anthropology and social theory. Culture, power, and the acting subject, Durham, London: Duke University Press (A John Hope Franklin Center Book).

Osumare, Halifu (2001): "Beat Streets in the Global Hood: Connective Marginalities in the Hip Hop Globe", in: Journal of American & Comparative Cultures 2, pp. 171-181.

Ott, Brian L. (2017): Affect in Critical Studies, Oxford: Oxford University Press.

Parreñas, Rhacel Salazar (2008): The Force of Domesticity. Filipina Migrants and Globalization, New York, NY: New York University Press.

Patel, Sujata (2014): "Is there a 'south' perspective to urban studies?", in: Oldfield/Parnell, The Routledge handbook on cities of the Global South, pp. 37-47.

Pennycook, Alastair (2007): Global Englishes and Transcultural Flows, London: Routledge.

Peters, Erica J. (2012): "Cuisine and Social Status Among Urban Vietnamese, 1888-1926", in: Nguyen-Marshall/Drummond/Bélanger, The Reinvention of distinction: modernity and the middle class in urban Vietnam, pp. 43-57.

Pettus, Ashley (2003): Between Sacrifice and Desire: National Identity and the Governing of Femininity in Vietnam, London and New York: Routledge.

Pham, Thi-Thanh-Hien/Labbé, Danielle (2018): "Spatial Logic and the Distribution of Open and Green Public Spaces in Hanoi: Planning in a Dense and Rapidly Changing City", in: Urban Policy and Research, 36(2), pp. 168-185.

Phinney, Harriet M. (2008): "Objects of Affection: Vietnamese Discourses on Love and Emancipation", in: Positions: Asia Critique 16(2), pp. 329-358.

Pink, Sarah (2009): Visual Interventions. Applied Visual Anthropology, New York, NY: Berghahn Books.

— (2015): Doing sensory ethnography, Los Angeles, CA: SAGE.

Poole, Deborah: (1997): Vision, Race, and Modernity, Princeton, NJ: Princeton University Press.

Posch, Lisa/Wagner, Claudia/Singer, Philipp et al. (2013): "Meaning as collective use: Predicting semantic hashtag categories on twitter", in: Daniel Schwabe (ed.), WWW '13 Companion: Proceedings of the 22nd International Conference on World Wide Web, Republic and Canton of Geneva: International World Wide Web Conferences Steering Committee.

Price-Styles, Alice (2015): "MC origins: rap and spoken word poetry", in: Justin A. Williams (ed.): The Cambridge companion to hip hop, Cambridge: Cambridge University Press, pp. 11-21.

Quijano, Anibal (2000): "Colonialidad del Poder y Clasificacion Social", in: Festschrift for Immanuel Wallerstein. Special issue, Journal of World Systems Research 5(2), pp. 342-386.

Reed, Susan A. (1998): "The Politics and Poetics of Dance", in: Annual Review of Anthropology 27, pp. 503-32.

Reed-Danahay, Deborah (1997): "Introduction", in: Deborah Reed-Danahay, Auto/ethnography: Rewriting the self and the social, New York, NY: Berg.

Reuter, Julia (2011): Geschlecht und Körper. Studien zur Materialität und Inszenierung gesellschaftlicher Wirklichkeit, Bielefeld: transcript.

Rose, Tricia (1994): Black noise. Rap music and black culture in contemporary America, Middletown, CT: Wesleyan University Press.

Rost, Katharina (2017): "Körper-Hören. Zu klanglichen Bewegungsspuren auf und in den Zuschau(-/hör)enden.", in: Sabine Karoß/Stephanie Schroedter (eds.), Klänge in Bewegung. Spurensuchen in Choreografie und Performance, Bielefeld: transcript.

Roy, Ananya (2009): "The 21st-century metropolis: New geographies of theory", in: Regional Studies 43(6), pp. 819-830.

— (2014): "Worlding the South: towards a post-colonial urban theory", in: Old-field/Parnell, The Routledge handbook on cities of the Global South, pp. 9-20.

Rubin, Herbert J./Rubin, Irene S. (2011): Qualitative interviewing. The art of hearing data. 3rd ed., Thousand Oaks, CA: Sage.

Rydstrøm, Helle (2003): Embodying morality. Growing up in rural northern Vietnam, Honolulu: University of Hawai'i Press.

— (2004): "Female and Male "Characters": Images of Identification and Self-Identification for Rural Vietnamese Children and Adolescents", in: Rydstrøm/ Drummond, Gender practices in contemporary Vietnam, pp. 74-95.

Saigoneer (2018): "In 'Công,' Suboi Delivers Full-Throated Anthem for Young Vietnamese Women", in: Saigoneer, 9 December 2018, available at: https://saigoneer.com/saigon-music-art/15191-video-in-c%C3%B4ng,-suboi-delivers-full-throated-anthem-for-young-vietnamese-women (accessed February 26, 2020).

Salemink, Oscar (2003): The ethnography of Vietnam's Central Highlanders: a historical contextualization, 1850–1990, Honolulu, HA: University of Hawaii Press.

Schafer, Raymond Murray (1969): The new soundscape. Don Mills: BMI Canada Limited.

Schechner, Richard (2000): Between theater and anthropology, Philadelphia, PA: University of Pennsylvania Press.

Schloss, Joe (2006): "The Art of Battling: An Interview with Zulu King Alien Ness", in: Chang, Total Chaos. The art and aesthetics of hip hop, pp. 27-32.

Schmitz-Bauerdick, Frauke (2017): "Vietnams Bekleidungsindustrie muss sich modernisieren", in: Germany Trade and Invest, Vietnam Branchenbericht Textilien, Bekleidung, 14 August 2017, available at: https://www.gtai.de/g tai-de/trade/branchen/branchenbericht/vietnam/vietnams-bekleidungsi ndustrie-muss-sich-modernisieren-9596 (accessed February 6, 2020).

— (2019): "Europäische Autobauer kämpfen in Vietnam mit erschwerten Handelsbedingungen", in: Germany Trade and Invest, Vietnam Branchenbericht Zollberatung, 29 January 2019, available at: https://www.gt ai.de/gtai-de/trade/branchen/branchenbericht/vietnam/europaeische-au tobauer-kaempfen-in-vietnam-mit-erschwerten-21762 (accessed February 28, 2020).

Schumacher, Thomas G. (2004): "This Is a Sampling Sport: Digital Sampling, Rap Music, and the Law in Cultural Production", in: Neal/Forman, That's the joint! The hip hop studies reader, pp. 443-458.

Schulz, Dorothea (2012): "Mapping Cosmopolitan Identities: Rap Music and Male Youth Culture in Mali", in: Eric S. Charry (ed.): Hip hop Africa. New African music in a globalizing world. Bloomington, Indianapolis, IN: Indiana University Press, pp. 129-146.

Schulze, Marion (2015): Hardcore & Gender. Soziologische Einblicke in eine globale Subkultur, Bielefeld: transcript.

Schwenkel, Christina (2011): "Youth culture and fading memories of war in Hanoi, Vietnam", in: Kathleen Gillogly/Kathleen M. Adams (eds.), Everyday Life in Southeast Asia, Bloomington, Indianapolis, IN: Indiana University Press, pp. 127-136.

Schwenkel, Christina/Leshkowich, Ann Marie (2012): "Guest Editors' Introduction: How Is Neoliberalism Good to Think Vietnam? How Is Vietnam Good to Think Neoliberalism?", in: Positions: Asia Critique 20(2), pp. 379-401.

Scott, James (1990): Domination and the arts of resistance: hidden transcripts, New Haven, CT: Yale University Press.

Sennett, Richard (1998): Der flexible Mensch: die Kultur des neuen Kapitalismus. New York, NY: W. Norton & Company.

Service Géographique de l'Indochine (1902): Plan de la ville de Hanoi. Edition d'Octobre 1902.

Sheets-Johnstone, Maxine (1999): The Primacy of Movement, Amsterdam: John Benjamins Publishing.

Shuker, Roy (2005): Popular Music: The Key Concepts, London, New York, NY: Routledge.

Sidnell, Jack/Shohet, Merav (2013): "The problem of peers in Vietnamese interaction", in: Journal of the Royal Anthropological Institute 19, pp. 618-638.

Sielke, Sabine (1998): "Self-Fashioning und Cross-Dressing: Strategien weiblicher Selbstinszenierung von der viktorianischen Verkleidungskunst zum postmodernen Zitatentheater*", in: Gertrud Lehnert (ed.), Mode, Weiblichkeit und Modernität, Berlin: Ebersbach & Simon, pp. 107-139.

— (2003): "Nature, Gender, Ecology, or: Mimicry as Agency?", in: Hans Bak/Walter W. Holbling (eds.), Nature's Nation Revisited: American Concepts of Nature from Wonder to Ecological Crisis, Amsterdam: Vu University Press, pp. 327-338.

— (2011): "Zwischen Anpassung, Täuschung und Irritation: Das Konzept der Mimikry in den Kulturwissenschaften - und wie es durch die Biologie herausgefordert wird", in: Anne-Rose Meyer/Sabine Sielke (eds.), Verschleierungstaktiken: Strategien von eingeschränkter Sichtbarkeit, Tarnung und Täuschung in Natur und Kultur, Frankfurt am Main: Peter Lang, pp. 225-62.

Silverstein, Michael (1976): "Shifters, linguistic categories, and cultural description", in: Keith H. Basso/Henry A. Selby (eds.), Meaning in Anthropology, Albuquerque, NM: University of New Mexico Press, pp. 11-55.

Simeziane, Sarah (2010): "Roma Rap and the Black Train: Minority Voices in Hungarian Hip Hop", in: Terkourafi, The languages of global hip hop, pp. 96-119.

Simone, AbdouMaliq (2019): "Precarious detachment: youth and modes of operating in Hyderabad and Jakarta", in: Setha Low (ed.), The Routledge handbook of anthropology, London, Routledge, pp. 27-40.

Skelton, Tracey (2002): "Research on Youth Transitions: Some Critical Interventions", in: Mark Cieslik/Gary Pollock (eds.), Young People in Risk Society: The Restructuring of Youth Identities and Transitions in Late Modernity, Burlington, VT: Ashgate, pp.100-16.

Skinner, Debra/Pach, Alfred/Holland, Dorothy (eds.) (1998): Selves in Time and Place: Identities, Experience, and History in Nepal, Lanham, MD: Rowman & Littlefield Publishers.

Sklar, Deidre (2000): "Reprise: On Dance Ethnography", in: Dance Research Journal 32(1), pp. 70-77.

Smith, Christopher Holmes (2003): "'I Don't Like to Dream about Getting Paid': Representations of Social Mobility and the Emergence of the Hip hop Mogul", in: Social Text 4(77), pp. 69-97.

Smitherman, Geneva (1997): "'The Chain Remain the Same' Communicative Practices in the Hip Hop Nation", in: Journal of Black Studies 28(1), pp. 3-25.

Soucy, Alexander (2000): "Vietnamese Warriors, Vietnamese Mothers. State Imperatives in the Portrayal of Women", in: Canadian Woman Studies/Les Cahiers De La Femme 19(4), pp. 121–126.

Spady, James/Eure, Joseph (1991): Nation Conscious Rap: The Hip Hop Vision, New York, NY: PC International Press/Black History Museum.

Spry, Tami (2006): "Performing Auto-ethnography: An Embodied Methodological Praxis", in: Sharlene Hesse-Biber/Patricia Leavy (eds), Emergent Methods in Social Research, Thousand Oaks, CA: Sage, pp. 183-211.

Star, Susan Leigh/Griesemer, James R. (1989): "Institutional Ecology, "Translations" and Boundary Objects: Amateurs and Professionals in Berkeley's Museum of Vertebrate Zoology 1907-39", in: Social Studies of Science, 19(3), pp. 387-420.

Star, Susan Leigh/Bowker, Geoffrey C./Neumann, Laura J. (2003): "Transparency beyond the individual level of scale: Convergence between Information Artifacts and communities of practice", in: Ann Peterson Bishop/Nancy A. VanHouse/Barbara P. Buttenfield (eds.), Digital Library Use: Social Practice in Design and Evaluation, London: MIT Press, pp. 241-269.

Street Style Lab 2019. "Tyrone Proctor", available at: http://www.streetstylela b.com/project/tyrone-proctor/ (accessed August 6, 2019).

Taylor, Philip (2001): Fragments from the Present. Searching for Modernity in Vietnam's South, Honolulu, HI: University of Hawaii Press.

Terkourafi, Marina (ed.) (2010): The languages of global hip hop, London: A&C Black.

Teo, Christian Russell (2015): "Lock 'n' load: A dive into Locking in the Lion City", Contented 22 June 2015, available at: https://contented.cc/2015/06/ lock-n-load-a-dive-into-locking-in-the-lion-city/ (accessed 16 July 2020).

Thayer, Carlyle (2009): "Vietnam and the Challenge of Political Civil Society", in: Contemporary Southeast Asia 31(1), pp. 1-27.

The Associated Press (2007): "Internet sex scandal snares young TV star; rivets Vietnam", in: The Associated Press, 24 October 2007, available at: http://www.iht.com/articles/ap/2007/10/25/asia/AS-GEN-Vietnam-Se x-Scandal.php (accessed October 24 2007).

The Economist (2018): "Vehicle demand remains robust in major ASEAN markets", in: The Economist Intelligence Unit, Industry Automotive, 24 December 2018, available at: http://www.eiu.com/industry/article/110749 0094/vehicle-demand-remains-robust-in-major-asean-markets/2018-12-24 (accessed February 28, 2020).

The Freshest Kids: A History of the B-Boy (2002) (USA, R: Israel).

Thomas, Mandy (2002): "Out of Control. Emergent Cultural Landscapes and Political Change in Urban Vietnam", in: Urban Studies 39(9), pp. 1611-1624.

Thompson, Robert Farris (1966): "Aesthetic of the Cool: West African Dance", in: African Forum 2(2), pp. 40-43, 64-67, 89-91.

Thu Thuy (2016): "Suboi - Tôi không muốn bị 'đầu độc'" in: Thanh Nien online, June 8th 2016, available at: https://thanhnien.vn/van-hoa/suboi-toi-khon g-muon-bi-dau-doc-710647.html (accessed February 10, 2020).

Tran, Angie Ngoc (2004): "What's women's work? Male negotiations and gender reproduction in the Vietnamese garment industry", in: Rydstrøm/Drummond, Gender practices in contemporary Vietnam, pp. 210-235.

Tran, Richard Quang-Anh (2014): "An epistemology of gender: historical notes on the homosexual body in contemporary Vietnam, 1986-2005", in: Journal of Vietnamese Studies 9(2), pp. 1-45.

Truitt, Allison (2012): "Banking on the Middle Class in Ho Chi Minh City", in: Nguyen-Marshall/Drummond/Bélanger, The Reinvention of Distinction, pp. 129-141.

Tung Phạm Hồng (2011): Thanh niên và lối sống của thanh niên Việt Nam trong quá trình đổi mới và hội nhập quốc tế. Nhà xuất bản Chính trị quốc gia.

Tusting, Karin/Barton, David (2005): Beyond communities of practice. Language, power, and social context, Cambridge, NY: Cambridge University Press.

United Nations (2018): World youth report. Youth and the 2030 agenda for sustainable development, United Nations, New York.

Urban Dictionary (2014): "Cookie Cutter Bitch", available at: https://www.urbandictionary.com/define.php?term=cookie%20cutter%20bitches (accessed 1 June 2021).

— (2019): "OG", available at: https://www.urbandictionary.com/define.php?term=OG (accessed 26 February 2021).

Valentin, Karen (2008): "Politicized Leisure in the Wake of Doi Moi: A Study of Youth in Hanoi", in: Dalsgaard/Hansen, Youth and the city in the global south, pp. 74-97.

Van Nguyen-Marshall/Drummond, Lisa B. Welch/Bélanger, Danièle (eds.) (2012): The Reinvention of distinction: modernity and the middle class in urban Vietnam. Dordrecht: Springer (ARI -Springer Asia Series).

Vann, Elizabeth F. (2012): "Afterword: Consumption and Middle-Class Subjectivity in Vietnam", in: Nguyen-Marshall/Drummond/Bélanger, The Reinvention of distinction: modernity and the middle class in urban Vietnam, pp. 157-170.

Vibe, Alona (2017): "Portrait: Deydey. Delphine Nguyen", in: Alona Vibe Photography & Journal, 12 Februrary 2017, available at: https://www.alonavibe.com/journal/2017/1/29/deydey (accessed 2 September 2020).

VietnamNetBridge (2012): "Model causes scandal at Hanoi Int'l Film Fest", in: VietnamNetBridge, 21 November 2012, available at: http://english.vietna

mnet.vn/fms/art-entertainment/53507/model-causes-scandal-at-hanoi-int-l-film-fest.html (accessed 6 June 2021).

Vietnam's Nutrition Association (Hội Dinh Dưỡng Việt Nam) (2017): "Nuôi con, đừng áp dụng tư duy nuôi lợn", available at: http://hoidinhduong.vn/be-yeu/nuoi-con-dung-ap-dung-tu-duy-nuoi-lon-905.html, (accessed 26 May 2020).

Wearesocial (2012): "We Are Social's Guide to Social, Digital and Mobile in Asia" (2nd Edition, Oct 2012), available at: https://www.slideshare.net/wearesocialsg/we-are-socials-guide-to-social-digital-mobile-in-asia-oct-2012/ (accessed 26 February 2021).

Wenger, Étienne (1998): Communities of practice: Learning, meaning, and identity, Cambridge, Cambridge University Press.

Wissmann, Torsten (2016): Geographies of urban sound, London, New York: Routledge.

Wolff, Janet (2006): "Reinstating Corporeality: Feminism and Body Politics", in: Desmond, Meaning in motion. New cultural studies of dance, pp. 81-110.

World Bank, Education Statistics (2018): http://datatopics.worldbank.org/education/country/vietnam (accessed 13 January 2020).

Wulff, Helena (2015): "The pains and peaks of being a ballerina in London", in: Gershon, A world of work. Imagined manuals for real jobs, pp. 207-219.

Yang, Lei/Sun, Tao/Zhang, Ming/Mei, Qiaozhu (2012): We know what @you #tag: does the dual role affect hashtag adoption?, WWW '12: Proceedings of the 21st international conference on World Wide Web.

Yasin, Jon (1999): "Rap in the African-American music tradition: cultural assertion and continuity", in: Arthur Spears (ed.), Race and Ideology: Language, Symbolism, and Popular Culture, Detroit, MI: Wayne State University Press.

Youtube (2014): "Tổng quan lịch sử phát triển Hiphop Việt Nam", available at: https://www.youtube.com/watch?v=Io_IUHtF3eI (accessed 7 June 2021).

Youtube (2015): "Phuc Sinh Cypher (Part 3)", available at: https://www.youtube.com/watch?v=riVekZKKwMI (accessed 10 February 2020).

Youtube (2016): "Kenzo X H&M Campaign", available at: https://www.youtube.com/watch?v=M16Tpt-gt7I (accessed 5 February 2020).

Zappavigna, Michele (2015): "Searchable talk: the linguistic functions of hashtags", in: Social Semiotics 25(3), pp. 274-291.

Zink, Annkatrin (2013): "Ho Chi Minh Megacity - Stadt der (Mega-) Möglichkeiten? Perspektiven der jungen Generation", in: Michael Waibel/

Hồ-chí-Minh (eds.), Ho Chi Minh MEGA City, Berlin: Regiospectra-Verl (14), pp. 97-122.

Social Sciences

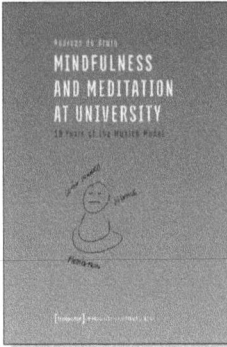

kollektiv orangotango+ (ed.)
This Is Not an Atlas
A Global Collection of Counter-Cartographies

2018, 352 p., hardcover, col. ill.
34,99 € (DE), 978-3-8376-4519-4
E-Book: free available, ISBN 978-3-8394-4519-8

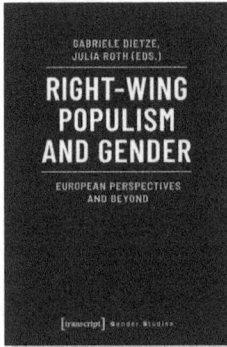

Gabriele Dietze, Julia Roth (eds.)
Right-Wing Populism and Gender
European Perspectives and Beyond

April 2020, 286 p., pb., ill.
35,00 € (DE), 978-3-8376-4980-2
E-Book: 34,99 € (DE), ISBN 978-3-8394-4980-6

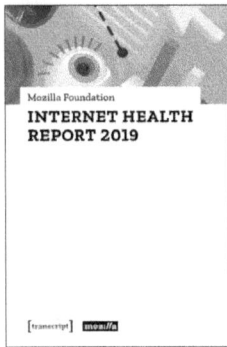

Mozilla Foundation
Internet Health Report 2019

2019, 118 p., pb., ill.
19,99 € (DE), 978-3-8376-4946-8
E-Book: free available, ISBN 978-3-8394-4946-2

**All print, e-book and open access versions of the titles in our list
are available in our online shop www.transcript-publishing.com**

Social Sciences

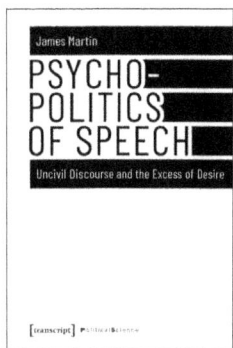

James Martin
Psychopolitics of Speech
Uncivil Discourse and the Excess of Desire

2019, 186 p., hardcover
79,99 € (DE), 978-3-8376-3919-3
E-Book:
PDF: 79,99 € (DE), ISBN 978-3-8394-3919-7

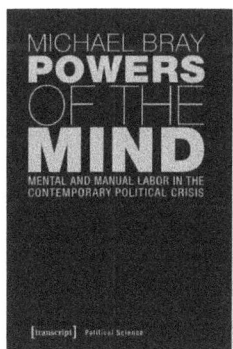

Michael Bray
Powers of the Mind
Mental and Manual Labor
in the Contemporary Political Crisis

2019, 208 p., hardcover
99,99 € (DE), 978-3-8376-4147-9
E-Book:
PDF: 99,99 € (DE), ISBN 978-3-8394-4147-3

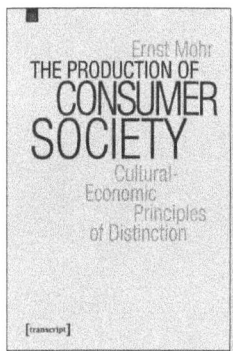

Ernst Mohr
The Production of Consumer Society
Cultural-Economic Principles of Distinction

April 2021, 340 p., pb., ill.
39,00 € (DE), 978-3-8376-5703-6
E-Book: available as free open access publication
PDF: ISBN 978-3-8394-5703-0

**All print, e-book and open access versions of the titles in our list
are available in our online shop www.transcript-publishing.com**

GPSR Authorized Representative: Easy Access System Europe, Mustamäe tee
50, 10621 Tallinn, Estonia, gpsr.requests@easproject.com

www.ingramcontent.com/pod-product-compliance
Lightning Source LLC
Chambersburg PA
CBHW070100030426
42335CB00016B/1954